ÜBER ORIGAMI

MORE THAN 100 ORIGAMI PROJECTS

BY DUY NGUYEN

FALL RIVER PRESS

New York

FALL RIVER PRESS

New York

An Imprint of Sterling Publishing
387 Park Avenue South
New York, NY 10016

Cover and interior title type: Shutterstock

ISBN 978-1-4351-5285-4

Distributed in Canada by Sterling Publishing
C/o Canadian Manda Group, 165 Dufferin Street
Toronto, Ontario, Canada M6K 3H6
Distributed in the United Kingdom by GMC Distribution Services
Castle Place, 166 High Street, Lewes, East Sussex, England BN7 1XU
Distributed in Australia by Capricorn Link (Australia) Pty. Ltd.
P.O. Box 704, Windsor, NSW 2756, Australia

For information about custom editions, special sales, and premium and corporate purchases,
please contact Sterling Special Sales at 800-805-5489 or specialsales@sterlingpublishing.com.

Manufactured in China

2 4 6 8 10 9 7 5 3 1

www.sterlingpublishing.com

TABLE OF CONTENTS

INTRODUCTION

Years ago,
when I began
to fold origami, it
was a struggle. I would
look at even the simplest
folds given at the beginning of the
book again and again. But I also looked
ahead at the diagram showing the next step of
whatever project I was folding to see how it *should*
look. As it turned out, that was the right thing to do.
Looking ahead at the "next step," the result of a fold,
is a very good way for a beginner to learn origami.

You will easily pick up this and other learning techniques as you follow
the step-by-step directions given here for making all kinds of origami
projects, from a submarine to an elephant, from dinosaurs to
monsters, from Elvis to Lincoln. Wherever your interests lie,
the variety of projects here will both challenge and satisfy.
And with these under your belt, there's nothing to
stop you from trying to create your own original
animals, myths, and fantasies.

So sit down, select some paper,
begin to fold...and enjoy
the wonderful art that
is origami!

Duy Nguyen

BASIC INSTRUCTIONS

Paper: Paper used in traditional origami is thin, keeps a crease well, and folds flat. Packets of specially designed sheets, about 6 and 8 inches square (15 and 21 cm), are available in various colors and patterns. A few of the projects given here call for rectangular size paper, but this shouldn't be a problem. You can use plain white, solid-color, or even wrapping paper with a design only on one side and cut the paper to size. Be aware, though, that some papers stretch slightly in length or width, which can cause folding problems, while others tear easily.

You will also find projects in this book that can be made with dollar bills. For these projects, fold whatever's in your wallet using the same basic folds shown on pages 10–13.

Beginners, or those concerned about getting their fingers to work tight folds, might consider using larger paper sizes. Regular paper may be too heavy to allow the many tight folds needed in creating more traditional origami figures, but fine for larger versions of these intriguing projects.

Glue: Use an easy-flowing but not loose paper glue. Use it sparingly; don't soak the paper. On delicate projects, a flat toothpick makes a good applicator. Be sure to allow the glued form time to dry. Avoid stick glue that, if it has become overly dry, can crease or damage your figure.

Technique: Fold with care. Position the paper, especially at corners, precisely and line edges up before creasing. Once you are sure of the fold, use a fingernail to make a clean, flat crease.

For more complex folds, create "construction lines." Fold and unfold, using simple mountain and valley folds, to pre-crease. This creates construction lines, and the finished fold is more likely to match the one shown in the book. Folds that look different, because the angles are slightly different, can throw you off. Don't get discouraged with your first efforts. In time, what your mind can create, your fingers can fashion.

Creativity: If you fold a favorite project several times, do you really want them all to look exactly alike? Once you are more comfortable in your folding ability, try adjusting certain folds to shape the form more to your liking, bringing each project to life in your hands.

Don't be afraid to add a personal touch, too. Use markers to add details or glue on bits and folds of paper to make a project more unique and realistic.

SYMBOLS AND LINES

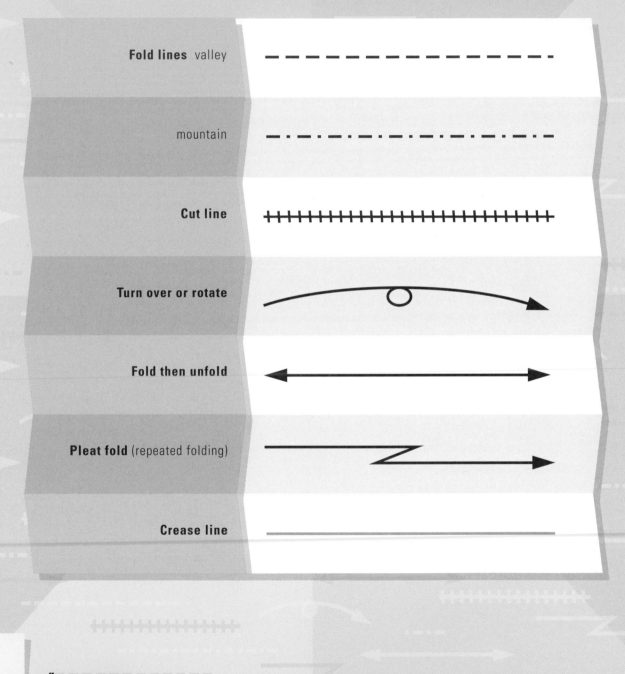

Fold lines valley

mountain

Cut line

Turn over or rotate

Fold then unfold

Pleat fold (repeated folding)

Crease line

SQUARING OFF PAPER

 1 Take a rectangular sheet of paper and valley fold it diagonally to opposite edge.

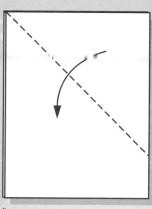

 2 Cut off excess on long side as shown.

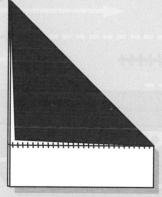

 3 Unfold, and sheet is square.

Squaring Off Paper

BASIC FOLDS

Kite Fold

1 Fold and unfold a square diagonally, making a center crease.

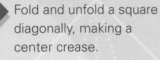

2 Fold both sides in to the center crease.

3 This is a kite fold.

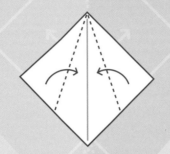

Valley Fold

1 Here, using the kite fold form toward you (forward), making a "valley."

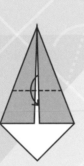

2 This fold forward is a valley fold.

Mountain Fold

1 Here, using the kite, fold form away from you (backward), making a "mountain."

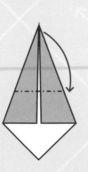

2 This fold backward is a mountain fold.

BASIC FOLDS

Inside Reverse Fold

1 Starting here with a kite, valley fold kite closed.

2 Valley fold as marked to crease, then unfold.

3 Pull tip in direction of arrow.

4 Appearance before completion.

5 You've made an inside reverse fold.

Outside Reverse Fold

1 Using closed kite, valley fold, unfold.

2 Fold inside out, as shown by arrows.

3 Appearance before completion.

4 You've made an outside reverse fold.

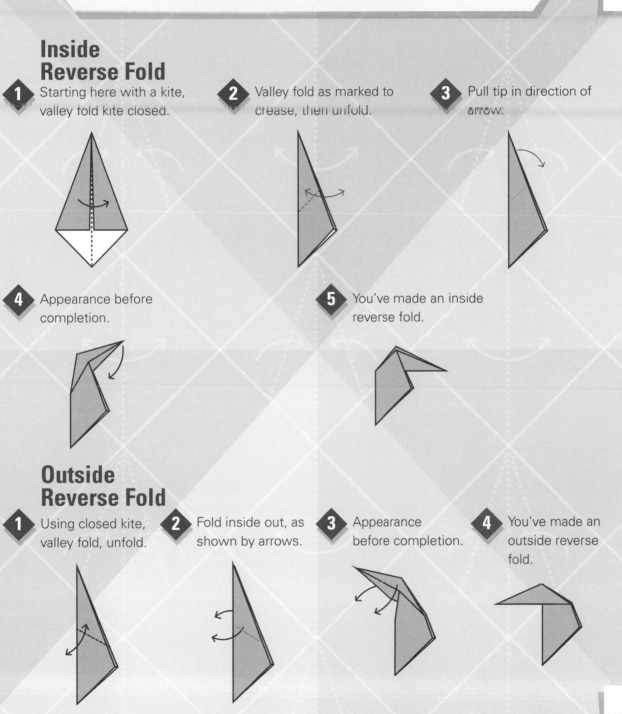

Basic Folds

BASIC FOLDS

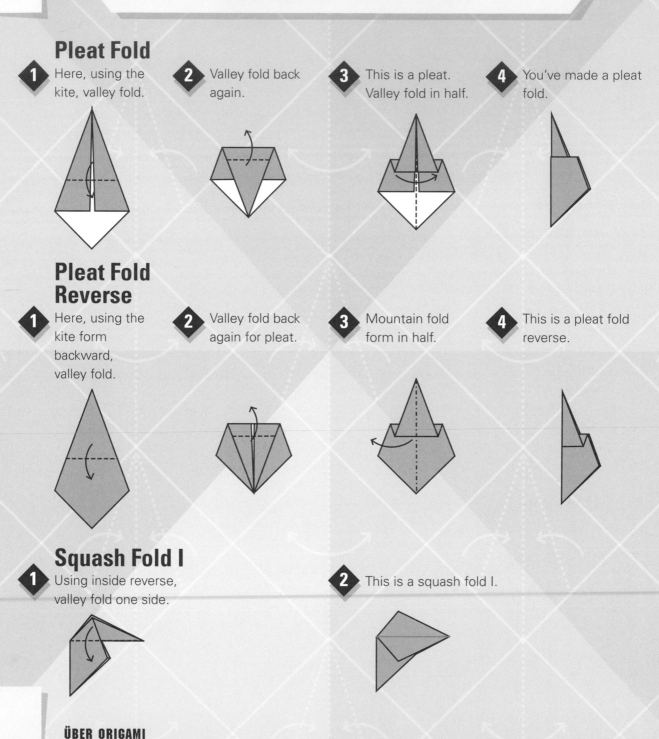

Pleat Fold

1 Here, using the kite, valley fold.

2 Valley fold back again.

3 This is a pleat. Valley fold in half.

4 You've made a pleat fold.

Pleat Fold Reverse

1 Here, using the kite form backward, valley fold.

2 Valley fold back again for pleat.

3 Mountain fold form in half.

4 This is a pleat fold reverse.

Squash Fold I

1 Using inside reverse, valley fold one side.

2 This is a squash fold I.

BASIC FOLDS

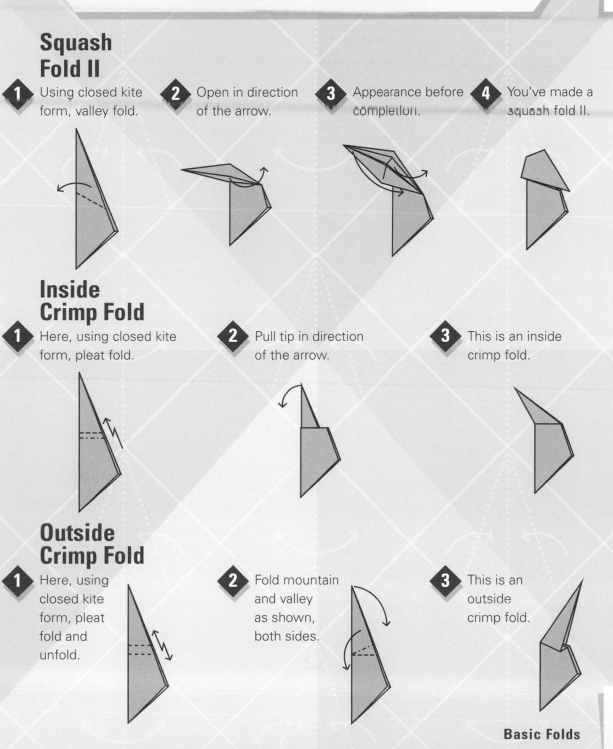

Squash Fold II

1 Using closed kite form, valley fold.

2 Open in direction of the arrow.

3 Appearance before completion.

4 You've made a squash fold II.

Inside Crimp Fold

1 Here, using closed kite form, pleat fold.

2 Pull tip in direction of the arrow.

3 This is an inside crimp fold.

Outside Crimp Fold

1 Here, using closed kite form, pleat fold and unfold.

2 Fold mountain and valley as shown, both sides.

3 This is an outside crimp fold.

Basic Folds

BASE FOLDS

Base folds are basic forms that do not in themselves produce origami, but serve as a basis, or jumping-off point, for a number of creative origami figures—some quite complex. As when beginning other crafts, learning to fold these base folds is not the most exciting part of origami. They are, however, easy to do, and will help you with your technique. They also quickly become rote, so much so that you can do many using different-colored papers while you are watching television or your mind is elsewhere. With completed base folds handy, if you want to quickly work up a form or are suddenly inspired with an idea for an original, unique figure, you can select an appropriate base fold and swiftly bring a new creation to life.

BASE FOLDS

Base Fold I

1 Fold and unfold in direction of arrow.

2 Fold both sides in to center crease, then unfold. Rotate.

3 Fold both sides in to center crease, then unfold.

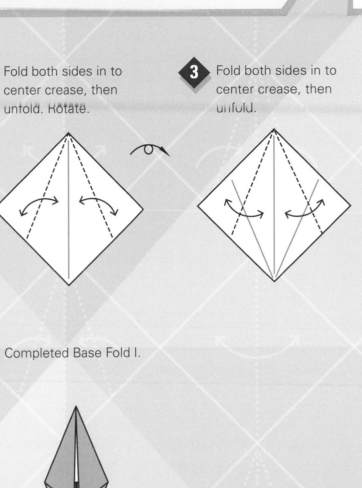

4 Pinch corners of square together and fold inward.

5 Completed Base Fold I.

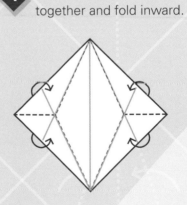

BASE FOLDS

Base Fold II

1 Valley fold.

2 Valley fold.

3 Squash fold.

4 Turn over to other side.

5 Squash fold.

6 Completed Base Fold II.

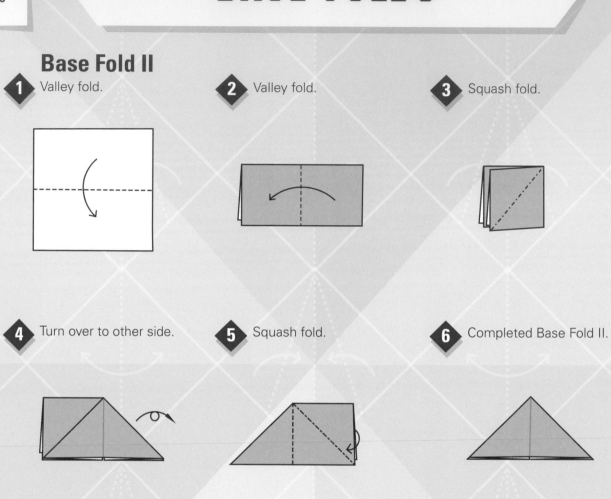

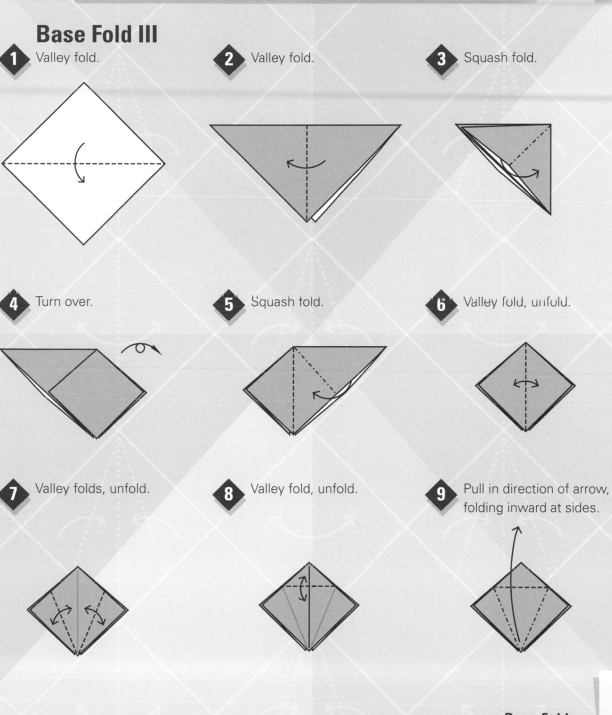

BASE FOLDS

Base Fold III

1 Valley fold.

2 Valley fold.

3 Squash fold.

4 Turn over.

5 Squash fold.

6 Valley fold, unfold.

7 Valley folds, unfold.

8 Valley fold, unfold.

9 Pull in direction of arrow, folding inward at sides.

Base Folds

BASE FOLDS

10 Appearance before completion of fold.

11 Fold completed. Turn over.

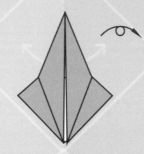

12 Valley folds, unfold.

13 Valley fold, unfold.

14 Repeat, again pulling in direction of arrow.

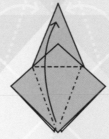

15 Appearance before completion.

16 Completed Base Fold III.

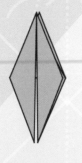

BASE FOLDS

Base Fold IV

1 Valley fold rectangle in half as shown. (Note: Base Fold IV paper size can be variable, but 4″ by 11″ is used for birds throughout book.)

2 Valley fold in direction of arrow.

3 Make cut as shown.

4 Unfold.

5 Unfold.

6 Valley fold in half.

7 Inside reverse folds to inner center crease.

8 Valley fold and unfold to crease.

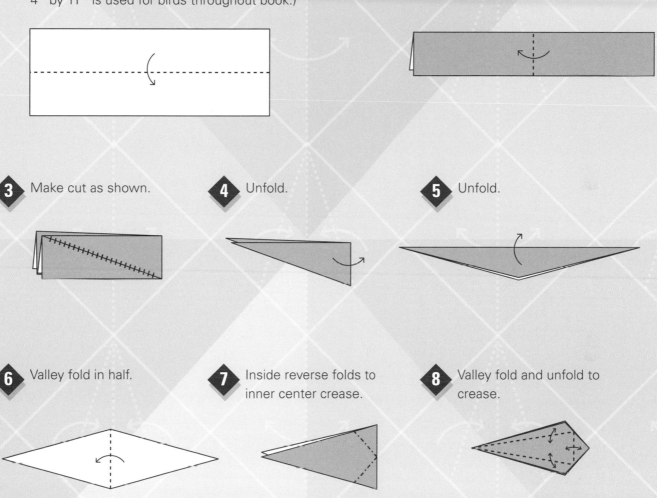

Base Folds

BASE FOLDS

9 Pull in direction of arrow and fold.

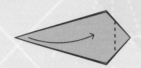

10 Appearance before completion.

11 Turn over.

12 Valley fold then unfold.

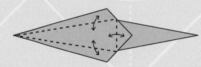

13 Pull in direction of arrow, and valley fold.

14 Completed Base Fold IV.

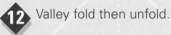

BASE FOLDS

Base Fold V

1 Start with Base Fold III.
Cut top layers.

2 Valley fold.

3 Turn over to other side.

4 Cut top layers.

5 Valley fold.

6 Inside reverse folds.

7 Turn over to other side.

8 Inside reverse folds.

9 Completed Base Fold V.

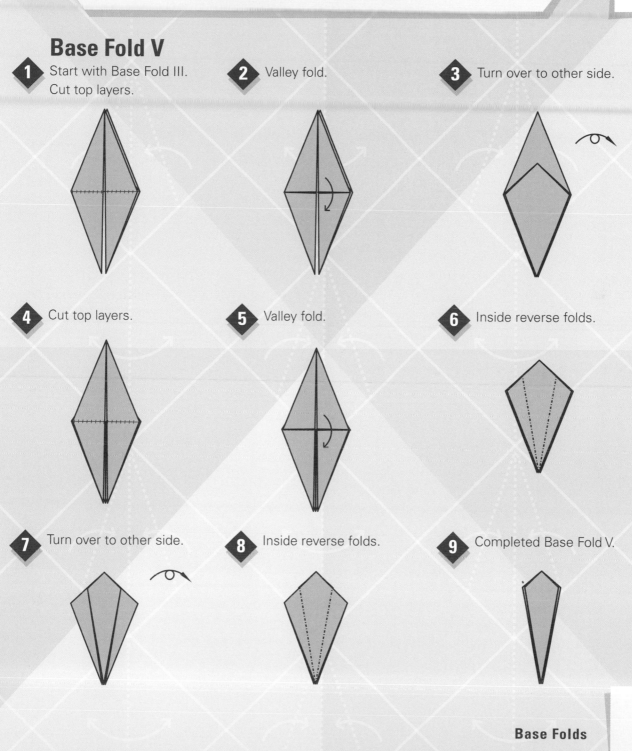

Base Folds

BASE FOLDS

Base Fold VI

1 Fold and unfold square.

2 Cut in half as shown.

3 Valley folds to crease.

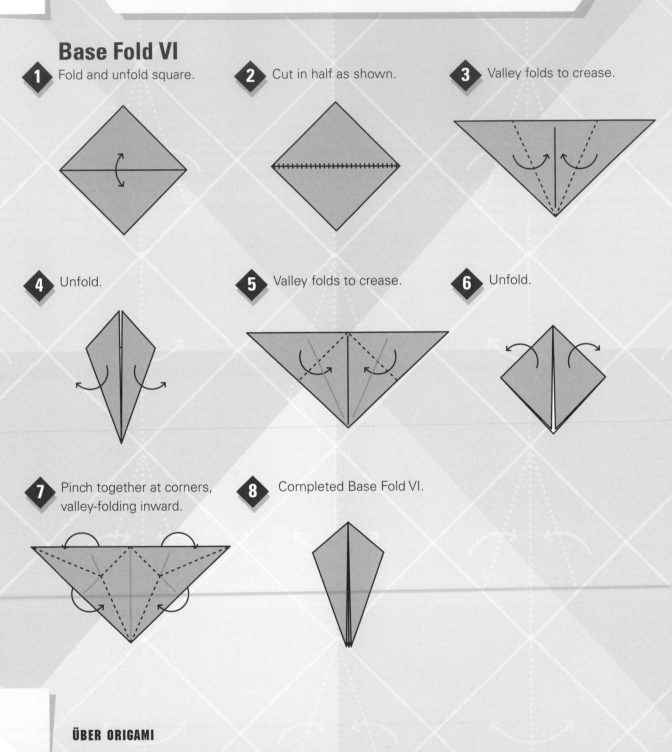

4 Unfold.

5 Valley folds to crease.

6 Unfold.

7 Pinch together at corners, valley-folding inward.

8 Completed Base Fold VI.

EASY DOES IT

Welcome to the world of origami! Start out your journey with some of these easy projects. Not only are these great to make, but they will also teach you a lot of folds you'll need to know later on.

FLOWER

1 Valley fold the square in half on the dashed line.

2 Valley fold the paper again on the dashed line, and unfold.

3 Valley fold and unfold again.

4 Using the creases, make inside reverse folds on both sides. The folds on both sides will be mountain folds.

5 Make inside reverse folds again.

6 Turn the form over.

7 Make two inside reverse folds on this side.

8 Now open up the folds a little.

9 What a lovely Flower you've made!

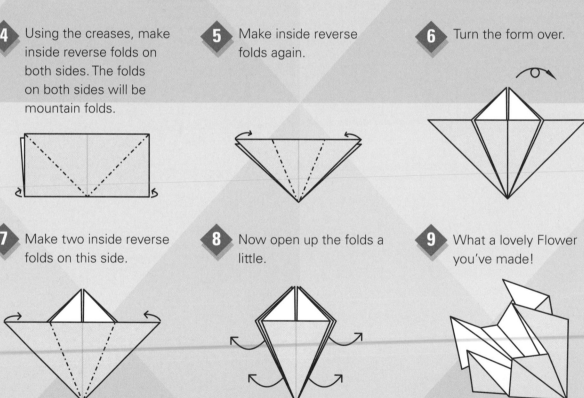

PUPPY

1 Valley fold the paper from corner to corner, diagonally.

2 Make an inside reverse fold on the dotted line.

3 Valley fold the top layer of paper on the dashed line.

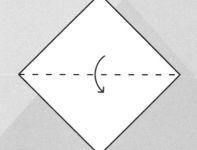

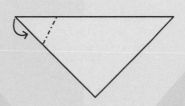

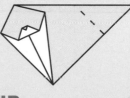

4 Make a valley fold upward on the dashed line.

5 Valley fold the tip to make the puppy's nose.

6 Valley fold the section on the right.

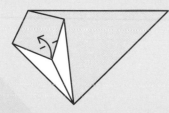

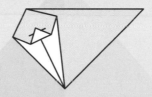

7 Turn the puppy to sit upright.

8 Here is the Puppy. Color nose and make eyes with markers.

TIP

Here's a way to make an inside or outside reverse fold easier to do. First, valley fold and then mountain fold the paper on the line and unfold it. Then, turn the creased folds on each side into mountain or valley folds. An inside reverse fold has mountain folds on both sides. An outside reverse fold has valley folds on both sides.

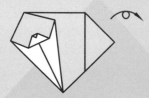

Puppy

CAT HEAD

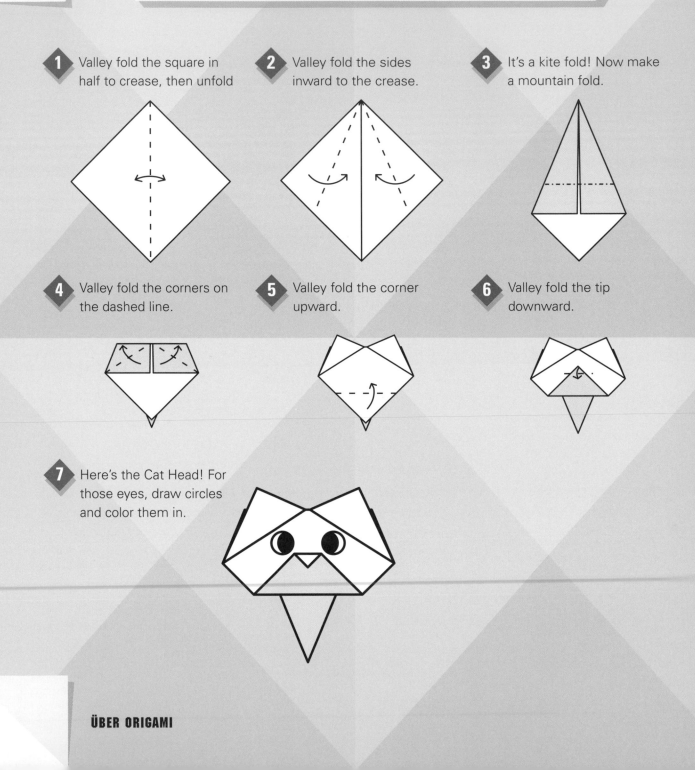

1 Valley fold the square in half to crease, then unfold

2 Valley fold the sides inward to the crease.

3 It's a kite fold! Now make a mountain fold.

4 Valley fold the corners on the dashed line.

5 Valley fold the corner upward.

6 Valley fold the tip downward.

7 Here's the Cat Head! For those eyes, draw circles and color them in.

BULL

1 Valley fold the square in half.

2 Mountain fold the form backward on the dotted line.

3 Make valley folds on the dashed lines (see next step).

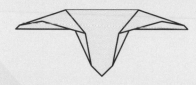

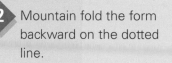

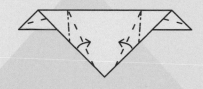

4 When it looks like this, squash the folds flat.

5 Valley fold each side to make the bull's horns, and valley fold the nose, too.

6 Mountain fold the bull in half on the dotted line and unfold.

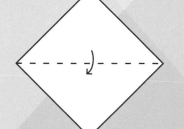

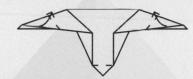

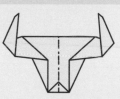

7 Look out! Here comes your Bull!

TIP

To move a fold just a little and make it stay there, squash it! It's called a squash fold. When a squash fold is on the inside, the lines don't show. When it is on the outside, you can see and follow the mountain and valley lines.

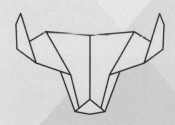

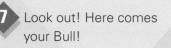

Bull

GOLDFISH

1 Valley fold a square in half diagonally.

2 Next make two valley folds on the dashed lines.

3 Valley fold the two flaps upward.

4 Then valley fold each side.

5 Now valley fold only one layer of paper upward.

6 Valley fold that same layer upward on the dashed line.

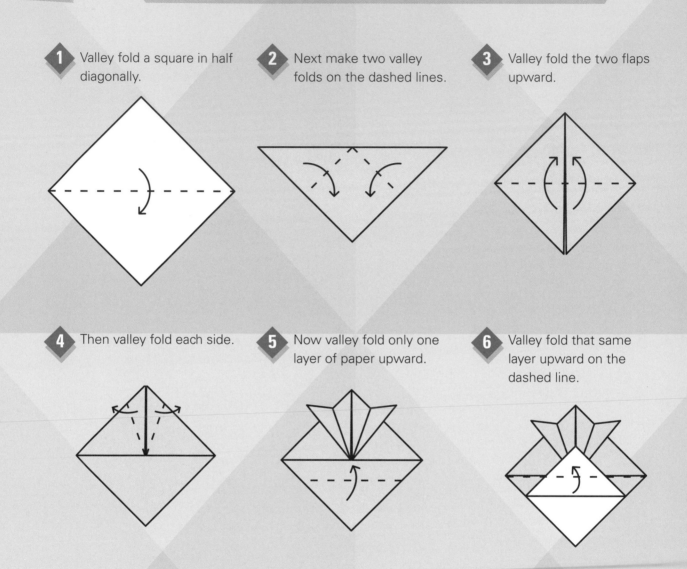

GOLDFISH

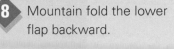

7 With your scissors, cut through the other layers as shown by the cut lines. Careful, don't cut too far!

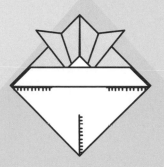

8 Mountain fold the lower flap backward.

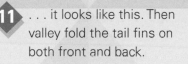

9 Pull open the front and back sections (see next step)

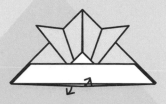

10 This is how it looks while you are pulling. Keep pulling until . . .

11 . . . it looks like this. Then valley fold the tail fins on both front and back.

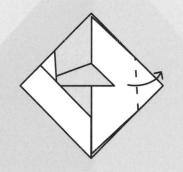

12 You've made a Goldfish!

Goldfish

BUTTERFLY

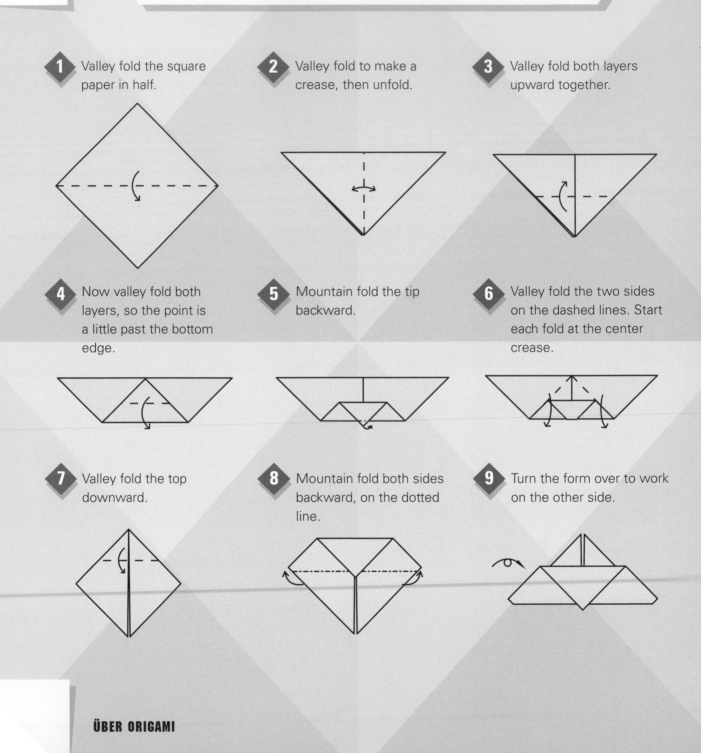

1 Valley fold the square paper in half.

2 Valley fold to make a crease, then unfold.

3 Valley fold both layers upward together.

4 Now valley fold both layers, so the point is a little past the bottom edge.

5 Mountain fold the tip backward.

6 Valley fold the two sides on the dashed lines. Start each fold at the center crease.

7 Valley fold the top downward.

8 Mountain fold both sides backward, on the dotted line.

9 Turn the form over to work on the other side.

BUTTERFLY

10 Pull the two sides outward a little (see next step) and squash fold (see the tip on page 27).

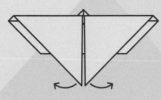

11 Valley fold the tips of the wings and the top point.

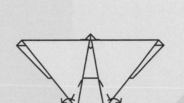

12 Valley fold in half, then unfold.

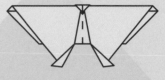

13 What a lovely Butterfly you've made!

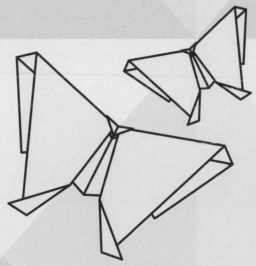

Butterfly

KING COBRA

1 Start with a square. Make a valley fold on the dashed line, then unfold it.

2 Make a valley fold on each of the dashed lines.

3 Now make two more valley folds.

4 And two more valley folds.

5 Now valley fold the form in half, on the dotted line.

6 Valley fold to crease, then turn it into an outside reverse fold.

7 Let's take a closer look.

8 Again, valley fold and turn it into an outside reverse fold.

9 Make another outside reverse fold right at the tip.

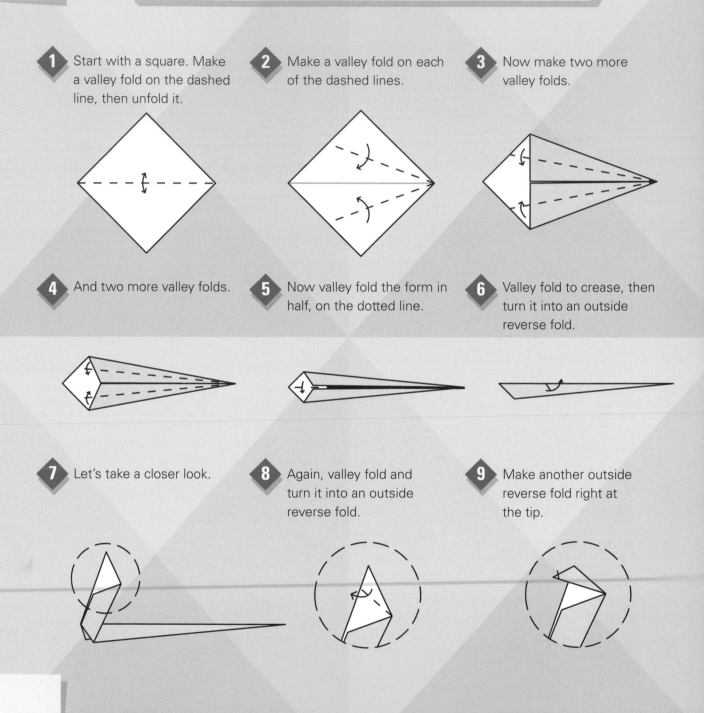

KING COBRA

 10 This is how it looks. Now let's do the body.

11 On the right side of the cobra, make a mountain fold.

12 Turning to the cobra's left side, make another mountain fold.

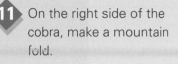

13 Go back to the right side and make another mountain fold.

14 On the dashed line, valley fold both sides to make the cobra's hood. Then shape the sharp folds of the snake's body into curves, so it looks more natural.

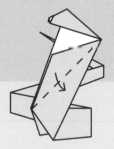

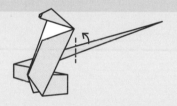

TIP

Add color to your white paper with highlighter, crayon, or paint. Or set your computer's printer to print out solid or patterned color paper for use in origami. You can even make two-sided color paper for special projects, like this King Cobra!

15 You've made a King Cobra!

ELEPHANT

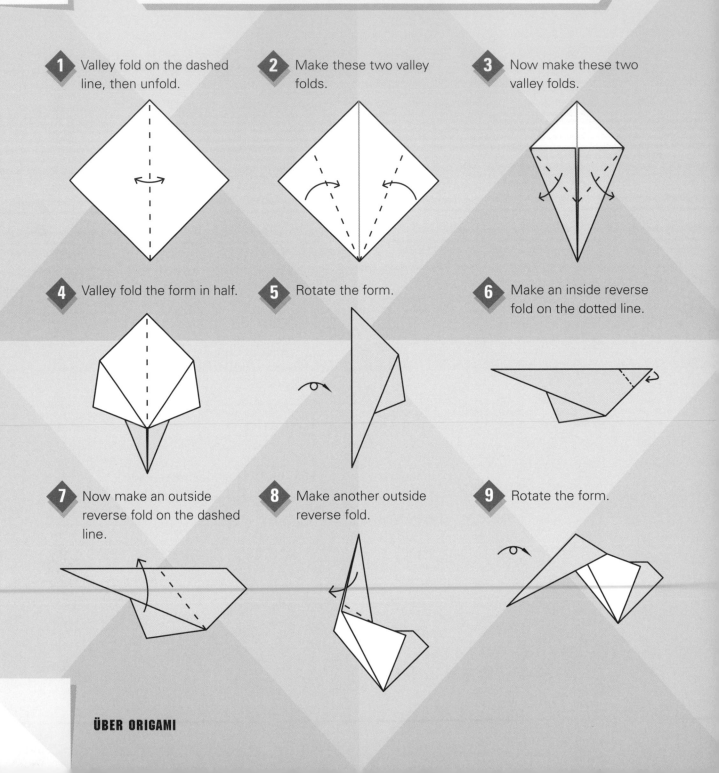

1 Valley fold on the dashed line, then unfold.

2 Make these two valley folds.

3 Now make these two valley folds.

4 Valley fold the form in half.

5 Rotate the form.

6 Make an inside reverse fold on the dotted line.

7 Now make an outside reverse fold on the dashed line.

8 Make another outside reverse fold.

9 Rotate the form.

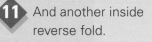

ELEPHANT

 10 Make an inside reverse fold on the dotted line to form the elephant's trunk.

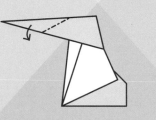

11 And another inside reverse fold.

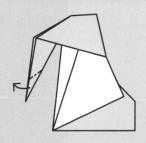

12 And another inside reverse fold to finish off the elephant's trunk.

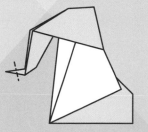

 13 Now valley fold both sides and unfold, to make the ears flap.

14 Here's your Elephant.

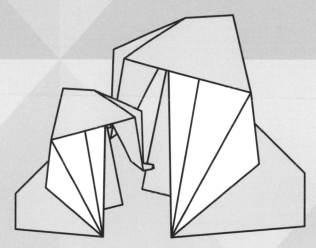

Elephant

FALCON

1 Valley fold a square diagonally.

2 Valley fold the top layer upward.

3 Then valley fold and unfold to crease.

4 Valley fold the right side against the center crease.

5 Valley fold back again on the dashed line.

6 Now do the same on the left side. Valley fold to the center crease . . .

7 . . . and then valley fold back toward the left.

8 Turn the form over.

9 Make a valley fold across the form as shown.

10 Now valley fold it back on the dashed line.

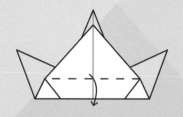

11 Make a beak on the falcon with a pleat fold (valley and mountain folds).

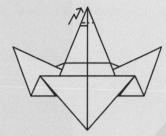

12 Mountain fold the form in half as shown by the arrow.

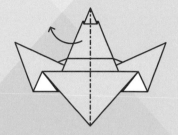

13 Rotate the falcon to the left (wings on top).

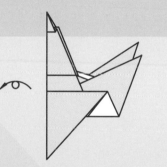

14 Let's take a closer look.

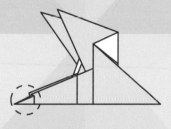

15 On the beak, make an outside reverse fold. Fold it at an angle, as shown by the dashed line.

16 This is how it looks; now let's finish the body.

17 Valley fold the front section down the length of the body.

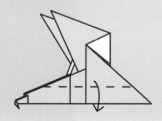

TIP

A pleat fold is made up of two folds done together. Follow the dotted (mountain) and dashed (valley) lines to see which way the folds go. Pleat folds are especially good for making birds' beaks.

FALCON

 18 Mountain fold the other side of the body to match.

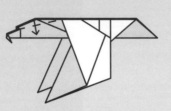 **19** Now let's shape the head. Valley fold the front side.

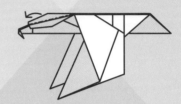 **20** Mountain fold the back side.

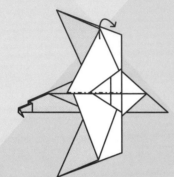

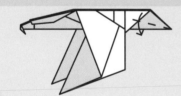 **21** Now, the tail. Valley fold the front side.

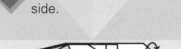 **22** Mountain fold the back side.

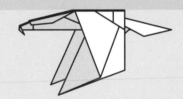 **23** Balance the wings out to the sides.

24 You've made a Falcon!

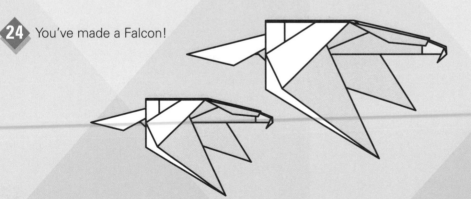

DUCK (EASY)

1 Valley fold a square in half.

2 Valley fold the top layer upward.

3 Does it look like this? Good! Now valley fold and unfold to crease.

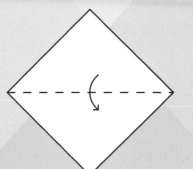

4 Valley fold one side. Line the paper up against the crease.

5 Now make a valley fold on the dashed line.

6 Valley fold the left side, like you did before on the right.

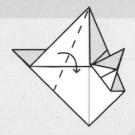

7 And valley fold back again.

8 Turn the form over.

9 Make a small pleat fold near the tip.

Duck (easy)

DUCK (EASY)

10 Valley fold in half.

11 Turn the form to the left.

12 Unfold both sides upward as shown.

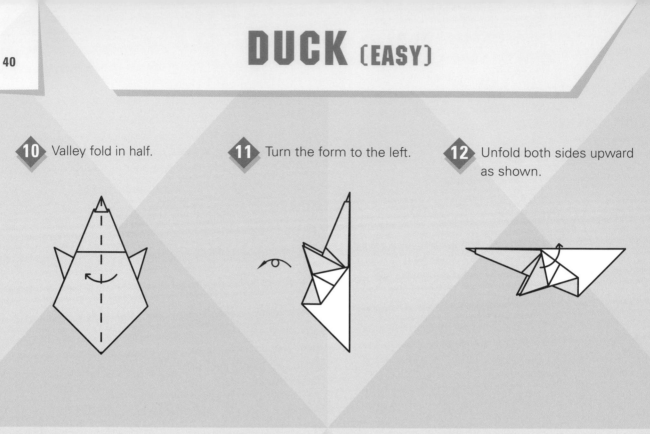

13 Make an outside reverse fold.

14 Mountain fold the top layer to the inside.

15 Valley fold the next layer.

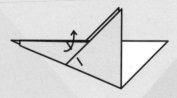

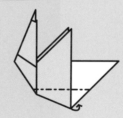

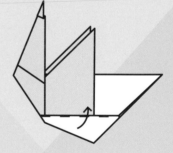

16 Tuck the flap inside.

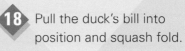 **17** Make an outside reverse fold for the neck.

18 Pull the duck's bill into position and squash fold.

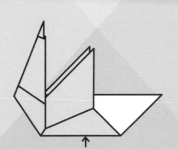

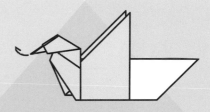

19 Make an inside reverse fold to start the tail.

 **20** Valley fold to the left.

21 Valley fold upward.

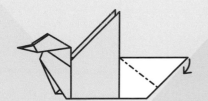

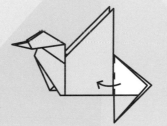

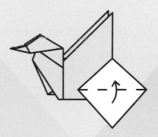

DUCK (EASY)

22 Valley fold tail.

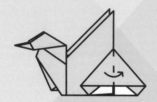

23 Pull the tip outward and squash fold.

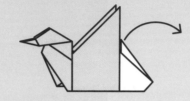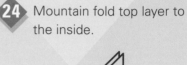

24 Mountain fold top layer to the inside.

25 Valley fold bottom layer forward and . . .

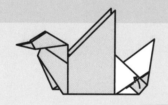

26 . . . hide flap inside (see arrow).

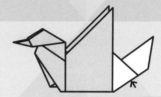

27 Valley fold both wings out to sides.

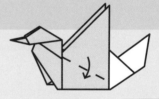

28 You've made a Duck.

ANIMAL KINGDOM

From an ankylosaur to a zebra, here is every beast and bird known to the origami animal kingdom.

TRICOLORED HERON

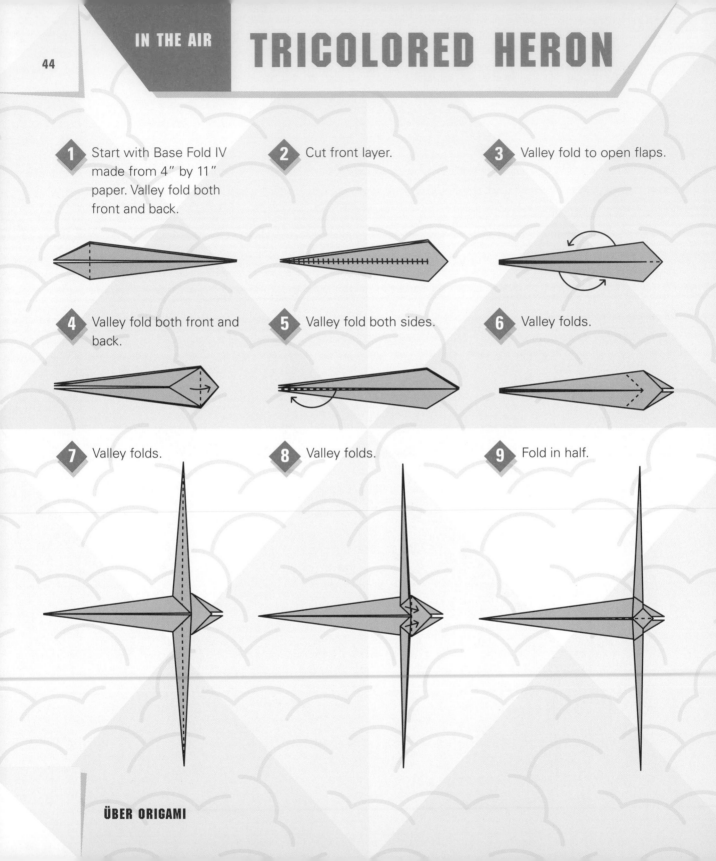

1 Start with Base Fold IV made from 4″ by 11″ paper. Valley fold both front and back.

2 Cut front layer.

3 Valley fold to open flaps.

4 Valley fold both front and back.

5 Valley fold both sides.

6 Valley folds.

7 Valley folds.

8 Valley folds.

9 Fold in half.

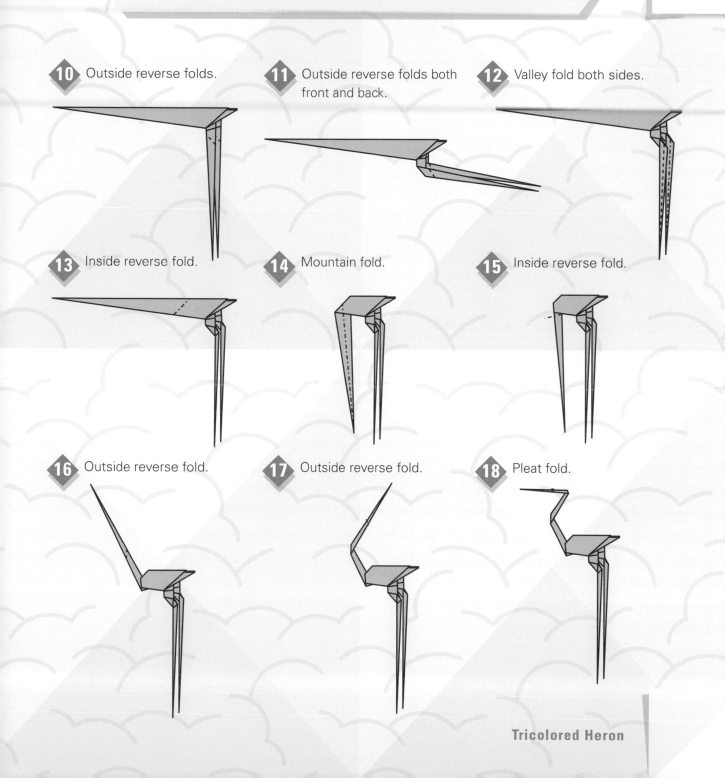

10 Outside reverse folds.

11 Outside reverse folds both front and back.

12 Valley fold both sides.

13 Inside reverse fold.

14 Mountain fold.

15 Inside reverse fold.

16 Outside reverse fold.

17 Outside reverse fold.

18 Pleat fold.

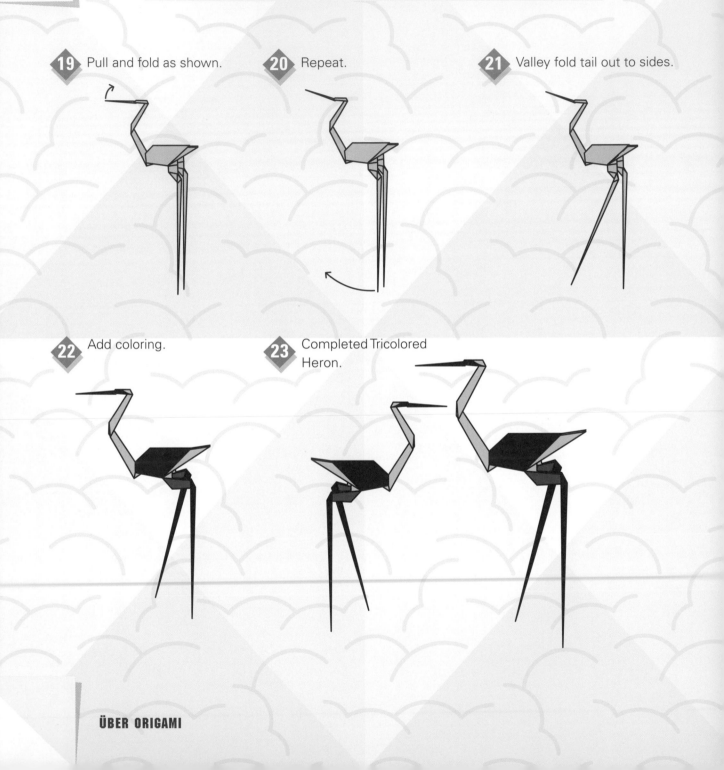

19 Pull and fold as shown.

20 Repeat.

21 Valley fold tail out to sides.

22 Add coloring.

23 Completed Tricolored Heron.

Part 1

1 Start with 5.5" by 4" paper. Cut as shown.

2 Separate the pieces, and select the center piece.

3 Valley fold and unfold.

4 Valley fold.

5 Pinch the corners together and valley fold the sides inward.

6 Unfold.

7 Make cuts as shown.

8 Pinch to valley fold center flap. Pull in direction of arrow.

9 Repeat the step 5 folds.

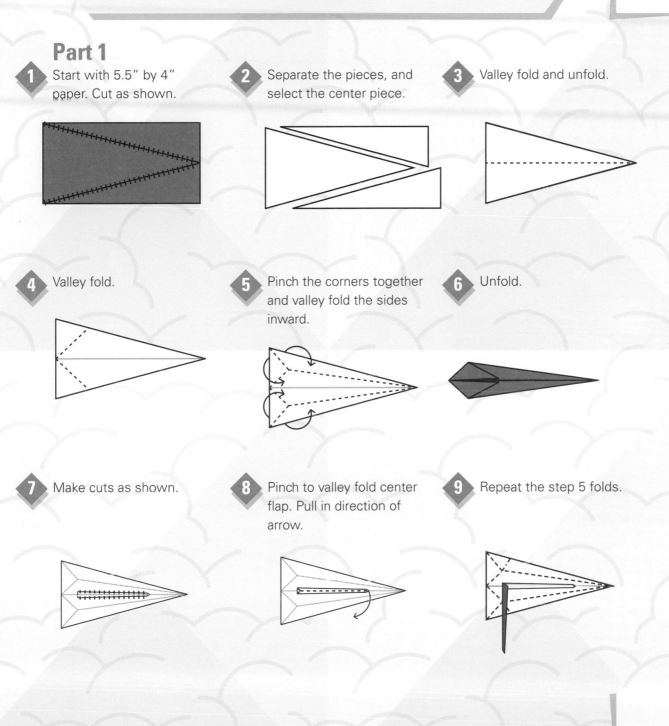

10 Mountain fold the lower portion in half upward, and pull the flap to the left.

11 Valley fold both front and back.

12 Inside reverse fold.

13 Crimp fold.

14 Inside reverse fold.

15 Inside reverse fold.

16 Crimp fold.

17 Completed part 1 of stork.

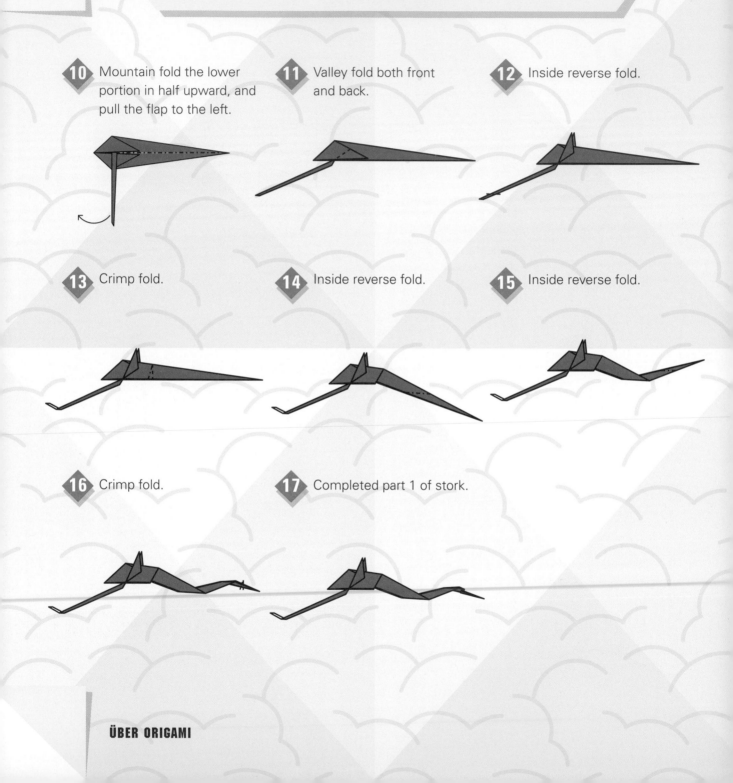

Part 2

1 Select a triangular piece. Valley fold and unfold

2 Valley fold.

3 Repeat with second piece. Completed wing sections.

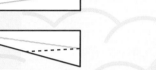

To Attach

1 Join all parts together and apply glue to hold.

2 Valley fold wings outward.

3 Mountain fold wings.

4 Make cuts as shown to trim and "feather" wings. Stretch wings outward.

5 Add coloring and detail.

6 Completed Stork.

HUMMINGBIRD

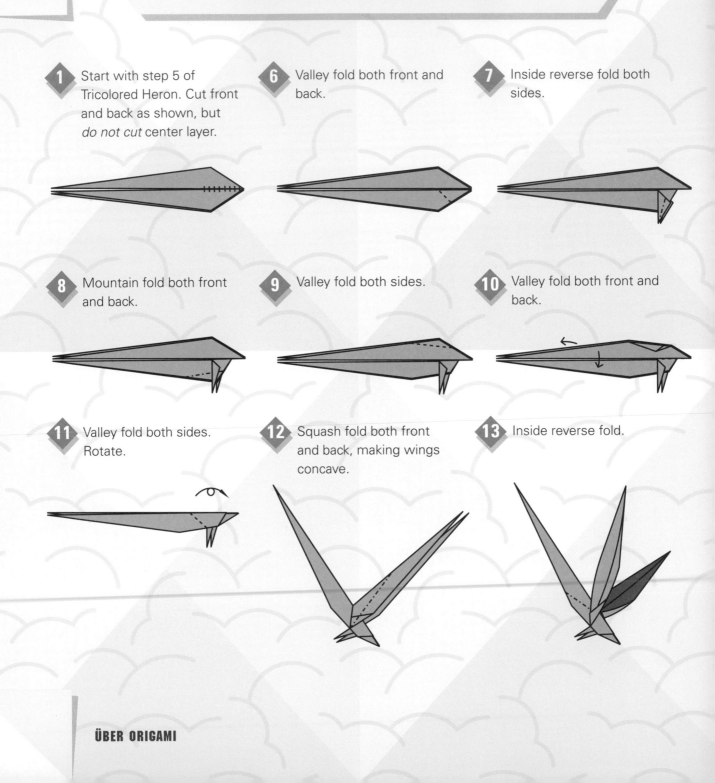

1 Start with step 5 of Tricolored Heron. Cut front and back as shown, but *do not cut* center layer.

6 Valley fold both front and back.

7 Inside reverse fold both sides.

8 Mountain fold both front and back.

9 Valley fold both sides.

10 Valley fold both front and back.

11 Valley fold both sides. Rotate.

12 Squash fold both front and back, making wings concave.

13 Inside reverse fold.

14 Outside reverse fold.

15 Crimp fold.

16 Pull and fold in direction of arrow.

17 Mountain fold both front and back.

18 Mountain fold both sides. Add coloring … and supply with flowers.

19 Completed Hummingbird.

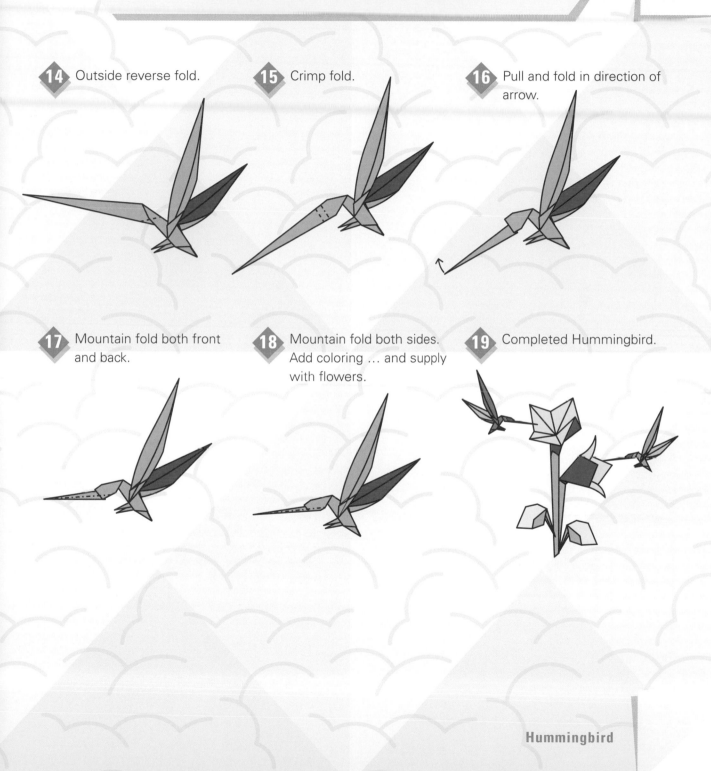

GOOSE

Standing Goose

1 Start with Base Fold IV, using 4″ by 11″ paper. Valley fold both sides.

2 Valley fold to open flaps.

3 Valley fold both front and back.

4 Valley fold back to step 2 position.

5 Make cut to front layer only.

6 Mountain fold.

7 Valley fold.

8 Valley fold.

9 Valley folds.

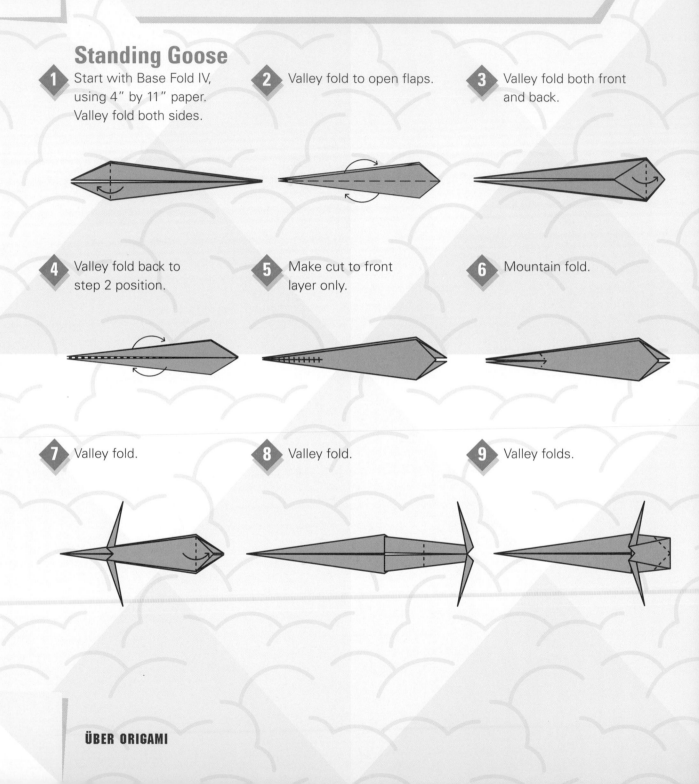

GOOSE

10 Valley fold.

11 Outside reverse fold.

12 Crimp fold.

13 Mountain fold.

14 Inside reverse fold.

15 Outside reverse fold.

16 Pull layers from inside flaps and squash fold open.

17 Pleat fold.

18 Pull and crimp.

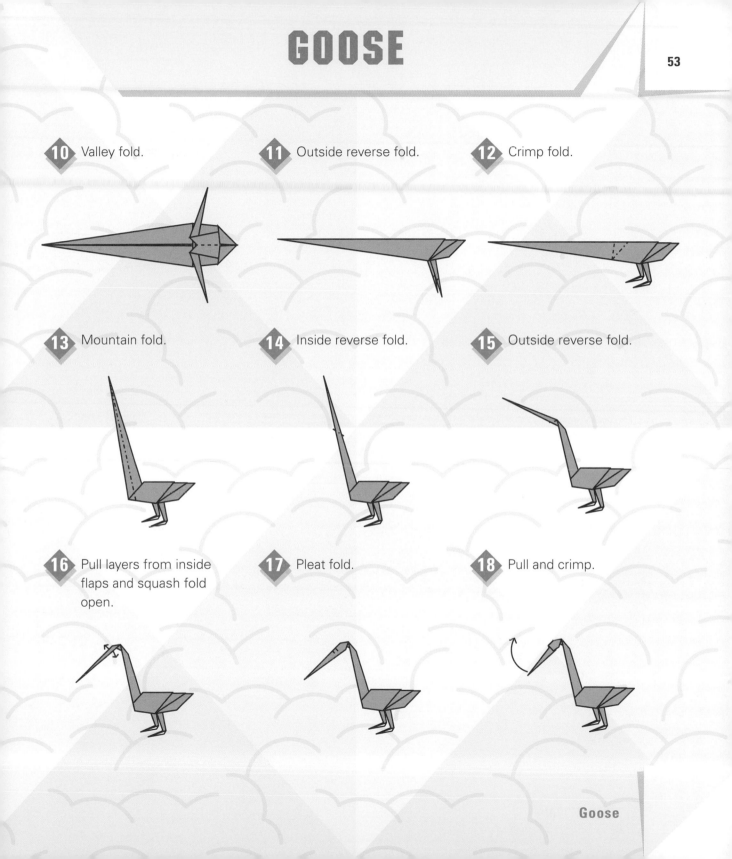

19 Cut as shown.

20 Mountain fold both sides.

21 Add coloring and pattern.

22 Completed Goose (standing).

Feeding Goose

1 Work through to step 14 of Standing Goose (pages 52–54). Inside reverse fold.

15 Inside reverse fold.

16 Inside reverse fold.

17 Cut front layer only, on each side.

18 Valley fold cut part on both sides.

GOOSE

 **19** Pleat fold.

 **20** Cut as shown.

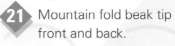 **21** Mountain fold beak tip front and back.

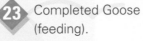

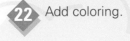 **22** Add coloring.

 **23** Completed Goose (feeding).

PELICAN

1 ## Part 1
Start with Base Fold IV. Valley fold both front and back.

2 Valley fold both sides to open flaps.

3 Valley folds, both front and back.

4 Valley folds back to step 2 position.

5 Cut front layer and valley fold cut parts.

6 Mountain fold in half.

7 Pull both sides as shown and squash fold into position.

8 Valley fold both front and back.

9 Make cuts both front and back.

10 Outside reverse fold.

11 Outside reverse fold.

12 Inside reverse fold.

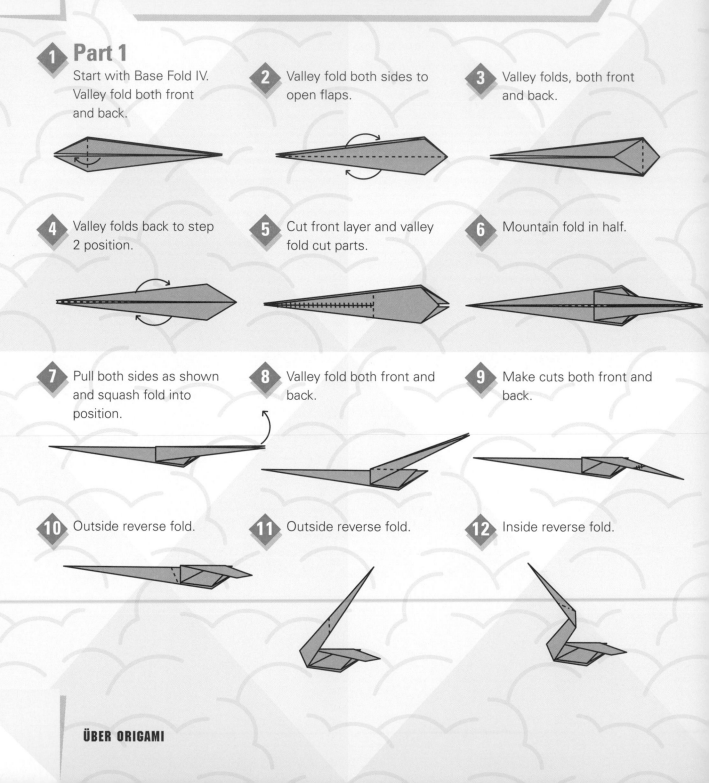

PELICAN

13 Outside reverse fold.

14 Valley fold both sides.

15 Unfold to balance both sides.

16 Completed part 1 of pelican.

Part 2

1 Start with Base Fold IV. Valley fold both sides.

2 Valley fold both sides to open flaps.

3 Valley folds, both front and back.

4 Valley folds back to step 2 position.

5 Make cut to front layer only.

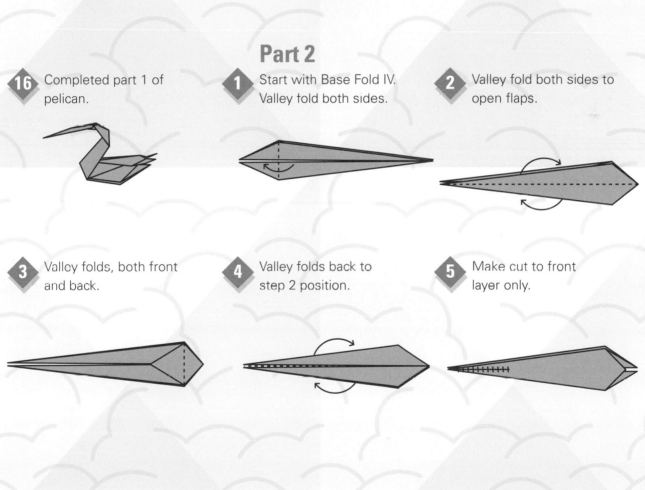

PELICAN

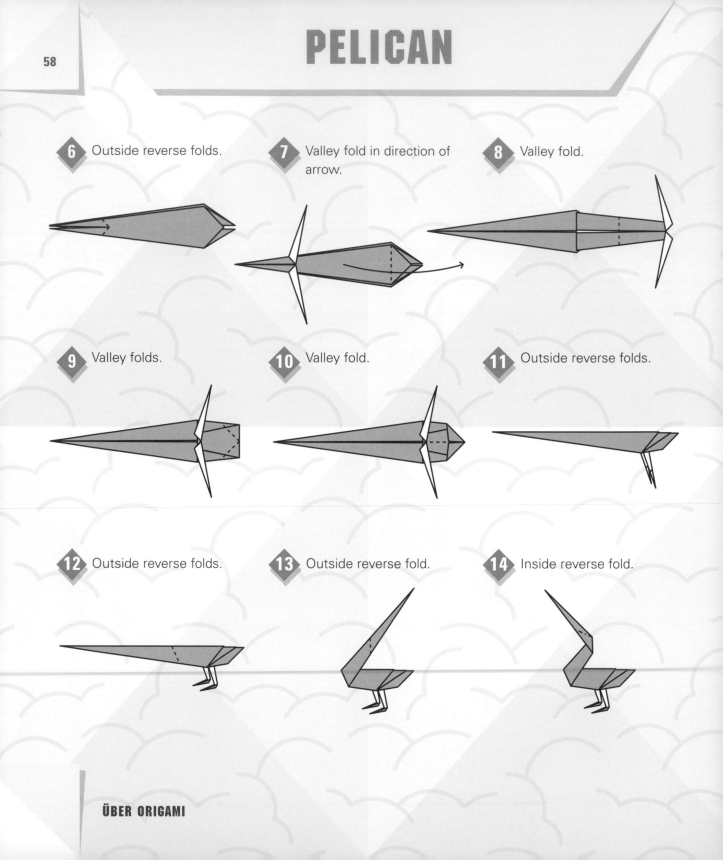

6 Outside reverse folds.

7 Valley fold in direction of arrow.

8 Valley fold.

9 Valley folds.

10 Valley fold.

11 Outside reverse folds.

12 Outside reverse folds.

13 Outside reverse fold.

14 Inside reverse fold.

PELICAN

15 Cut outer layer on both sides.

16 Valley fold both cut parts.

17 Outside reverse fold.

18 Completed part 2 of pelican.

To Attach

1 Join both parts together as shown and apply glue to hold.

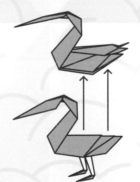

2 Cut both tips to shape beak.

3 Completed Pelican.

CARDINAL

Part 1

1 Start with Base Fold III. Valley fold in half.

2 Inside reverse fold both flaps together.

3 Crimp fold outer flap only.

4 Inside reverse fold.

5 Valley fold front and back.

6 Valley fold both sides.

7 Squash fold both sides.

8 Rotate.

9 Completed part 1 of cardinal.

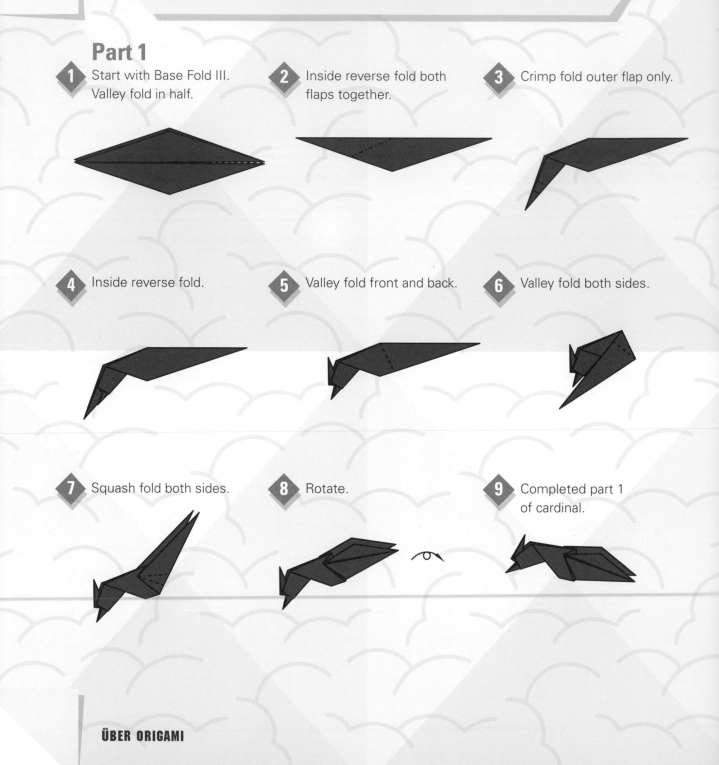

Part 2

1 Start with Base Fold III. Valley fold top flap to the left.

2 Valley fold.

3 Valley fold.

4 Make cuts as shown.

5 Valley fold cut parts.

6 Valley fold.

7 Valley fold.

8 Valley fold in half.

9 Inside reverse fold, both front and back.

10 Valley fold both sides.

11 Mountain folds.

12 Inside reverse fold both sides.

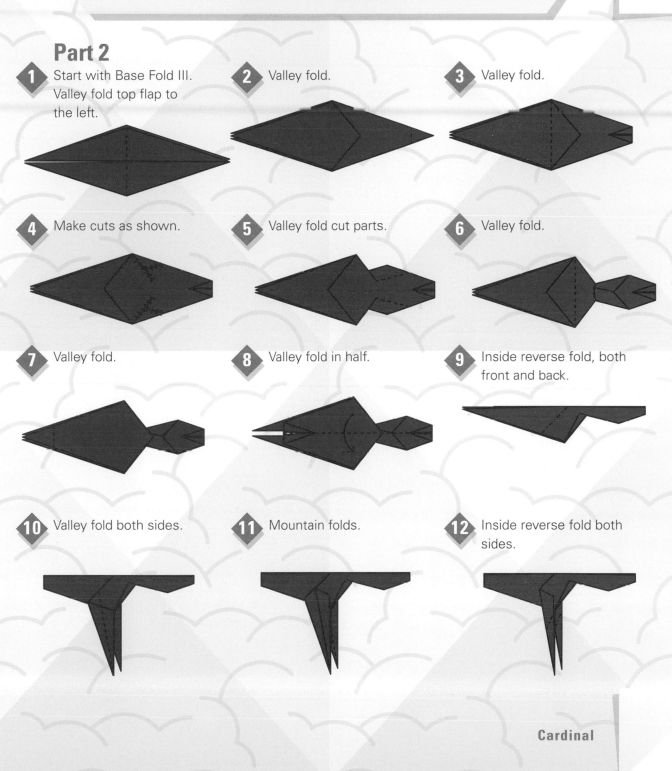

CARDINAL

13 Outside reverse folds.

14 Inside reverse fold both sides.

15 Inside reverse fold both sides.

To Attach

16 Completed part 2 of cardinal.

1 Join both parts together as shown and apply glue to hold.

2 Add colors and patterning to completion.

3 Completed Cardinal.

PARROT

Part 1

1 Start with Base Fold IV. Inside reverse folds.

2 Mountain fold both sides.

3 Valley fold both sides.

4 Inside reverse folds.

5 Mountain fold in half.

6 Outside reverse fold top layer.

7 Cut as shown.

8 Rotate.

9 Inside reverse fold.

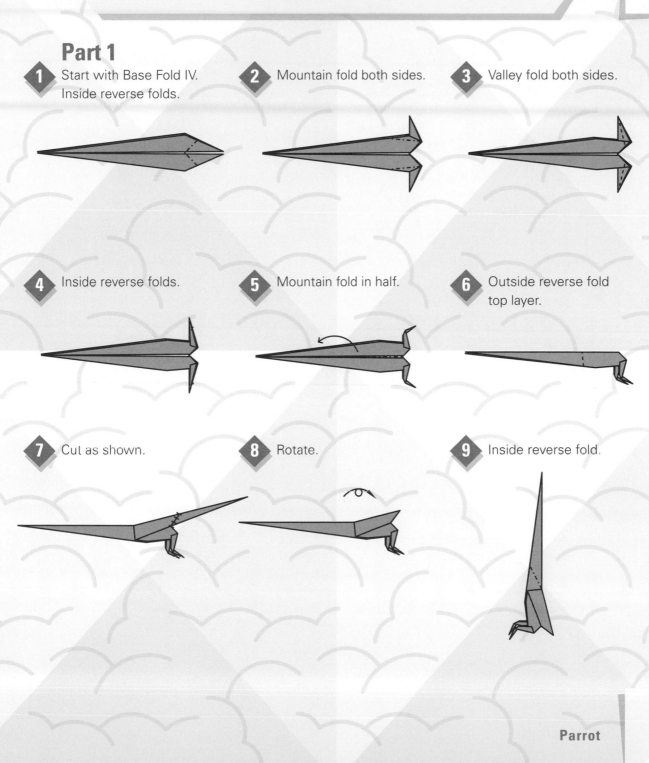

PARROT

10 Outside reverse fold.

11 Pleat fold.

12 Pull and squash to crimp.

13 Inside reverse fold.

14 Cut through all layers.

15 Cut on fold to separate.

16 Completed part 1 of parrot.

Part 2

1 Start with Base Fold IV. Valley fold both sides.

2 Valley fold front and back to open flaps.

PARROT

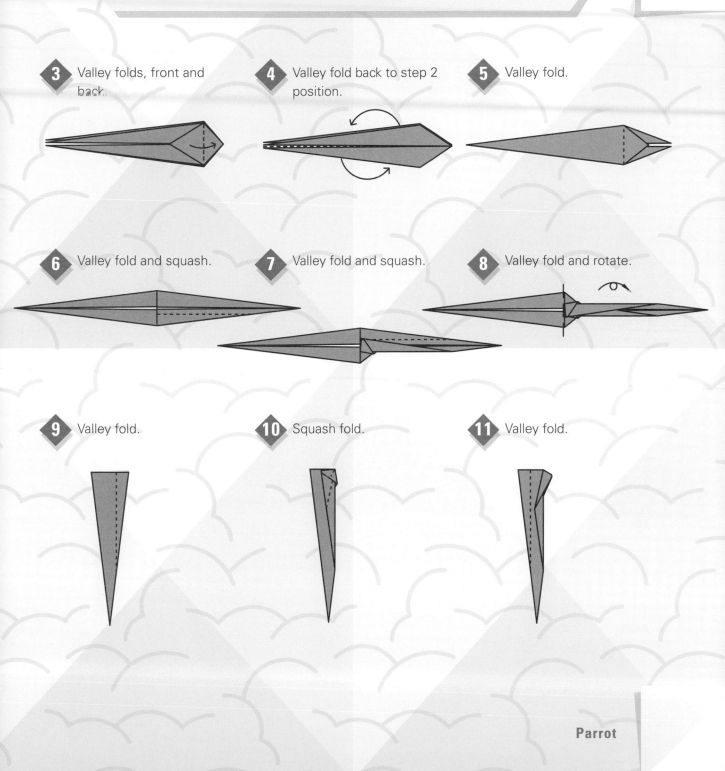

3 Valley folds, front and back.

4 Valley fold back to step 2 position.

5 Valley fold.

6 Valley fold and squash.

7 Valley fold and squash.

8 Valley fold and rotate.

9 Valley fold.

10 Squash fold.

11 Valley fold.

Parrot

PARROT

 Squash fold.

 Valley fold in half.

14 Completed part 2 of parrot.

To Attach

1 Join both parts together as shown and apply glue to hold.

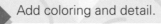 Add coloring and detail.

3 Completed Parrot.

DUCK

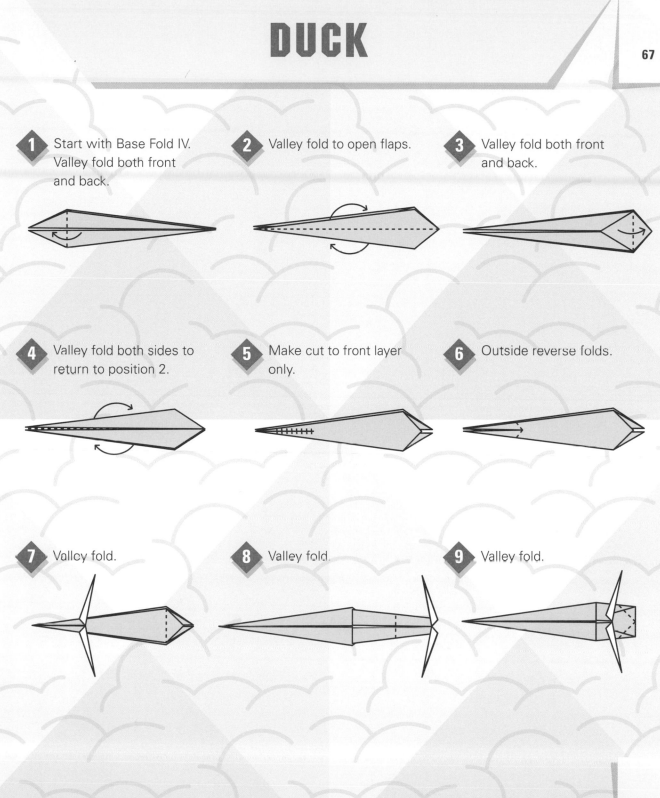

1 Start with Base Fold IV. Valley fold both front and back.

2 Valley fold to open flaps.

3 Valley fold both front and back.

4 Valley fold both sides to return to position 2.

5 Make cut to front layer only.

6 Outside reverse folds.

7 Valley fold.

8 Valley fold.

9 Valley fold.

DUCK

10 Valley fold in half.

11 Outside reverse folds.

12 See blow-ups for detail.

13 Inside reverse both sides.

14 Mountain fold both sides.

15 Valley fold each foot to side.

16 Valley fold both sides.

17 Back to full view.

18 Crimp fold.

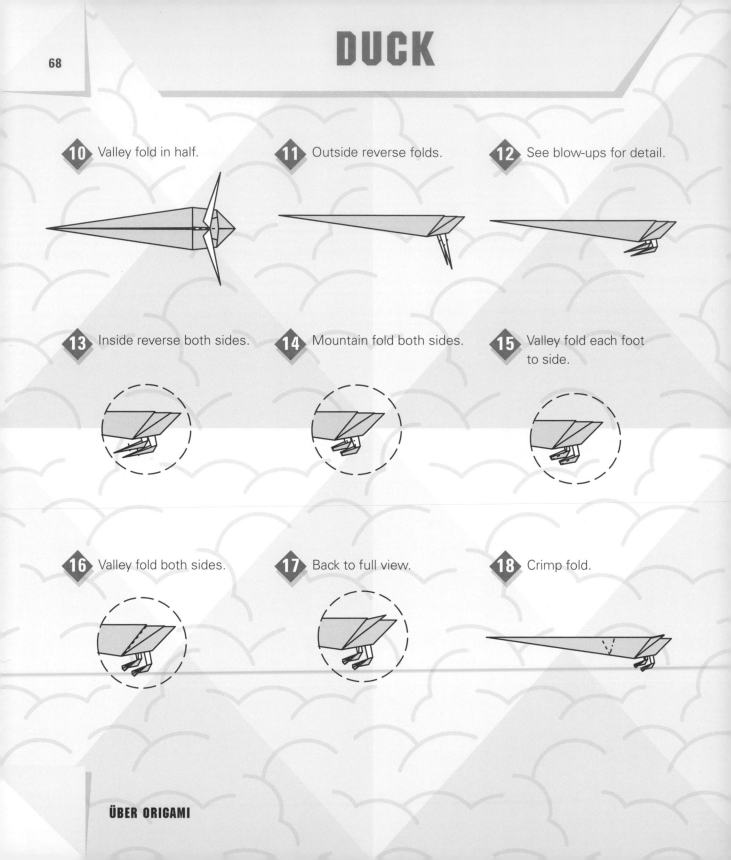

DUCK

19 Inside reverse fold.

20 Outside reverse fold.

21 Pleat fold.

22 Pull in direction of arrow and crimp fold.

23 Cut as shown.

24 Valley fold both sides and rotate upright.

25 Add color and detail.

26 Completed Duck.

Duck

PENGUIN

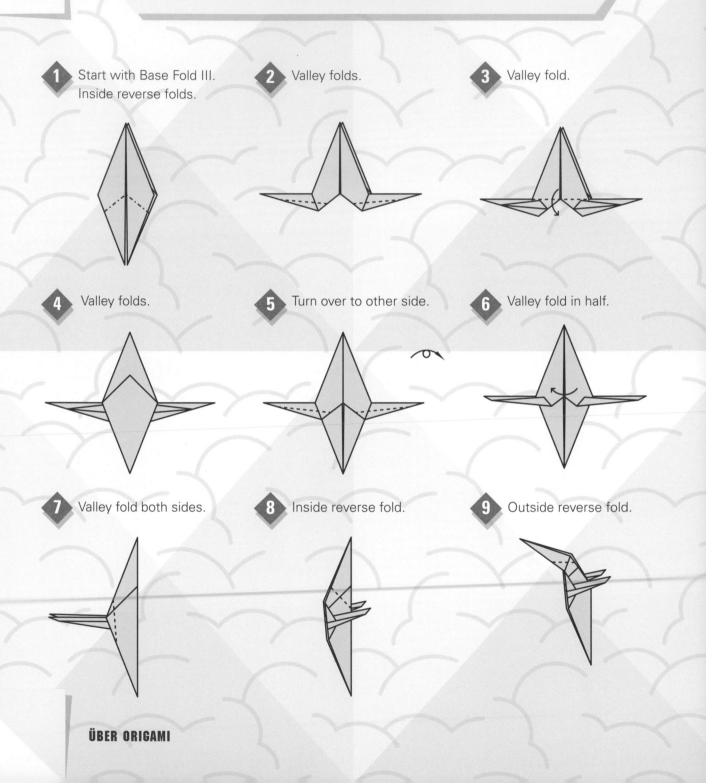

1 Start with Base Fold III. Inside reverse folds.

2 Valley folds.

3 Valley fold.

4 Valley folds.

5 Turn over to other side.

6 Valley fold in half.

7 Valley fold both sides.

8 Inside reverse fold.

9 Outside reverse fold.

PENGUIN

10 Pleat fold.

11 Cut as shown.

12 Mountain fold both sides.

13 Add coloring if you wish.

14 Completed Penguin.

TURKEY

1 Start with Base Fold III and valley fold both sides.

2 Valley fold.

3 Make cuts as shown, then valley folds.

4 Valley fold both front and back.

5 Make cuts front and back.

6 Valley fold cut parts both sides.

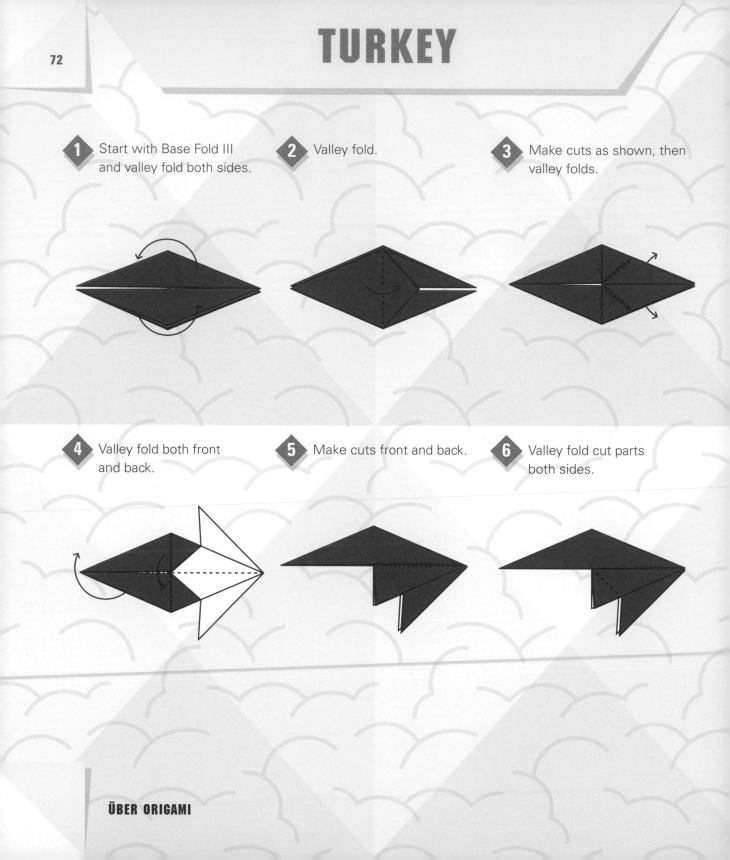

TURKEY

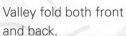

7 Valley fold both front and back.

8 Outside reverse folds front and back.

9 Outside reverse folds front and back.

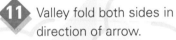

10 Inside reverse folds front and back.

11 Valley fold both sides in direction of arrow.

12 Valley folds front and back.

TURKEY

13 Valley folds front and back.

14 Valley folds front and back.

15 Cuts as shown, to both sides.

16 Mountain folds front and back.

17 Outside reverse folds.

18 Outside reverse fold.

19 Cut edge, then valley fold.

20 Mountain fold.

21 Completed Turkey.

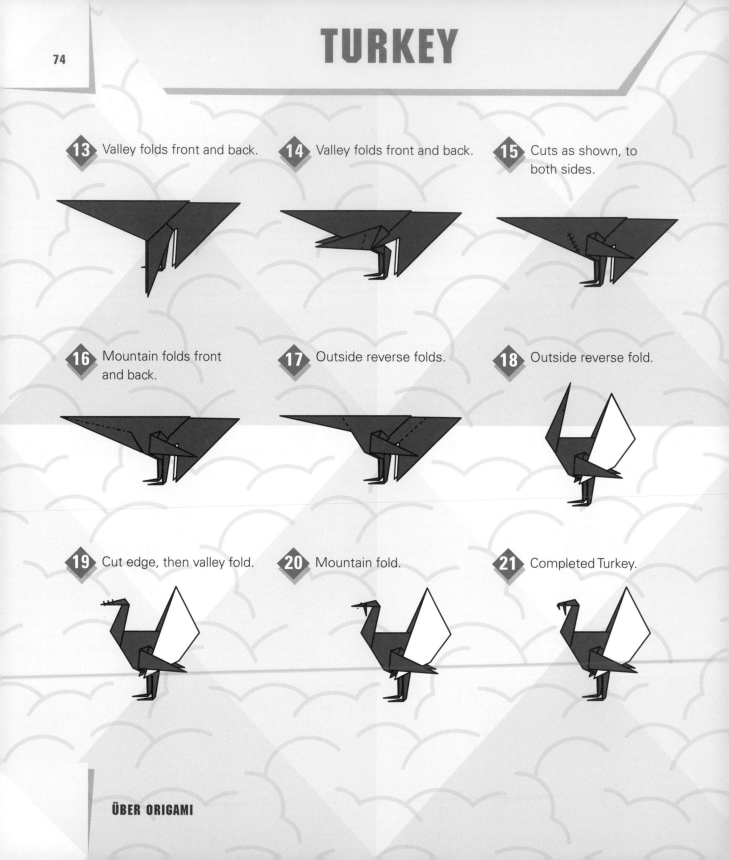

Part 1

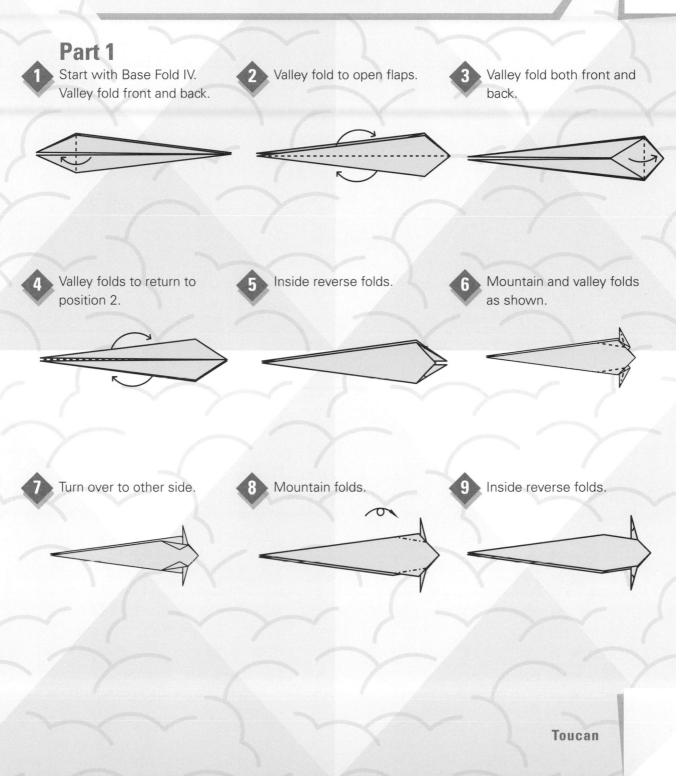

1 Start with Base Fold IV. Valley fold front and back.

2 Valley fold to open flaps.

3 Valley fold both front and back.

4 Valley folds to return to position 2.

5 Inside reverse folds.

6 Mountain and valley folds as shown.

7 Turn over to other side.

8 Mountain folds.

9 Inside reverse folds.

TOUCAN

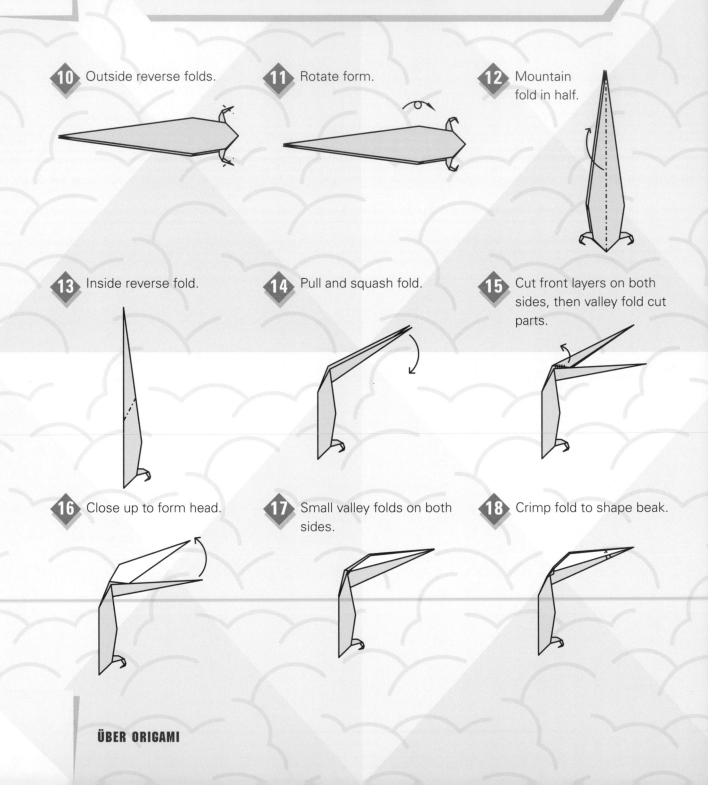

10 Outside reverse folds.

11 Rotate form.

12 Mountain fold in half.

13 Inside reverse fold.

14 Pull and squash fold.

15 Cut front layers on both sides, then valley fold cut parts.

16 Close up to form head.

17 Small valley folds on both sides.

18 Crimp fold to shape beak.

TOUCAN

Part 2

19 Completed part 1 of toucan.

1 Start with Base Fold IV. Valley fold both sides.

2 Valley fold both sides to open flaps.

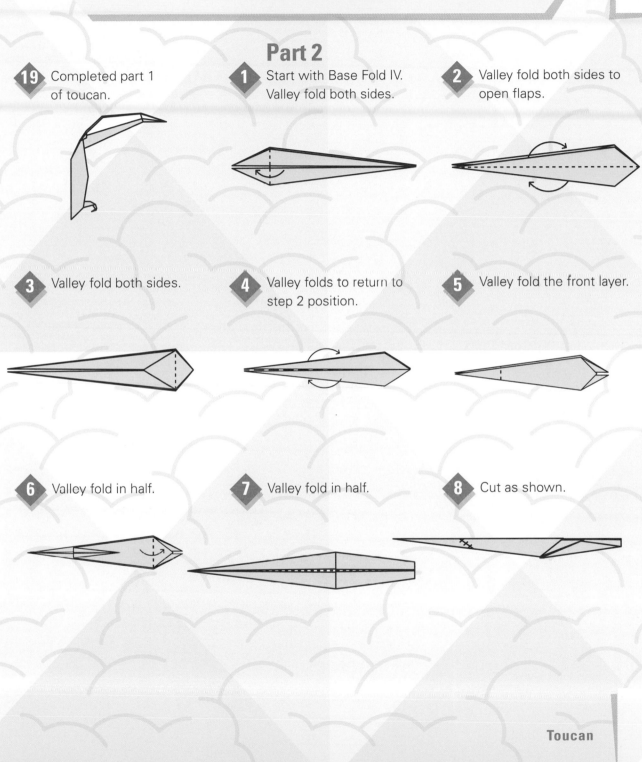

3 Valley fold both sides.

4 Valley folds to return to step 2 position.

5 Valley fold the front layer.

6 Valley fold in half.

7 Valley fold in half.

8 Cut as shown.

TOUCAN

9 Inside reverse fold.

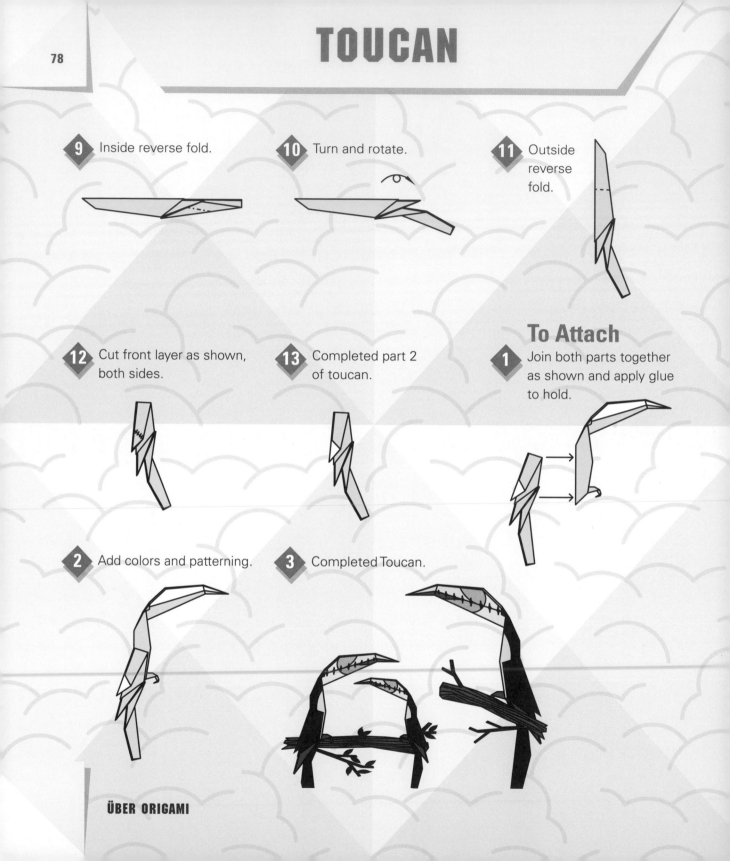

10 Turn and rotate.

11 Outside reverse fold.

12 Cut front layer as shown, both sides.

13 Completed part 2 of toucan.

To Attach

1 Join both parts together as shown and apply glue to hold.

2 Add colors and patterning.

3 Completed Toucan.

COCKATOO

Part 1

1 Start with Base Fold IV. Valley folds front and back.

2 Valley fold both sides to open flaps.

3 Valley folds both front and back.

4 Valley fold both sides to return to step 2 position.

5 Inside reverse folds.

6 Valley folds both front and back.

7 Inside reverse folds.

8 Valley fold in half.

9 Rotate form.

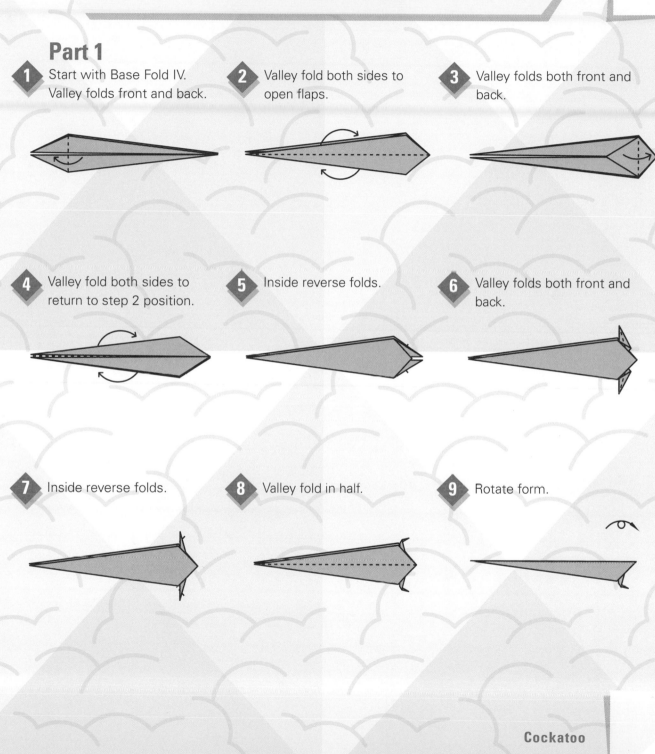

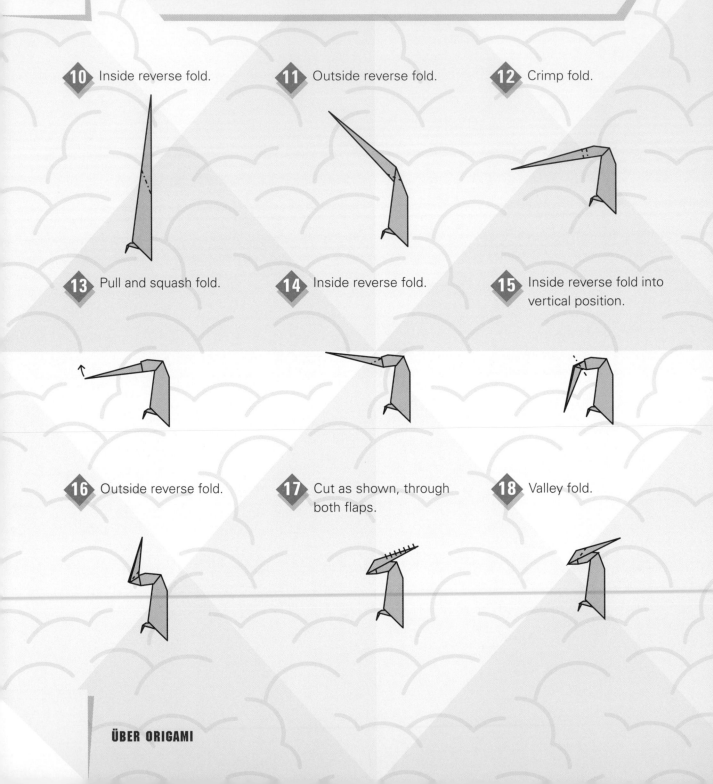

10 Inside reverse fold.

11 Outside reverse fold.

12 Crimp fold.

13 Pull and squash fold.

14 Inside reverse fold.

15 Inside reverse fold into vertical position.

16 Outside reverse fold.

17 Cut as shown, through both flaps.

18 Valley fold.

COCKATOO

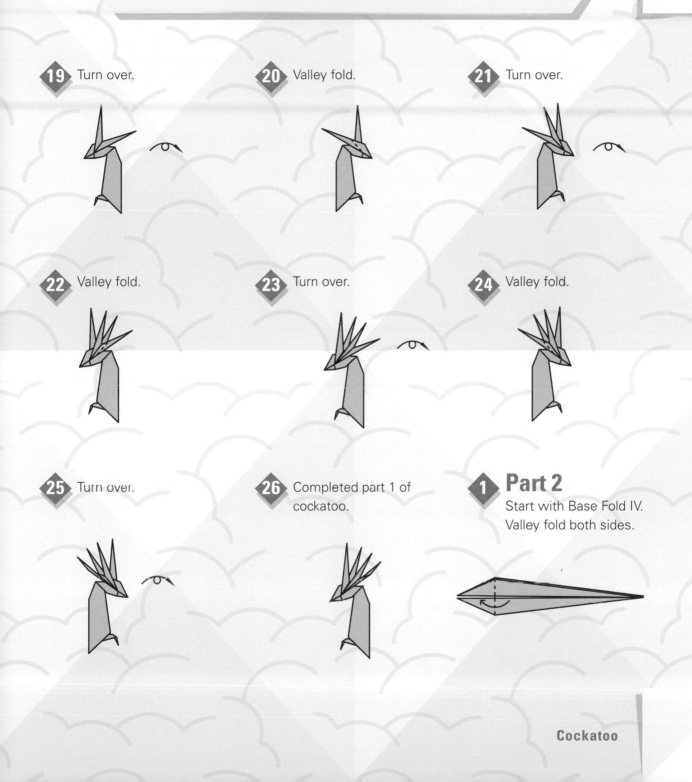

19 Turn over.

20 Valley fold.

21 Turn over.

22 Valley fold.

23 Turn over.

24 Valley fold.

25 Turn over.

26 Completed part 1 of cockatoo.

1 **Part 2**
Start with Base Fold IV. Valley fold both sides.

COCKATOO

2 Valley fold both sides to open flaps.

3 Valley fold both sides.

4 Valley fold sides back to step 2 position.

5 Valley fold as shown by arrow.

6 Make cuts as shown.

7 Valley fold in half.

8 Outside reverse fold.

9 Rotate.

10 Valley fold wings and inside reverse fold tail.

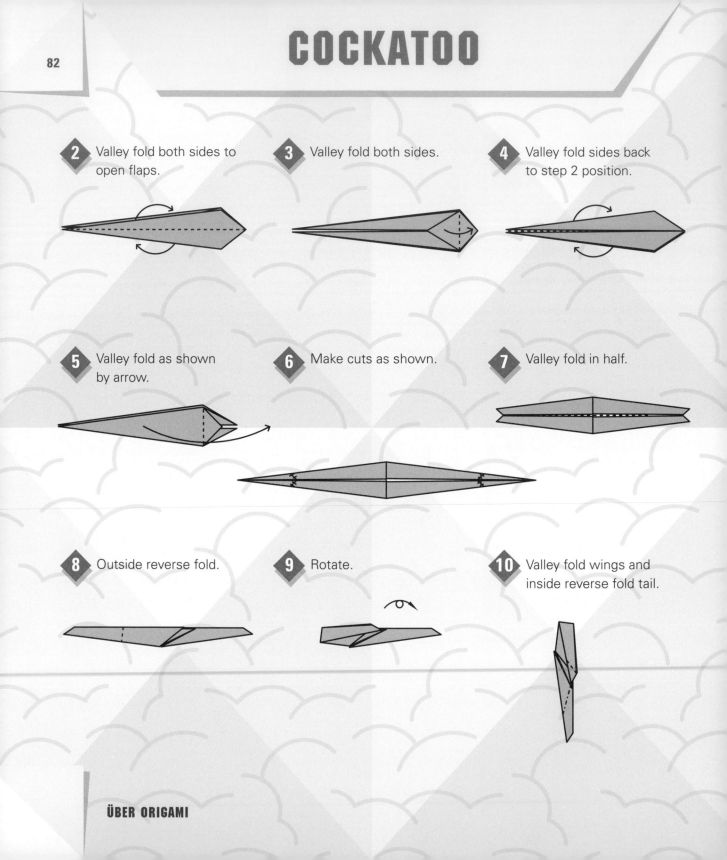

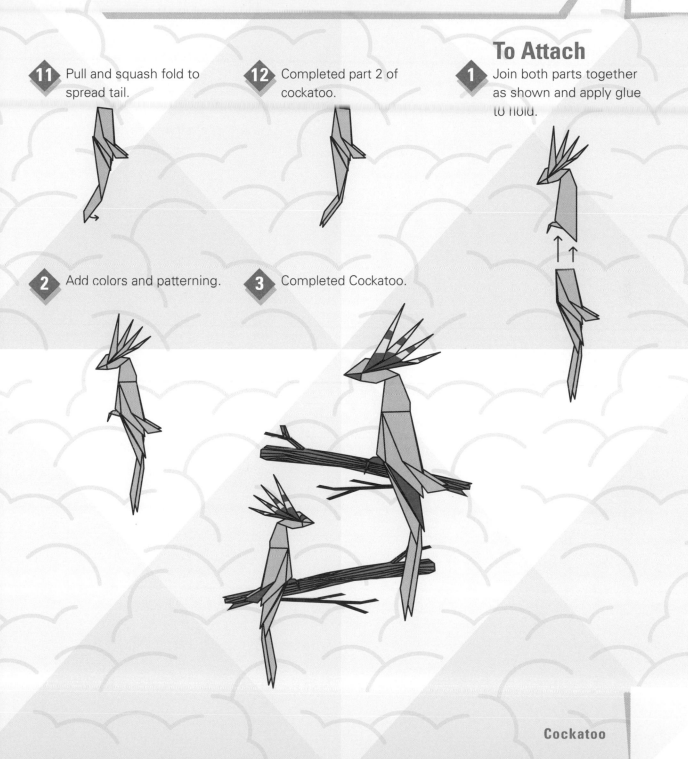

11 Pull and squash fold to spread tail.

12 Completed part 2 of cockatoo.

To Attach

1 Join both parts together as shown and apply glue to hold.

2 Add colors and patterning.

3 Completed Cockatoo.

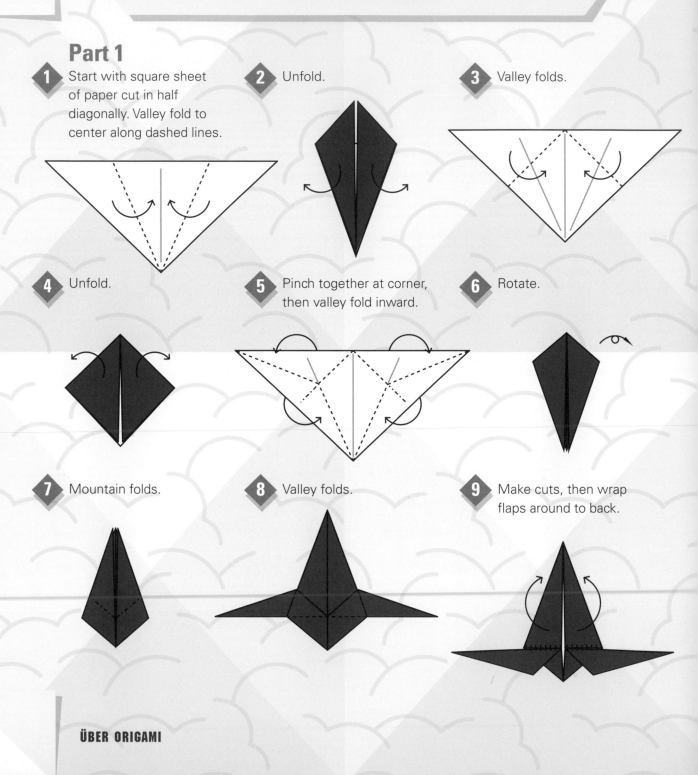

VULTURE

Part 1

1 Start with square sheet of paper cut in half diagonally. Valley fold to center along dashed lines.

2 Unfold.

3 Valley folds.

4 Unfold.

5 Pinch together at corner, then valley fold inward.

6 Rotate.

7 Mountain folds.

8 Valley folds.

9 Make cuts, then wrap flaps around to back.

VULTURE

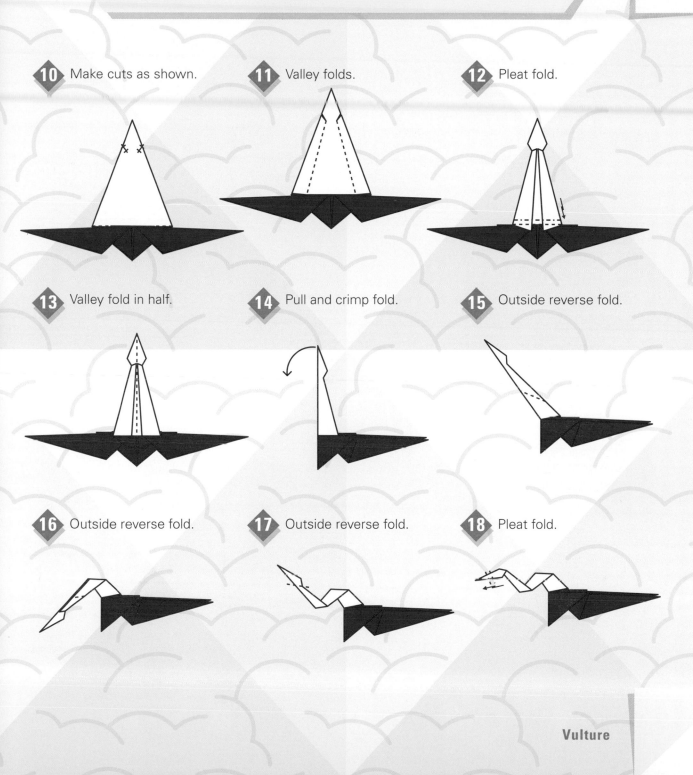

10 Make cuts as shown.

11 Valley folds.

12 Pleat fold.

13 Valley fold in half.

14 Pull and crimp fold.

15 Outside reverse fold.

16 Outside reverse fold.

17 Outside reverse fold.

18 Pleat fold.

Vulture

VULTURE

19 Inside reverse fold.

20 Mountain folds through inside, front and back.

21 Valley folds front and back.

22 Inside reverse fold.

23 Mountain folds front and back.

24 Make cuts as shown.

25 Complete part 1 (front) of vulture.

Part 2

1 Start with step 6 of Part 1, then mountain fold in half and rotate.

7 Valley folds to left, both sides.

VULTURE

8 Valley and squash folds both sides.

9 Mountain folds front and back.

10 Inside reverse fold.

11 Valley folds.

12 Outside reverse fold.

13 Mountain folds front and back.

14 Outside reverse folds.

15 Outside reverse folds.

16 Valley folds to front and back, each foot.

VULTURE

17 Outside reverse fold, for back claws.

18 Complete part 2 (rear) of vulture.

To Attach

1 Join head and wings (part 1) to body. Glue to secure.

2 Completed Vulture.

WILD DUCK

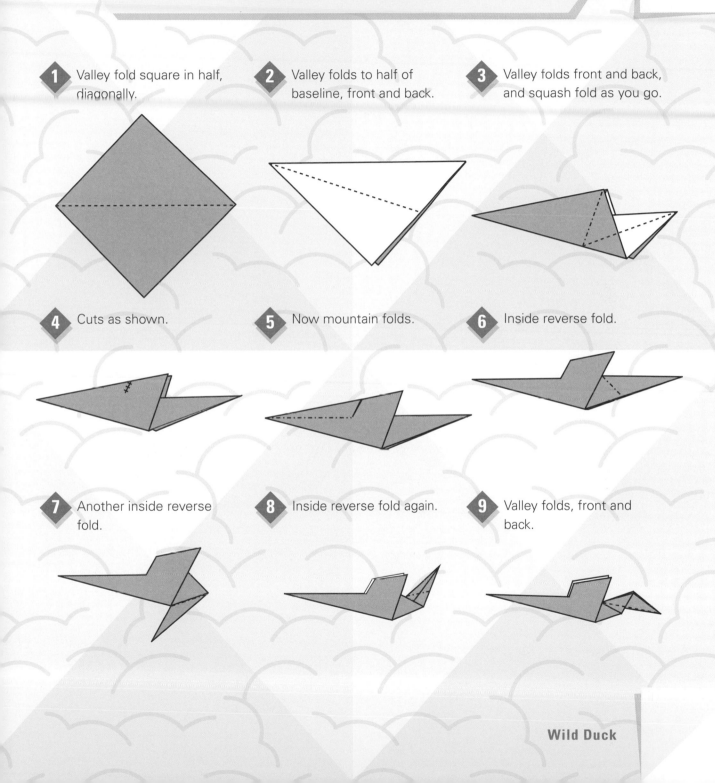

1 Valley fold square in half, diagonally.

2 Valley folds to half of baseline, front and back.

3 Valley folds front and back, and squash fold as you go.

4 Cuts as shown.

5 Now mountain folds.

6 Inside reverse fold.

7 Another inside reverse fold.

8 Inside reverse fold again.

9 Valley folds, front and back.

Wild Duck

WILD DUCK

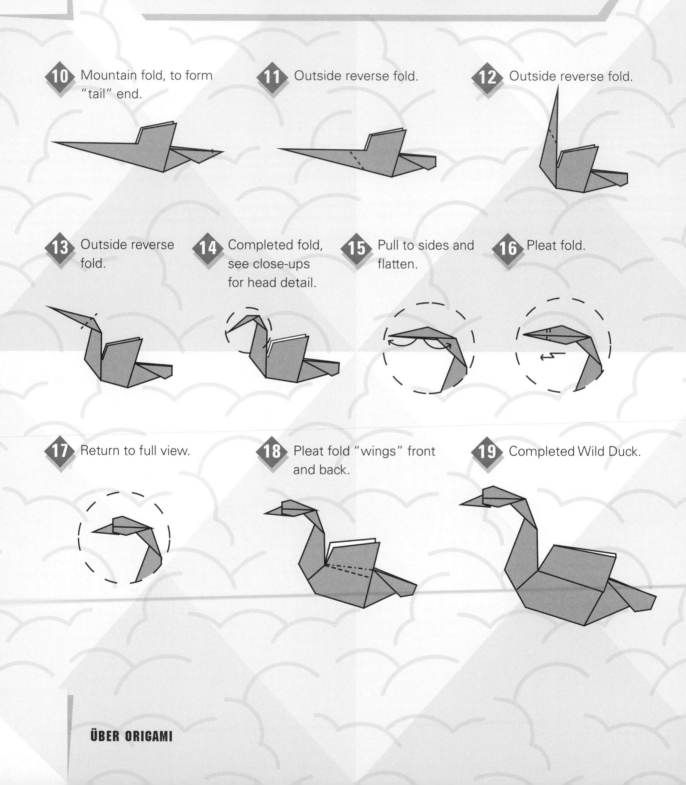

10 Mountain fold, to form "tail" end.

11 Outside reverse fold.

12 Outside reverse fold.

13 Outside reverse fold.

14 Completed fold, see close-ups for head detail.

15 Pull to sides and flatten.

16 Pleat fold.

17 Return to full view.

18 Pleat fold "wings" front and back.

19 Completed Wild Duck.

FLAMINGO

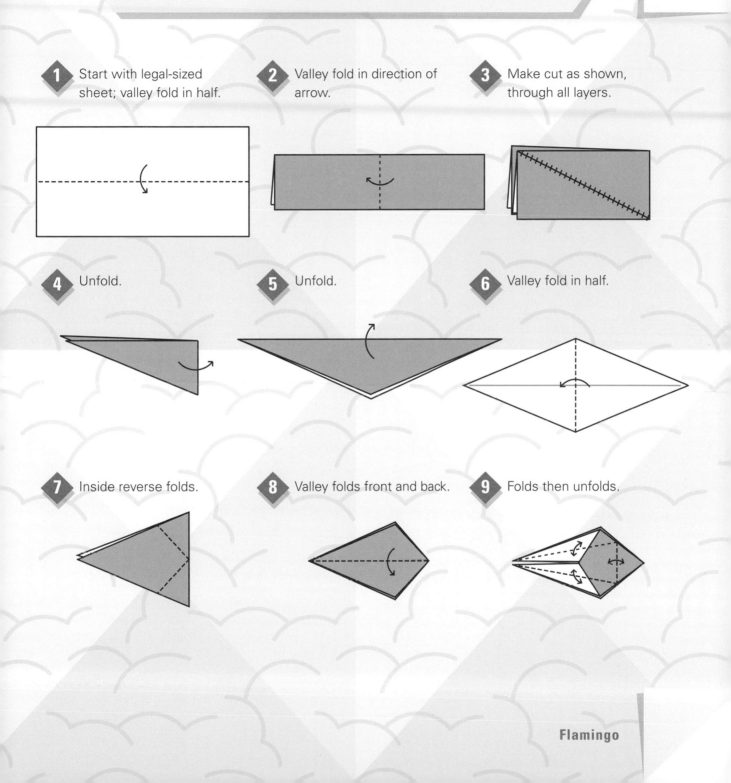

1 Start with legal-sized sheet; valley fold in half.

2 Valley fold in direction of arrow.

3 Make cut as shown, through all layers.

4 Unfold.

5 Unfold.

6 Valley fold in half.

7 Inside reverse folds.

8 Valley folds front and back.

9 Folds then unfolds.

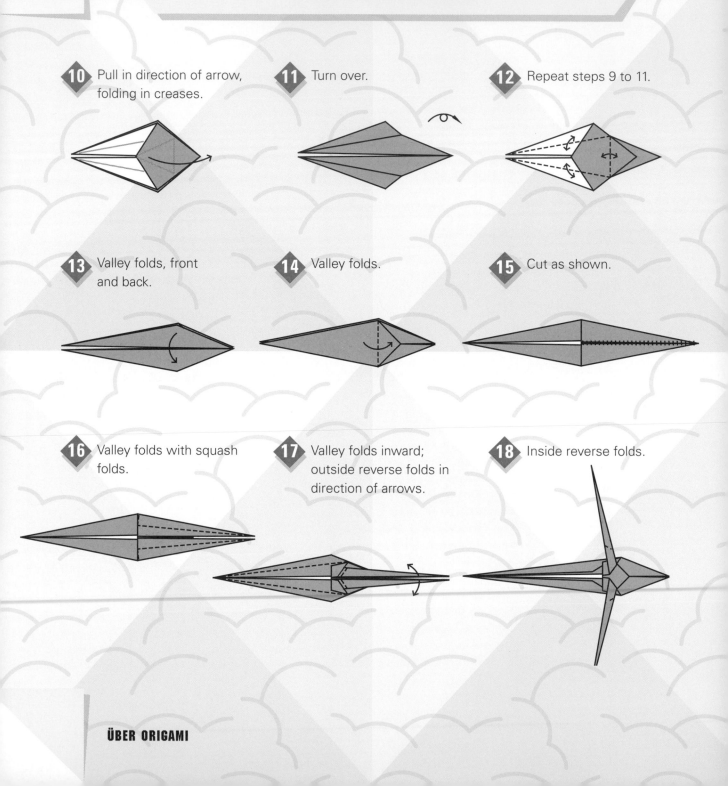

10 Pull in direction of arrow, folding in creases.

11 Turn over.

12 Repeat steps 9 to 11.

13 Valley folds, front and back.

14 Valley folds.

15 Cut as shown.

16 Valley folds with squash folds.

17 Valley folds inward; outside reverse folds in direction of arrows.

18 Inside reverse folds.

FLAMINGO

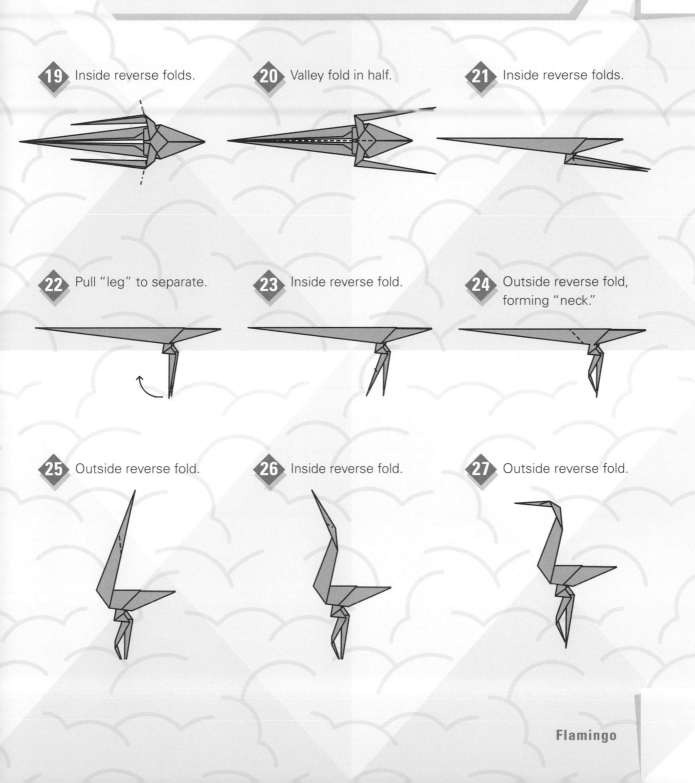

19 Inside reverse folds.

20 Valley fold in half.

21 Inside reverse folds.

22 Pull "leg" to separate.

23 Inside reverse fold.

24 Outside reverse fold, forming "neck."

25 Outside reverse fold.

26 Inside reverse fold.

27 Outside reverse fold.

Flamingo

FLAMINGO

28 Pull paper out to sides and flatten to form "head."

29 Pleat fold for "beak."

30 Inside reverse fold.

31 Completed Flamingo... and friends.

ELECTRIC EEL

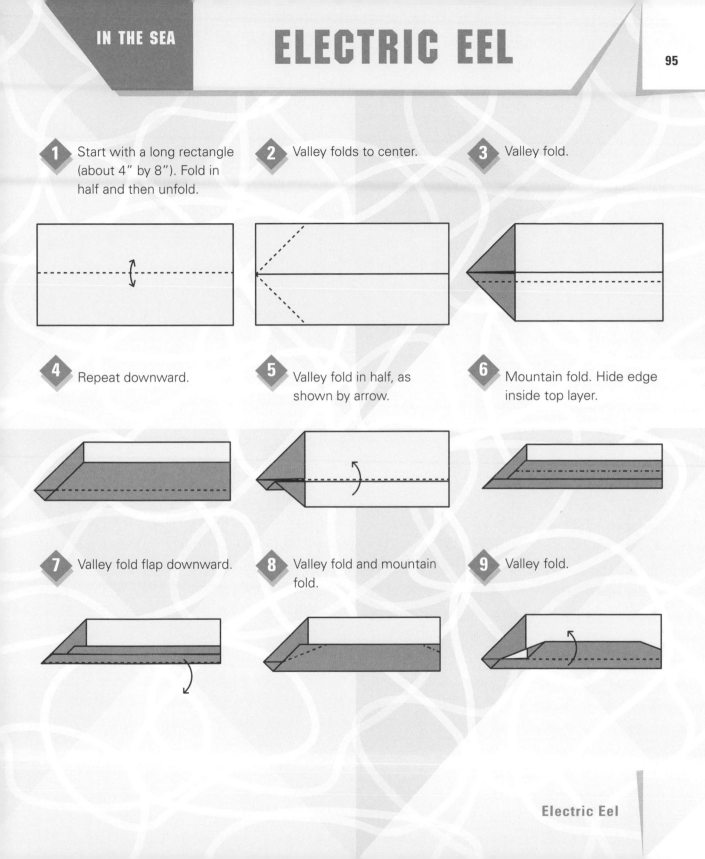

1 Start with a long rectangle (about 4" by 8"). Fold in half and then unfold.

2 Valley folds to center.

3 Valley fold.

4 Repeat downward.

5 Valley fold in half, as shown by arrow.

6 Mountain fold. Hide edge inside top layer.

7 Valley fold flap downward.

8 Valley fold and mountain fold.

9 Valley fold.

ELECTRIC EEL

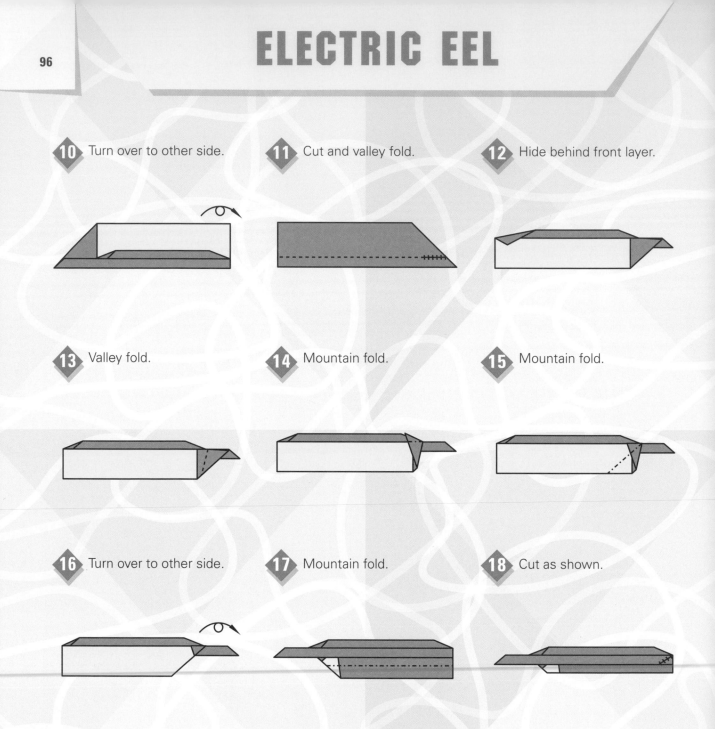

10 Turn over to other side.

11 Cut and valley fold.

12 Hide behind front layer.

13 Valley fold.

14 Mountain fold.

15 Mountain fold.

16 Turn over to other side.

17 Mountain fold.

18 Cut as shown.

ELECTRIC EEL

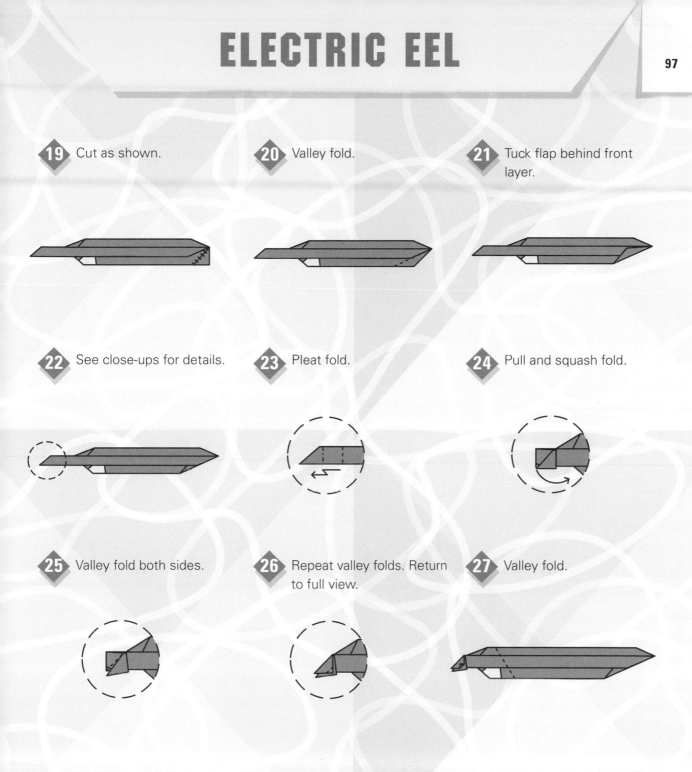

19 Cut as shown.

20 Valley fold.

21 Tuck flap behind front layer.

22 See close-ups for details.

23 Pleat fold.

24 Pull and squash fold.

25 Valley fold both sides.

26 Repeat valley folds. Return to full view.

27 Valley fold.

ELECTRIC EEL

28 Valley fold.

29 Valley fold.

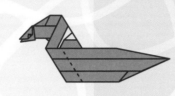

30 Valley fold.

31 Press and pull firmly at the folds to form into curves.

32 Completed Electric Eel.

Part 1

1 Start with Base Fold III. Pleat fold through all layers.

2 Repeat pleat fold through layers.

3 Make cuts as shown (to top layer only).

4 Valley folds.

5 Valley fold in half.

6 Pull and crimp fold.

7 Pull and crimp fold.

8 Mountain fold.

9 Valley folds.

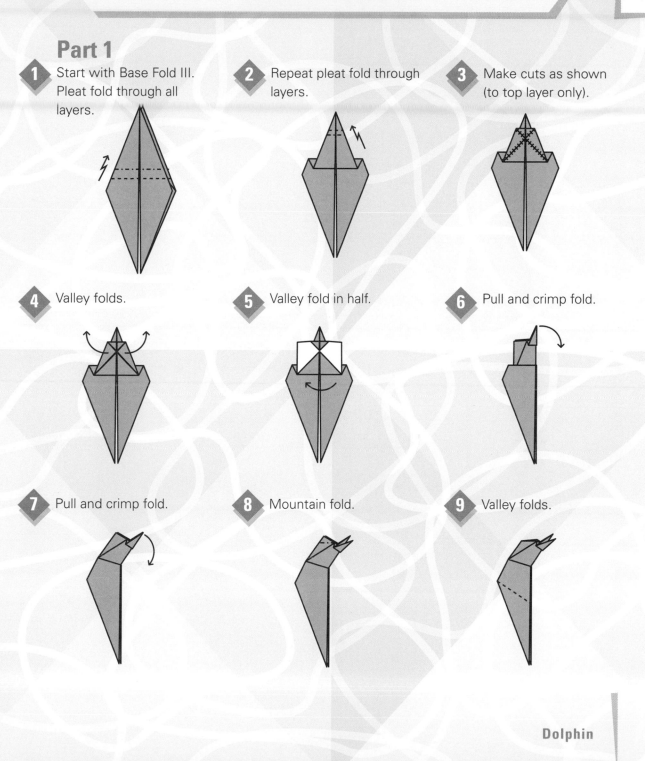

Dolphin

DOLPHIN

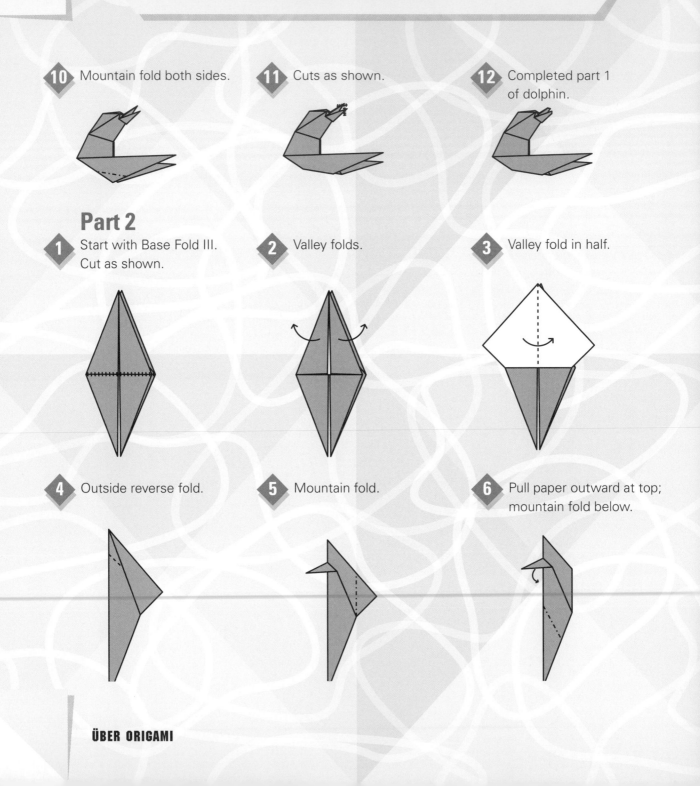

10 Mountain fold both sides.

11 Cuts as shown.

12 Completed part 1 of dolphin.

Part 2

1 Start with Base Fold III. Cut as shown.

2 Valley folds.

3 Valley fold in half.

4 Outside reverse fold.

5 Mountain fold.

6 Pull paper outward at top; mountain fold below.

7 Outside reverse at top. Mountain fold below.

8 Valley fold and glue into position.

9 Completed part 2 of dolphin.

To Attach

1 Join both parts together as shown.

2 Valley fold both sides.

3 Completed Dolphin.

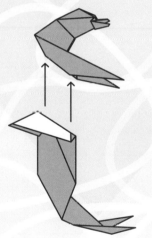

STINGRAY

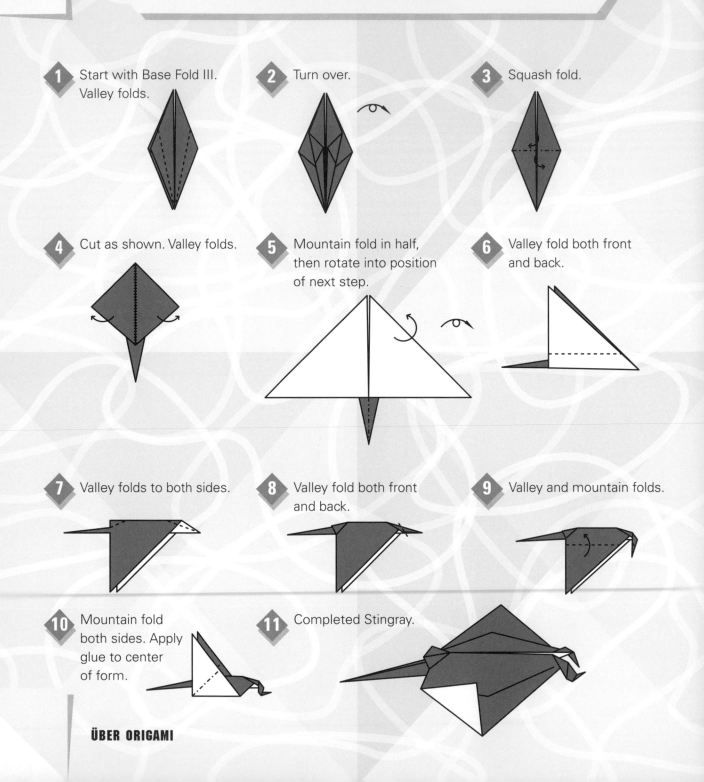

1 Start with Base Fold III. Valley folds.

2 Turn over.

3 Squash fold.

4 Cut as shown. Valley folds.

5 Mountain fold in half, then rotate into position of next step.

6 Valley fold both front and back.

7 Valley folds to both sides.

8 Valley fold both front and back.

9 Valley and mountain folds.

10 Mountain fold both sides. Apply glue to center of form.

11 Completed Stingray.

HAMMERHEAD SHARK

1 Start with Base Fold III. Valley one flap and repeat behind.

2 Cut as shown front and back.

3 Valley fold flap back again. Repeat behind.

4 Valley folds upward.

5 Valley folds.

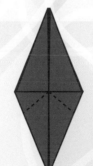

6 Turn over to other side.

7 Valley fold.

8 Turn over to other side.

9 Valley folds.

Hammerhead Shark

10 Pull inner layer out.

11 Valley folds.

12 Make cuts, then valley fold.

13 Valley fold in half. Rotate.

14 Cuts as shown.

15 Valley folds both front and back.

16 Outside reverse fold. Valley fold.

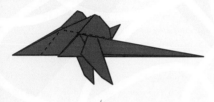

17 Cut edge as shown.

18 Valley fold both front and back.

19 Squash fold both front and back.

20 Valley fold sides outward, to balance.

21 Make cut as shown.

HAMMERHEAD SHARK

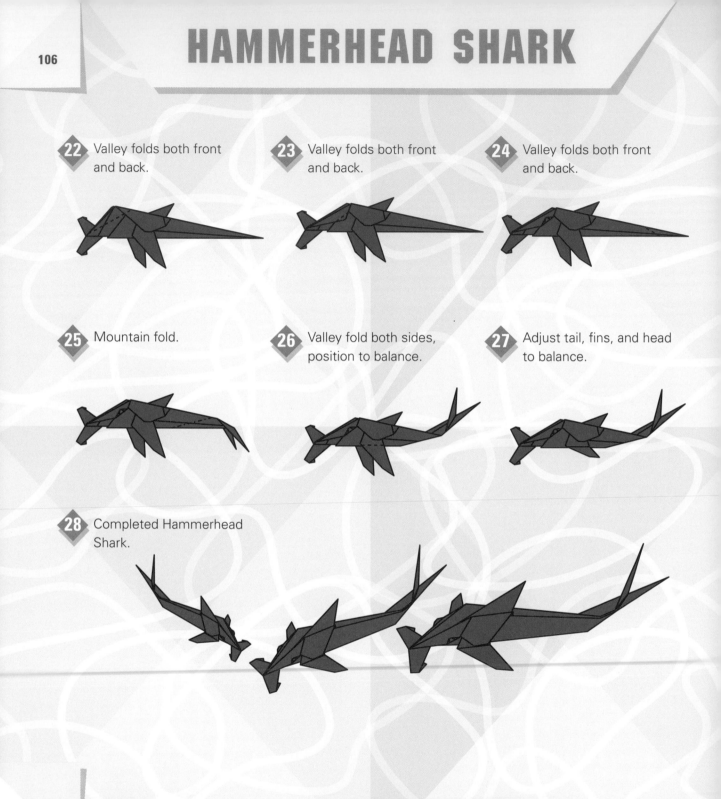

22 Valley folds both front and back.

23 Valley folds both front and back.

24 Valley folds both front and back.

25 Mountain fold.

26 Valley fold both sides, position to balance.

27 Adjust tail, fins, and head to balance.

28 Completed Hammerhead Shark.

HORSESHOE CRAB

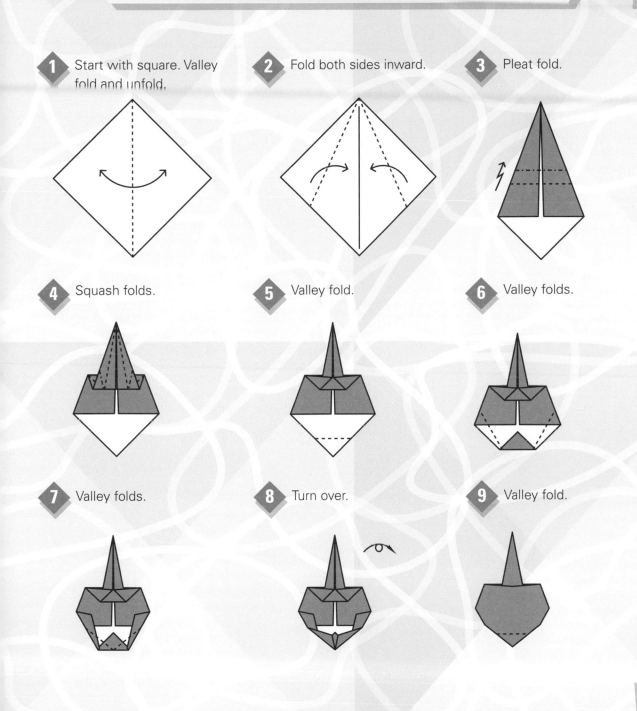

1 Start with square. Valley fold and unfold.

2 Fold both sides inward.

3 Pleat fold.

4 Squash folds.

5 Valley fold.

6 Valley folds.

7 Valley folds.

8 Turn over.

9 Valley fold.

Horseshoe Crab

HORSESHOE CRAB

10 Mountain fold in half.

11 Rotate.

12 Crimp fold.

13 Mountain folds both sides.

14 Valley fold and unfold.

15 Unfold to flatten.

16 Completed Horseshoe Crab.

ANGELFISH

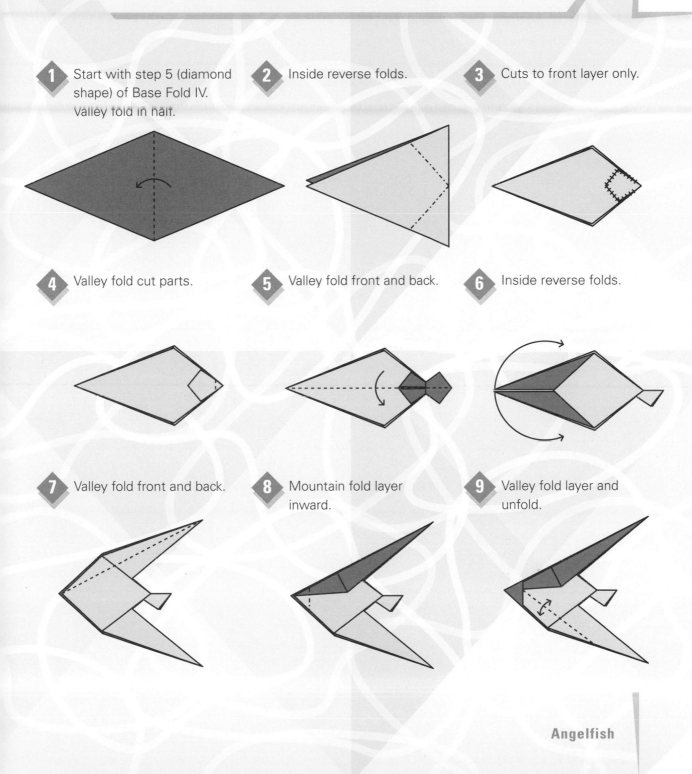

1 Start with step 5 (diamond shape) of Base Fold IV. Valley fold in half.

2 Inside reverse folds.

3 Cuts to front layer only.

4 Valley fold cut parts.

5 Valley fold front and back.

6 Inside reverse folds.

7 Valley fold front and back.

8 Mountain fold layer inward.

9 Valley fold layer and unfold.

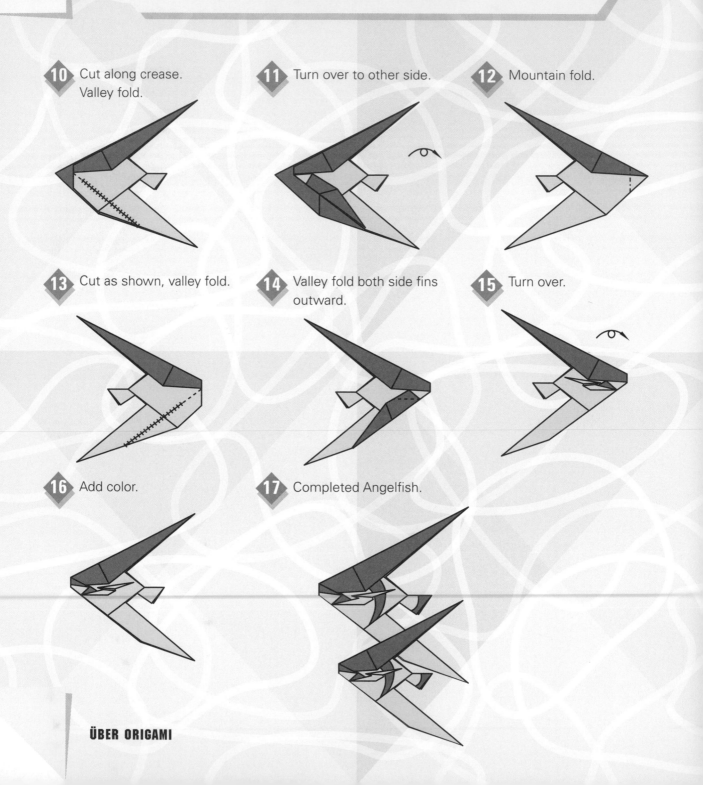

ANGELFISH

10 Cut along crease. Valley fold.

11 Turn over to other side.

12 Mountain fold.

13 Cut as shown, valley fold.

14 Valley fold both side fins outward.

15 Turn over.

16 Add color.

17 Completed Angelfish.

LIONFISH

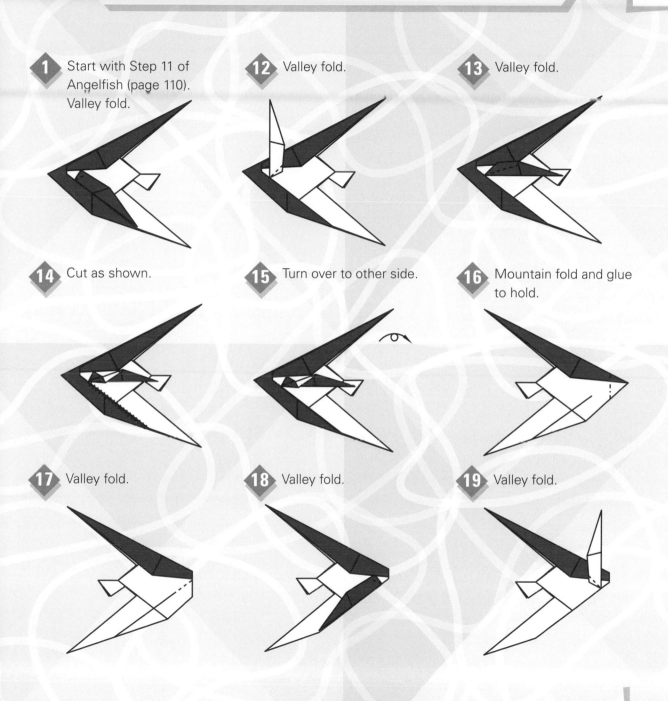

1 Start with Step 11 of Angelfish (page 110). Valley fold.

12 Valley fold.

13 Valley fold.

14 Cut as shown.

15 Turn over to other side.

16 Mountain fold and glue to hold.

17 Valley fold.

18 Valley fold.

19 Valley fold.

Lionfish

LIONFISH

20 Valley fold.

21 Cut top layer as shown.

22 Valley unfold both front and back.

23 Valley fold both sides.

24 Valley folds front and back.

25 Cut as shown to both sides.

26 Repeat cuts, to lower section.

27 Valley fold front and back.

28 Repeat.

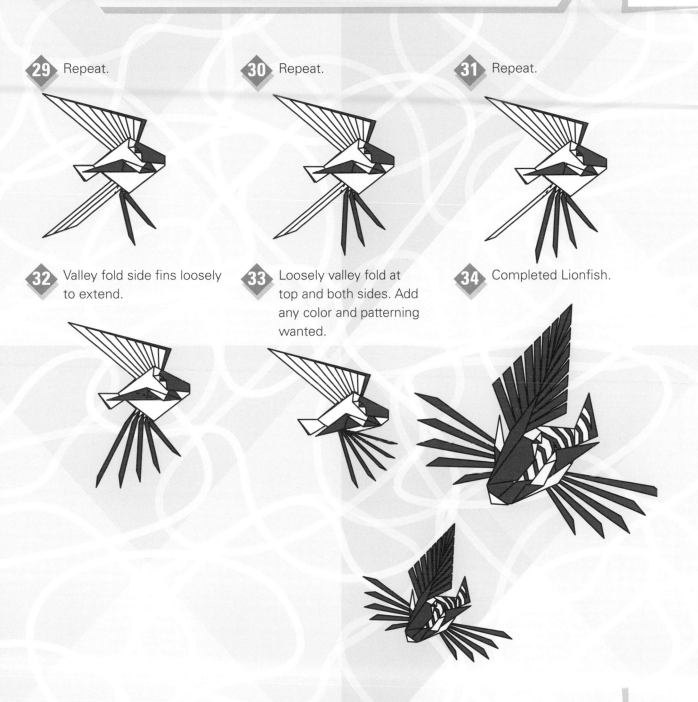

29 Repeat.

30 Repeat.

31 Repeat.

32 Valley fold side fins loosely to extend.

33 Loosely valley fold at top and both sides. Add any color and patterning wanted.

34 Completed Lionfish.

SEA HORSE

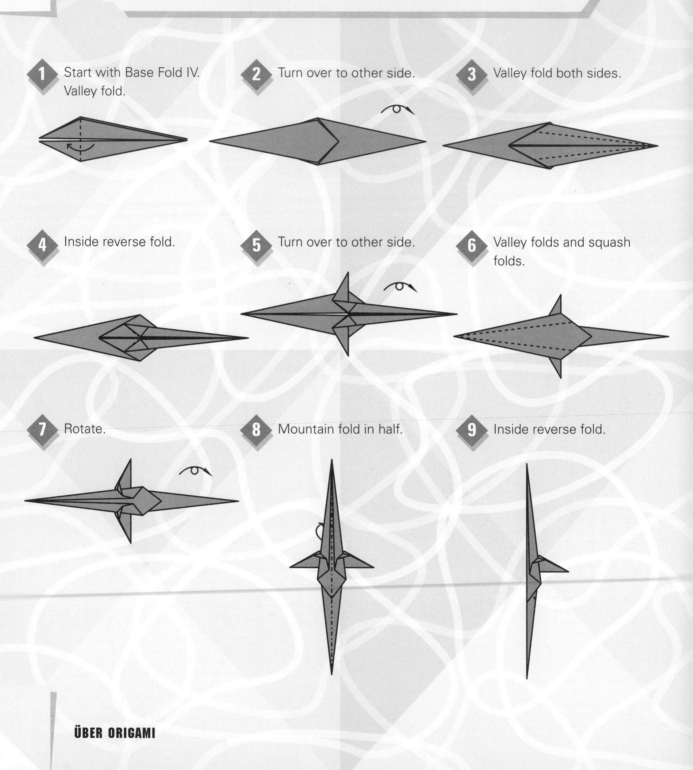

1 Start with Base Fold IV. Valley fold.

2 Turn over to other side.

3 Valley fold both sides.

4 Inside reverse fold.

5 Turn over to other side.

6 Valley folds and squash folds.

7 Rotate.

8 Mountain fold in half.

9 Inside reverse fold.

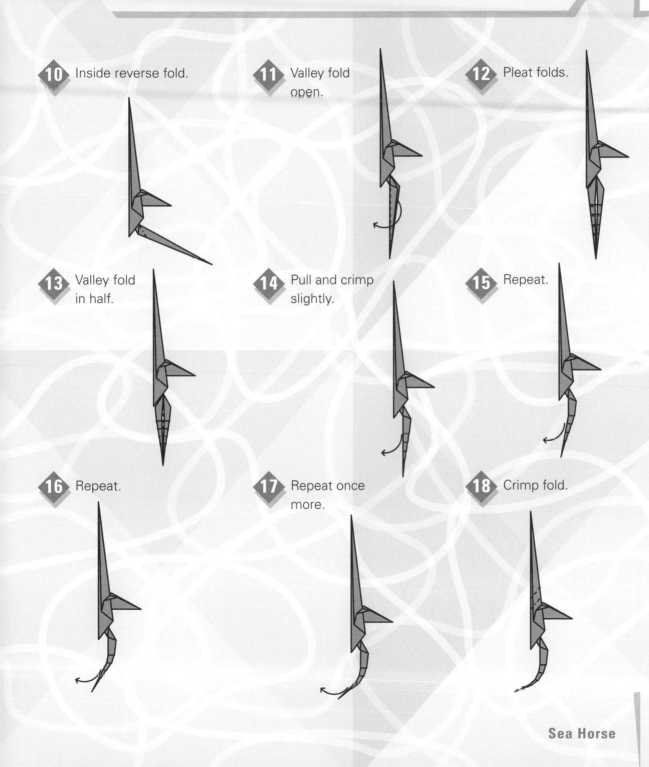

10 Inside reverse fold.

11 Valley fold open.

12 Pleat folds.

13 Valley fold in half.

14 Pull and crimp slightly.

15 Repeat.

16 Repeat.

17 Repeat once more.

18 Crimp fold.

Sea Horse

19 Outside reverse fold.

20 Inside and outside reverse folds.

21 Valley fold both sides.

22 Pleat fold and crimp into position.

23 Outside reverse folds.

24 Inside reverse fold.

25 Completed Sea Horse.

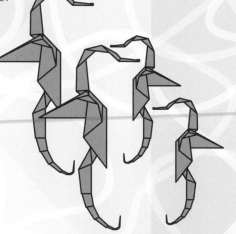

BABY TIGER SHARK

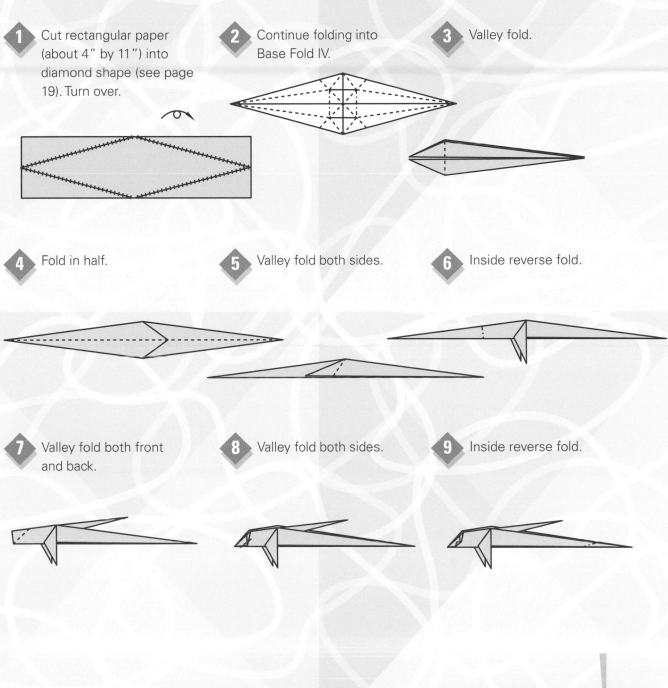

1 Cut rectangular paper (about 4" by 11") into diamond shape (see page 19). Turn over.

2 Continue folding into Base Fold IV.

3 Valley fold.

4 Fold in half.

5 Valley fold both sides.

6 Inside reverse fold.

7 Valley fold both front and back.

8 Valley fold both sides.

9 Inside reverse fold.

Baby Tiger Shark

BABY TIGER SHARK

10 Valley fold both front and back.

11 Valley fold and unfold to crease.

12 Pull and press creased lines to form a natural body curve.

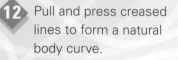

13 Completed Baby Tiger Shark.

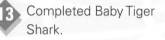

HUMPBACK WHALE

Part 1

1 Cut rectangular paper (about 4" by 11") into diamond shape (see page 19). Turn over.

2 Continue folding into Base Fold IV.

3 Valley fold.

4 Turn over.

5 Cuts to front layer.

6 Valley folds.

7 Valley fold.

8 Fold in half.

9 Cut as shown.

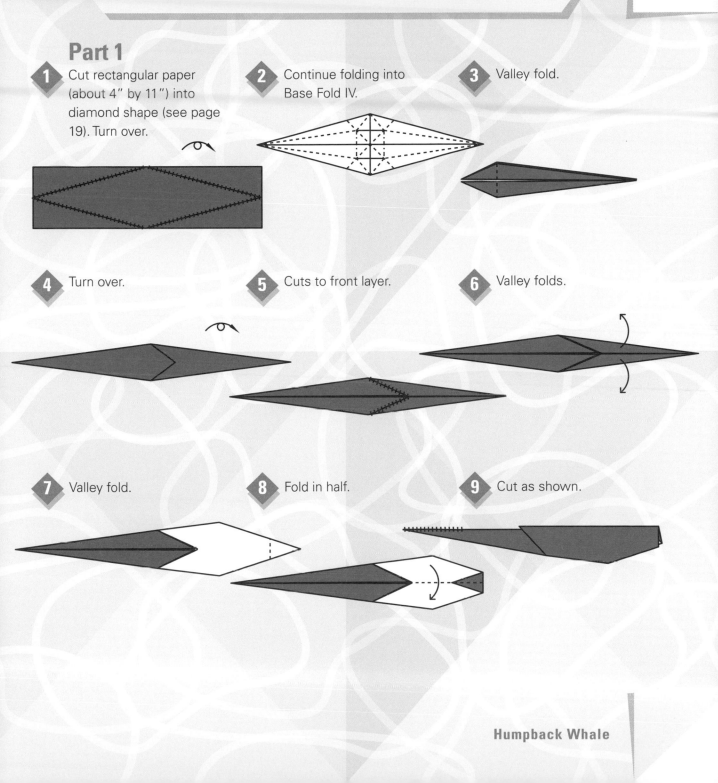

Humpback Whale

10 Valley fold.

11 Mountain fold.

12 Completed part 1 of whale.

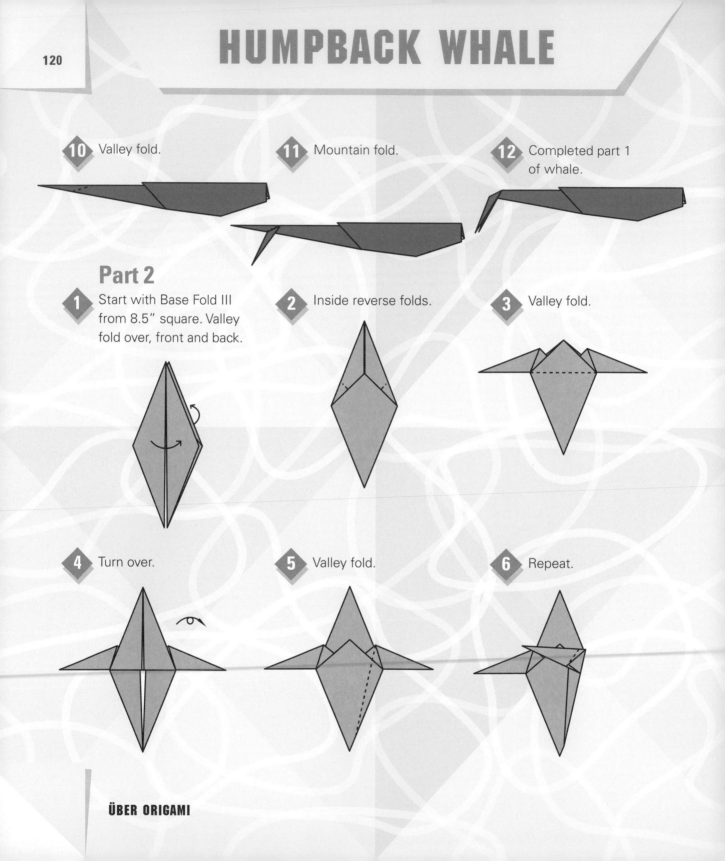

Part 2

1 Start with Base Fold III from 8.5" square. Valley fold over, front and back.

2 Inside reverse folds.

3 Valley fold.

4 Turn over.

5 Valley fold.

6 Repeat.

HUMPBACK WHALE

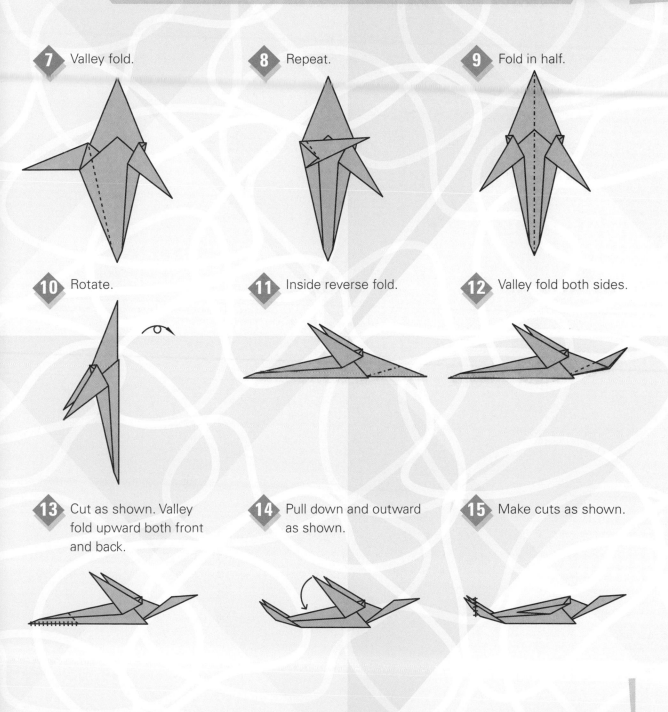

7 Valley fold.

8 Repeat.

9 Fold in half.

10 Rotate.

11 Inside reverse fold.

12 Valley fold both sides.

13 Cut as shown. Valley fold upward both front and back.

14 Pull down and outward as shown.

15 Make cuts as shown.

HUMPBACK WHALE

To Attach

16 Completed part 2 of whale.

1 Position part 2 of whale into part 1. Glue to secure.

2 Use steps 11 and 12 of Baby Tiger Shark (page 118) to curve tail section.

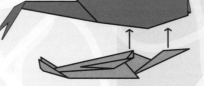

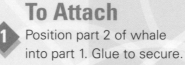

3 Completed Humpback Whale.

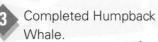

KING CRAB

Part 1

1 Cut rectangular paper (about 4″ by 11″) into diamond shape (see page 19). Turn over.

2 Continue folding into Base Fold IV.

3 Valley fold both front and back.

4 Cut as shown on both sides.

5 Valley fold long flaps to right. Then valley fold first layer up and back layer down.

6 Valley fold.

7 Mountain fold.

8 Rotate.

9 Valley folds.

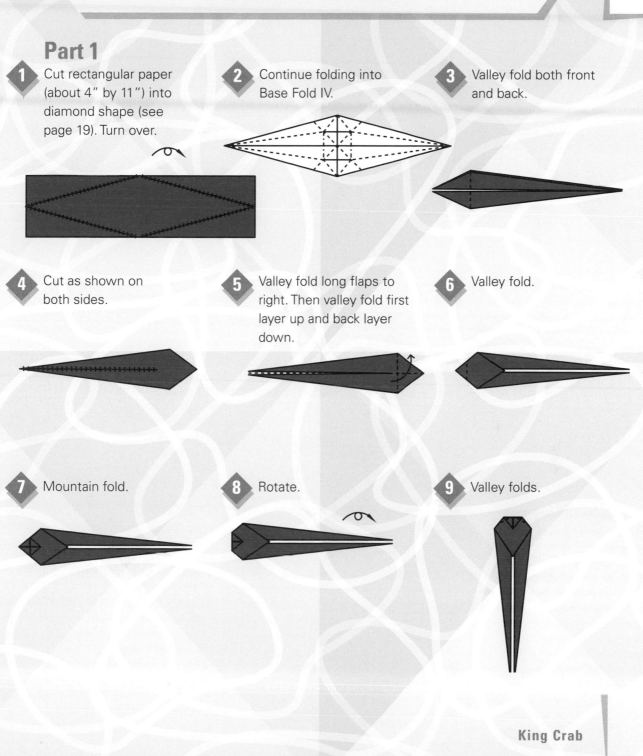

King Crab

KING CRAB

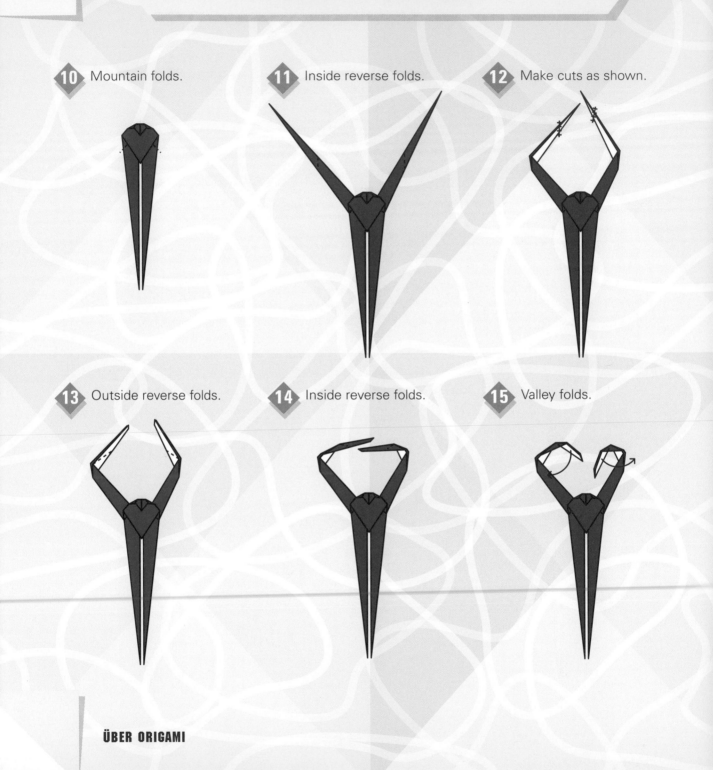

10 Mountain folds.

11 Inside reverse folds.

12 Make cuts as shown.

13 Outside reverse folds.

14 Inside reverse folds.

15 Valley folds.

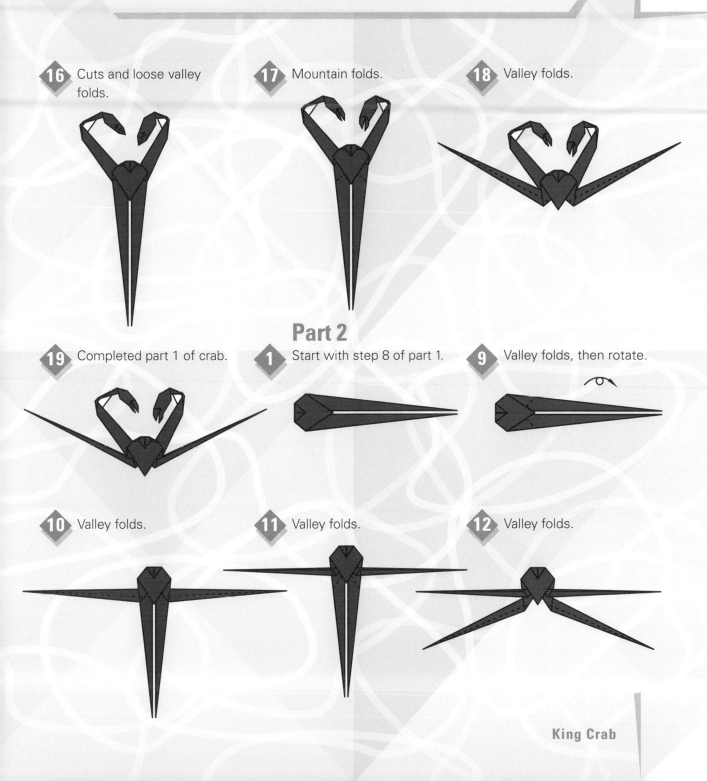

16 Cuts and loose valley folds.

17 Mountain folds.

18 Valley folds.

19 Completed part 1 of crab.

Part 2

1 Start with step 8 of part 1.

9 Valley folds, then rotate.

10 Valley folds.

11 Valley folds.

12 Valley folds.

KING CRAB

To Attach

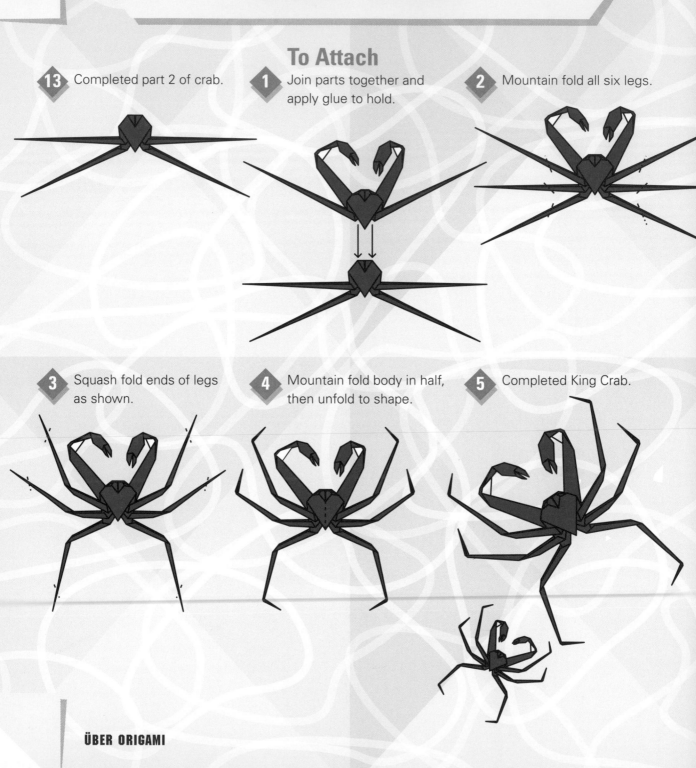

13 Completed part 2 of crab.

1 Join parts together and apply glue to hold.

2 Mountain fold all six legs.

3 Squash fold ends of legs as shown.

4 Mountain fold body in half, then unfold to shape.

5 Completed King Crab.

SQUID

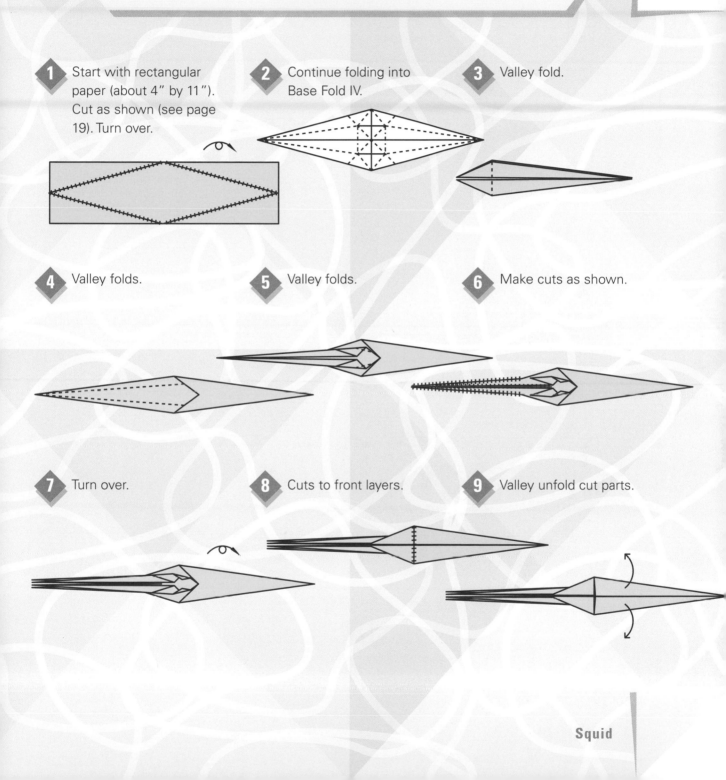

1. Start with rectangular paper (about 4" by 11"). Cut as shown (see page 19). Turn over.

2. Continue folding into Base Fold IV.

3. Valley fold.

4. Valley folds.

5. Valley folds.

6. Make cuts as shown.

7. Turn over.

8. Cuts to front layers.

9. Valley unfold cut parts.

Squid

SQUID

10 Valley fold in half.

11 Inside reverse fold.

12 Repeat inside reverse fold.

13 Valley fold both front and back.

14 Add curves to tentacles.

15 Completed Squid.

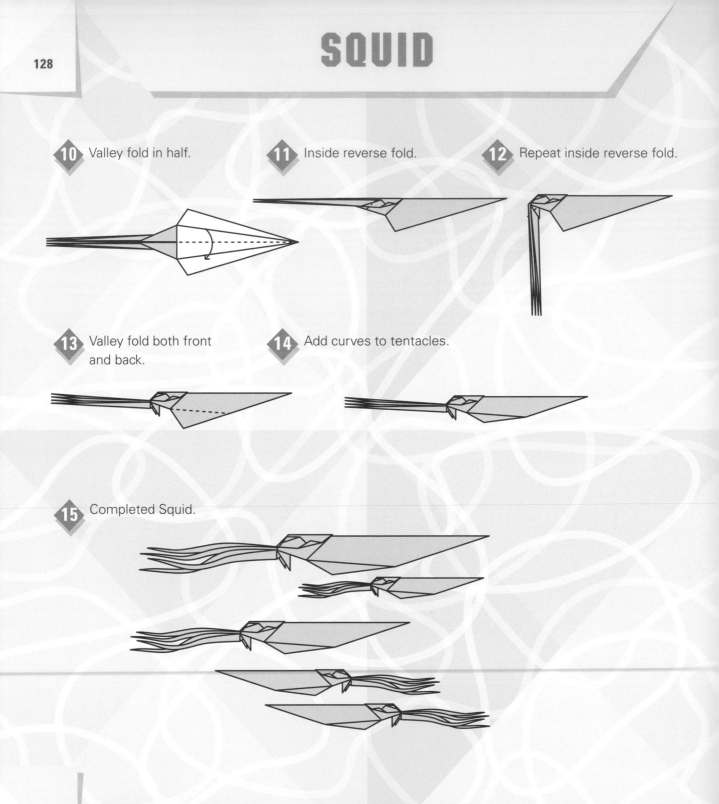

BLUE SHARK

Part 1

1 Cut rectangular paper (about 4" by 11") into diamond shape (see page 19). Turn over.

2 Continue folding into Base Fold IV.

3 Valley fold.

4 Turn over.

5 Cuts to front layer.

6 Valley unfolds.

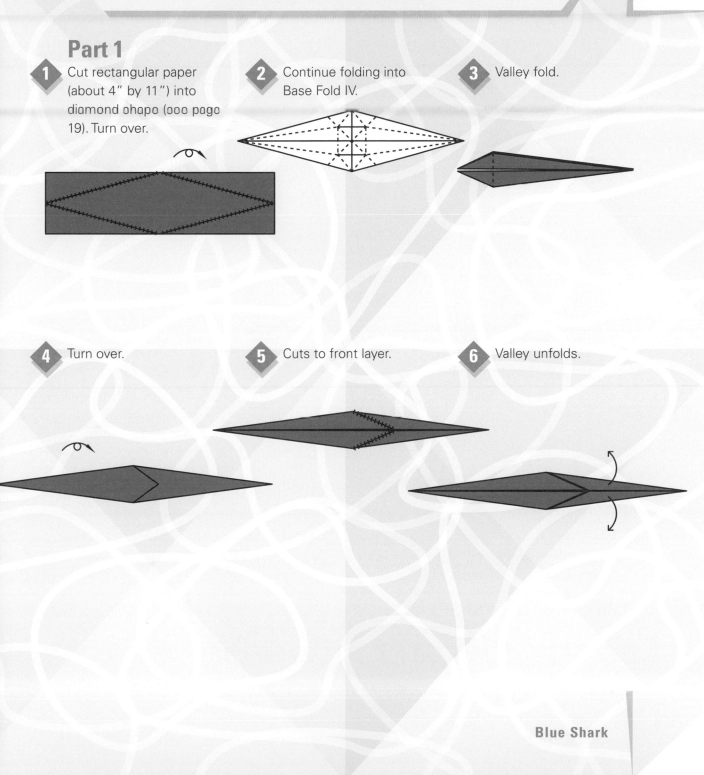

BLUE SHARK

7 Valley fold.

8 Valley folds.

9 Cuts as shown.

10 Valley folds, then mountain fold in half.

11 Valley fold both sides.

12 Valley fold.

13 Completed part 1 of shark.

Part 2

1 Cut rectangular paper (about 4″ by 11″) into diamond shape (see page 19). Turn over.

2 Continue folding into Base Fold IV.

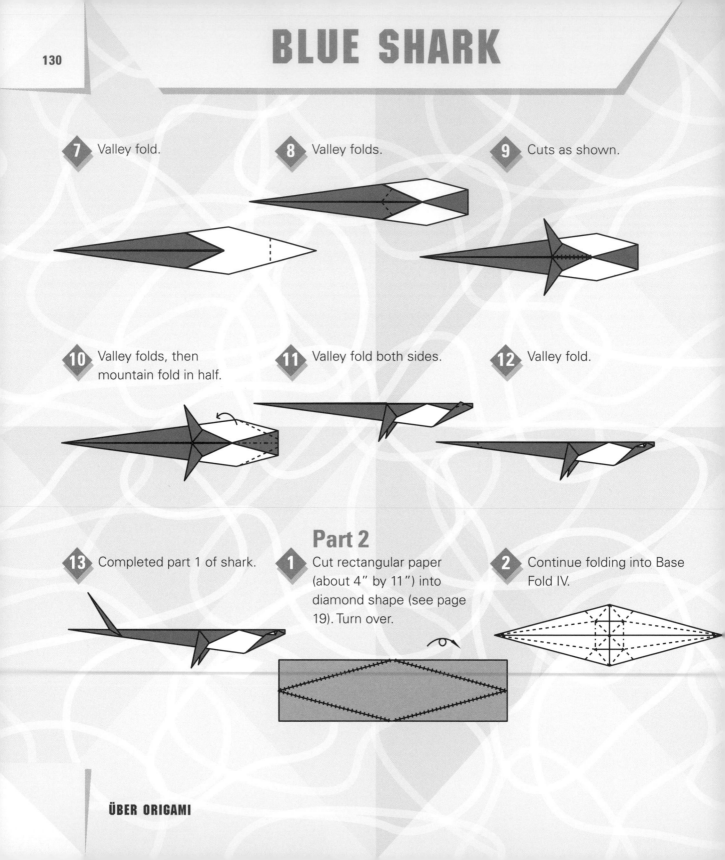

BLUE SHARK

3 Valley folds. Repeat behind.

4 Valley fold.

5 Cuts as shown. Valley open cut parts.

6 Cut, and mountain fold cut parts.

7 Cut off ends as shown.

8 Inside reverse to form fin, then valley fold in half.

9 Mountain folds.

10 Cut as shown.

11 Completed part 2 of shark.

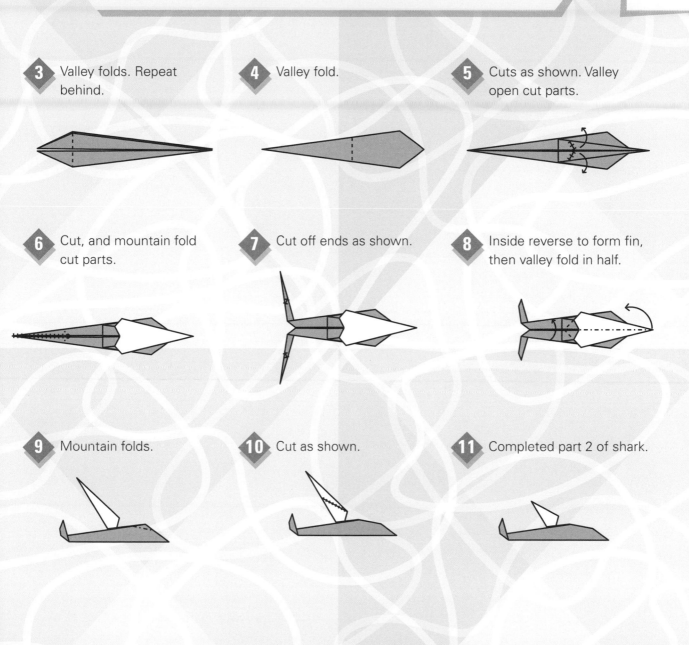

BLUE SHARK

To Attach

1 Insert part 2 fin through opening in part 1 and apply glue to hold.

2 Mountain fold to inside.

3 Valley fold to front. Apply glue to hold.

4 Completed Blue Shark.

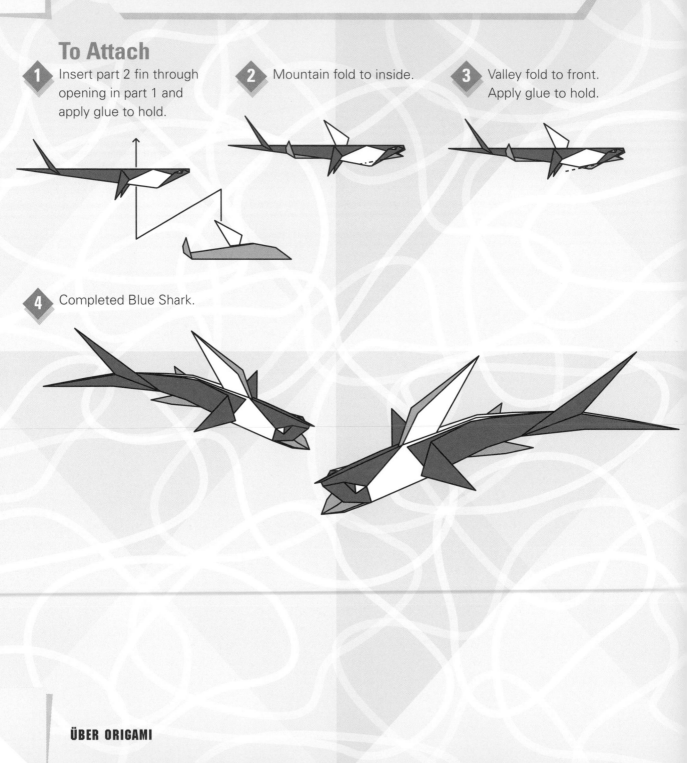

OCTOPUS

Part 1

1 Cut rectangular paper (about 4" by 11") into diamond shape (see page 19). Turn over.

2 Valley fold.

3 Valley fold and unfold.

4 Cut as shown.

5 Inside reverse folds.

6 Pull and valley fold along dashed line.

7 Turn over to other side.

8 Cut as shown.

9 Valley folds.

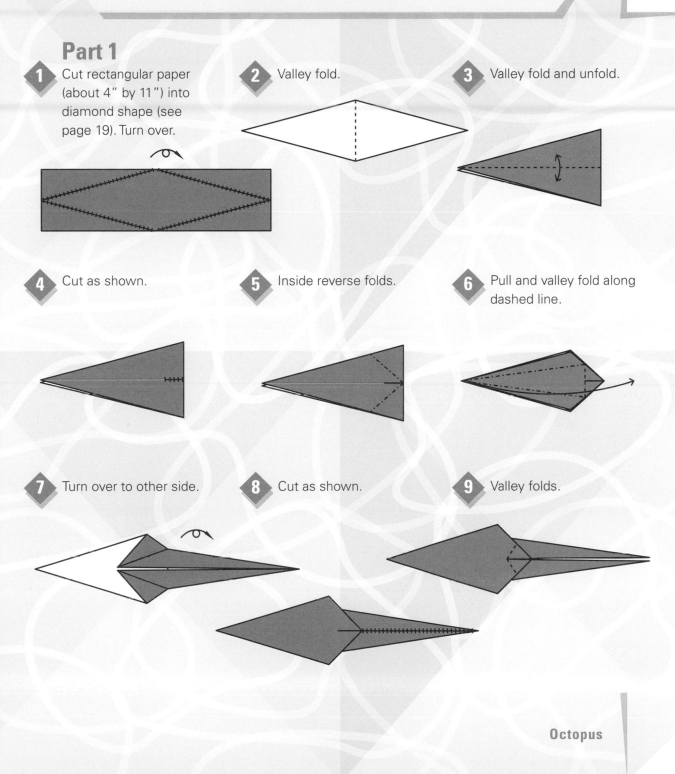

OCTOPUS

10 Squash folds.

11 Valley fold in half.

12 Outside reverse fold.

13 Inside reverse fold.

14 Outside reverse fold.

15 Valley fold both front and back.

16 Squash fold both front and back.

17 Valley fold both sides, and rotate.

18 Mountain fold both front and back.

Part 2

19 Completed part 1 of octopus.

1 Base Fold IV. Valley folds.

2 Valley fold both sides.

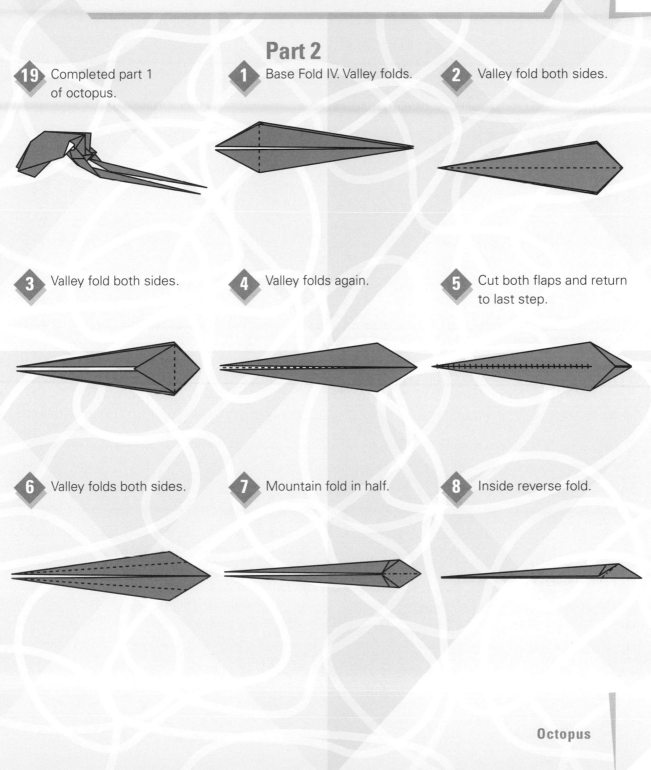

3 Valley fold both sides.

4 Valley folds again.

5 Cut both flaps and return to last step.

6 Valley folds both sides.

7 Mountain fold in half.

8 Inside reverse fold.

9 Completed part 2 of octopus.

To Attach

1 Join both parts together as shown and apply glue to hold.

2 Valley fold back tentacles. Mountain fold front tentacles.

3 Mountain folds as shown.

4 Spread out tentacles to completion.

5 Completed Octopus.

1 Start with Base Fold III. Valley fold.

2 Cut as shown.

3 Cut front layer only.

4 Valley fold.

5 Fold in half.

6 Rotate.

7 Cut as shown.

8 Mountain fold front and back to inside.

9 Valley fold.

Hyena

HYENA

10 Pleat fold.

11 Valley fold in half.

12 Inside reverse fold.

13 Outside reverse fold.

14 Outside reverse fold.

15 Cut tip slightly as shown.

16 Valley fold both sides.

17 Valley fold.

18 Cut front layers only as shown.

19 Valley folds.

20 Valley fold.

21 Valley fold both sides.

22 Inside reverse folds.

23 Valley fold both sides.

24 Valley folds.

25 Inside reverse folds.

26 Inside reverse folds, then rotate.

27 Mountain folds front and back.

HYENA

28 Mountain folds again.

29 Outside reverse folds.

30 Pull and squash tail into position.

31 Completed Hyena.

HIPPOPOTAMUS

HIPPOPOTAMUS

Part 1

1. Start with Base Fold III. Inside reverse folds.

2. Cuts as shown.

3. Inside reverse folds.

4. Squash folds to front.

5. Valley folds.

6. Valley fold top layers and crimp feet outward.

7. Open out as shown.

8. Valley fold in half, then rotate.

9. Pleat fold.

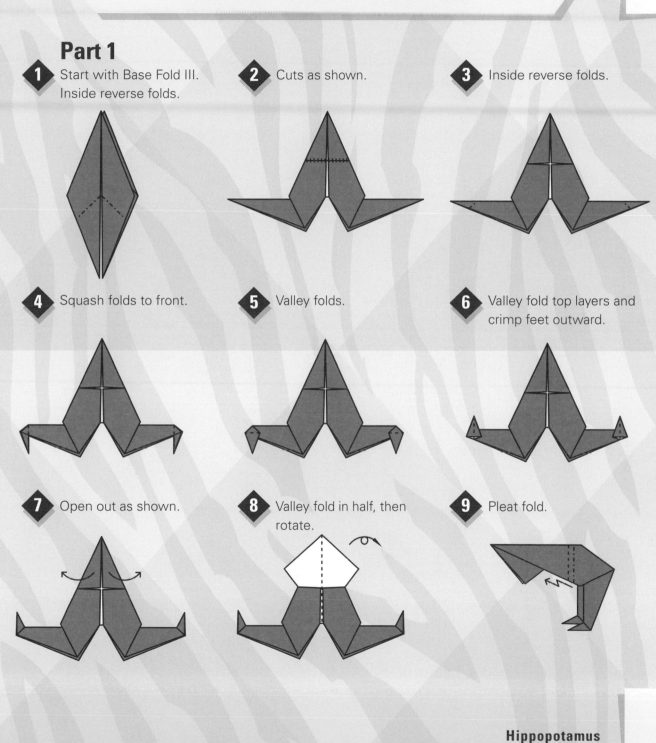

Hippopotamus

HIPPOPOTAMUS

10 Unfold folds.

11 Pleat fold.

12 Pleat fold.

13 Outside reverse fold.

14 Cut as shown.

15 Outside reverse fold.

16 Squash fold ears forward.

17 Completed part 1 (front) of hippopotamus.

HIPPOPOTAMUS

Part 2

1 Start with Base Fold III. Valley fold

2 Turn over.

3 Cuts as shown.

4 Valley folds.

5 Mountain fold in half.

6 Rotate.

7 Inside reverse fold.

8 Valley folds both front and back.

9 Inside reverse fold.

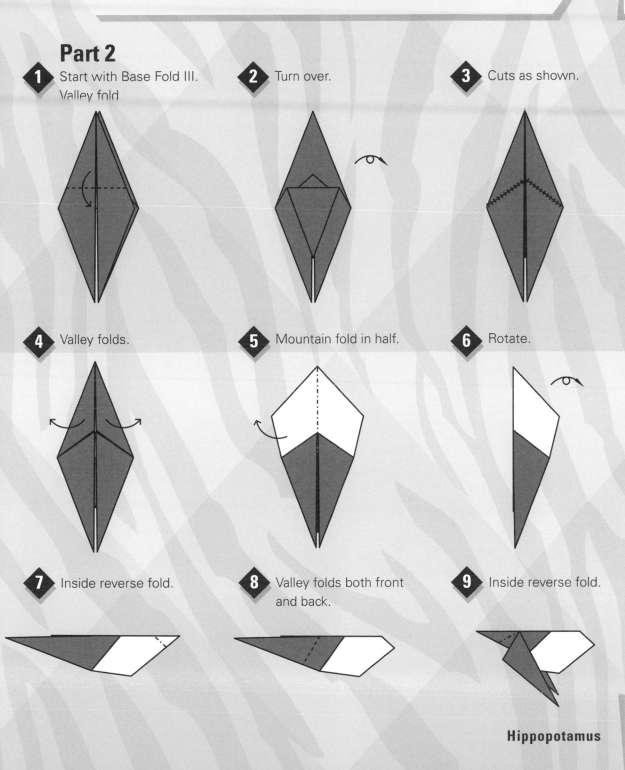

Hippopotamus

HIPPOPOTAMUS

10 Valley fold both sides.

11 Secure tail behind layers.

12 Cut as shown.

13 Inside reverse folds.

15 Inside reverse folds and rotate.

16 Completed part 2 (rear) of hippopotamus.

To Attach

1 Join both parts together as shown and apply glue to hold.

2 Completed Hippopotamus.

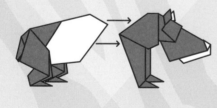

GIRAFFE

Part 1

1 Start with Base Fold IV, then valley fold.

2 Make cuts as shown. Rotate.

3 Mountain fold in half.

4 Cut as shown, then outside reverse fold.

5 Inside reverse fold.

6 Cut as shown.

7 Inside reverse folds, both sides.

8 Add patterning or color.

9 Completed part 1 (front) of giraffe.

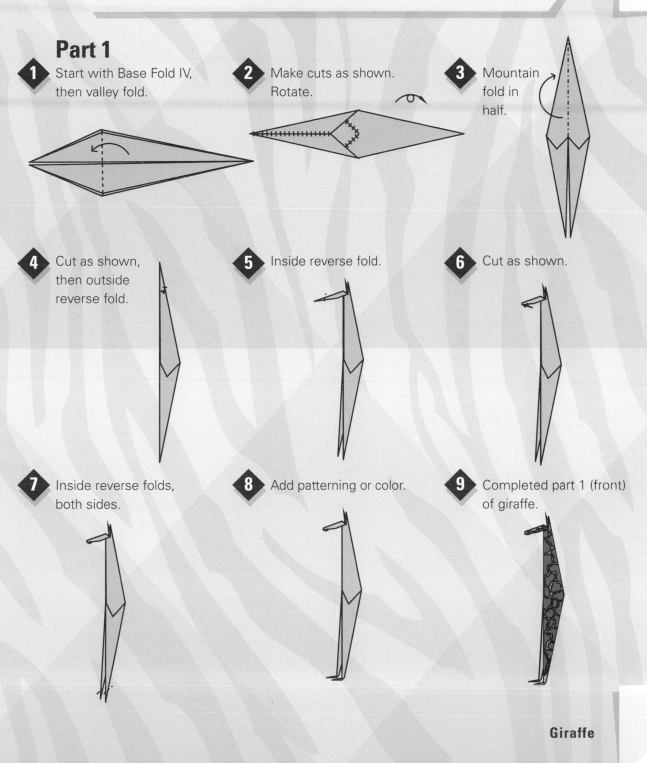

Giraffe

GIRAFFE

Part 2

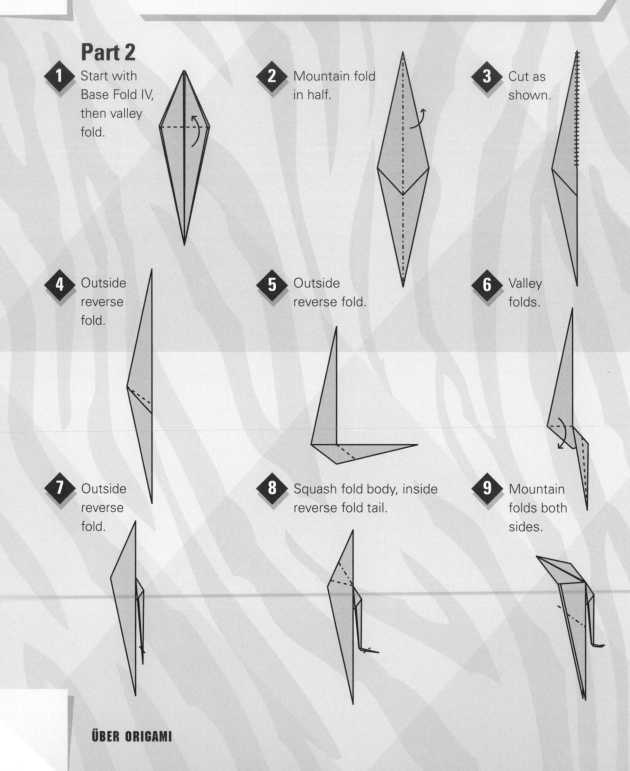

1 Start with Base Fold IV, then valley fold.

2 Mountain fold in half.

3 Cut as shown.

4 Outside reverse fold.

5 Outside reverse fold.

6 Valley folds.

7 Outside reverse fold.

8 Squash fold body, inside reverse fold tail.

9 Mountain folds both sides.

10 Repeat mountain folds.

11 Outside reverse folds.

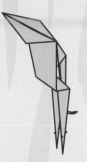

12 Add patterning or color to completion.

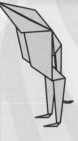

13 Completed part 2 (rear) of giraffe.

To Attach

1 Join both parts together as shown. Apply glue to hold.

2 Completed Giraffe.

GORILLA

Part 1

1 Start with square sheet cut diagonally, then valley fold.

2 Inside reverse folds.

3 Valley folds.

4 Turn over to other side.

5 Valley folds and squash folds.

6 Pleat fold.

7 Squash folds.

8 Valley fold.

9 Valley fold.

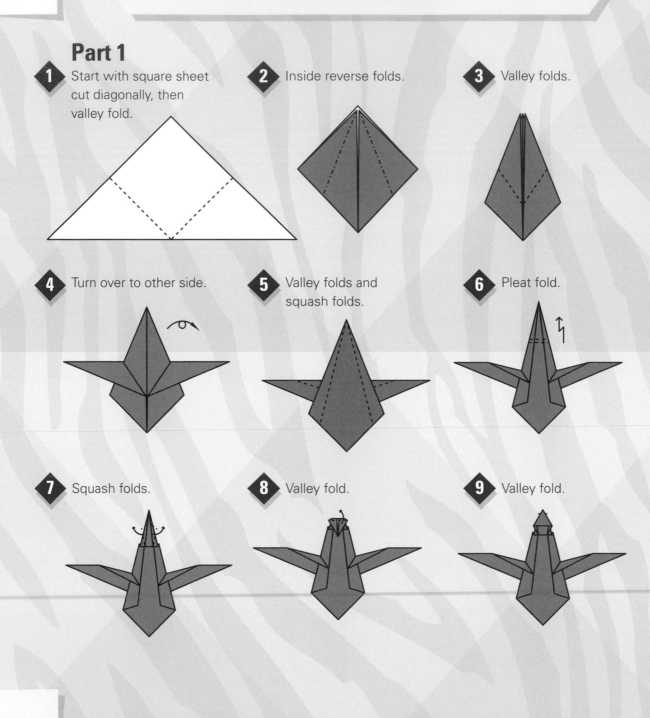

GORILLA

10 Mountain fold.

11 Valley fold.

12 Cut as shown.

13 Cuts as shown.

14 Inside reverse folds.

15 Outside reverse folds.

16 Valley folds.

17 Mountain fold in half.

18 Pull and crimp head into position.

Gorilla

GORILLA

19 Pull and crimp open.

20 Unfold in direction of arrow.

21 Valley fold both sides to extend arms.

22 Completed part 1 (top) of gorilla.

Part 2

1 Start with step 3 of part 1, then valley fold.

4 Turn over to other side.

5 Valley fold.

6 Valley fold in half.

7 Valley fold both front and back.

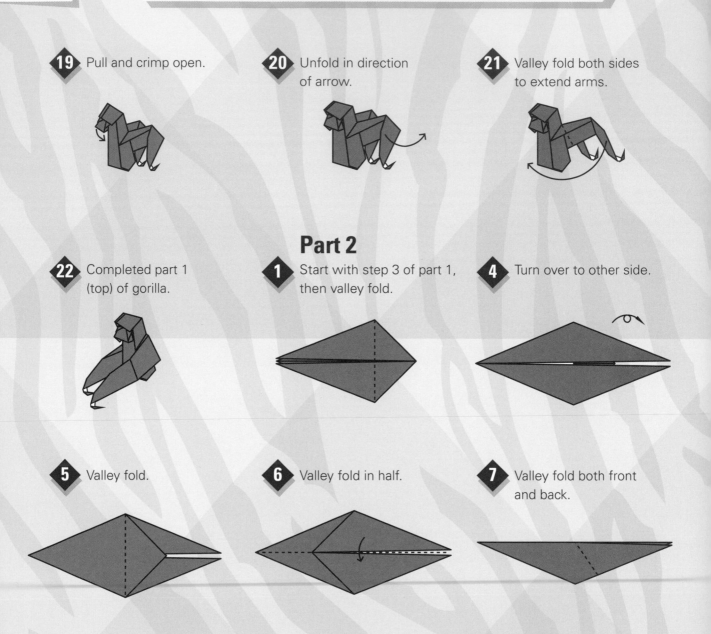

GORILLA

8 Mountain fold both front and back.

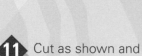

9 Repeat.

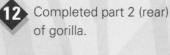

10 Inside reverse fold.

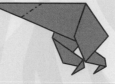

11 Cut as shown and rotate.

12 Completed part 2 (rear) of gorilla.

To Attach

1 Join the two parts together as shown and apply glue to hold.

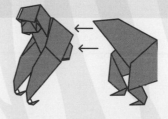

2 Completed Gorilla.

Gorilla

LION

Part 1

1 Start with Base Fold III. Valley fold.

2 Cut as shown.

3 Valley fold.

4 Rotate.

5 Inside reverse fold.

6 Outside reverse fold.

7 Repeat.

8 Cut as shown.

9 Valley folds front and back.

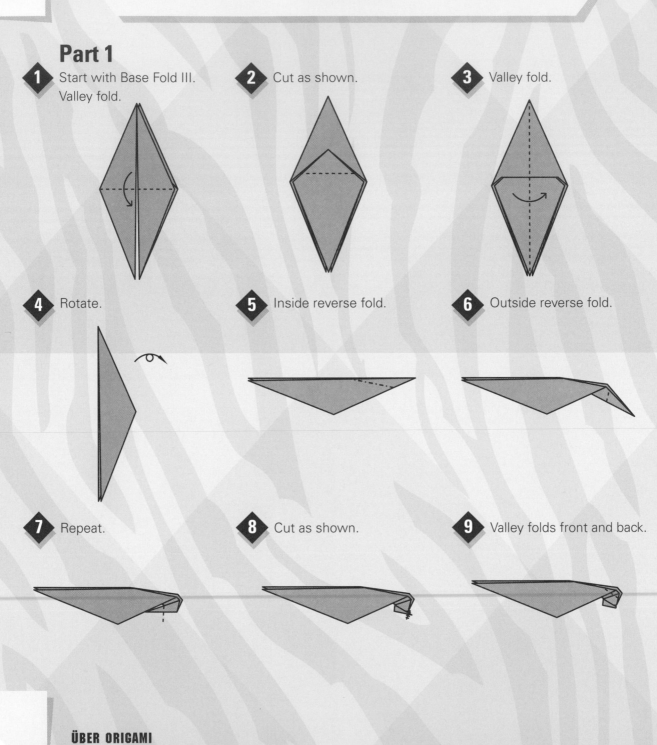

LION

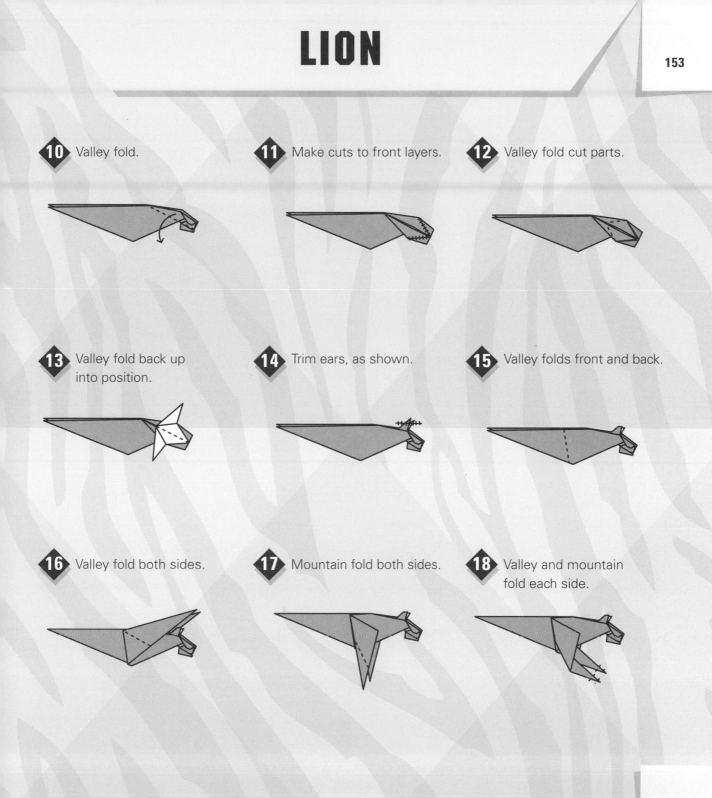

10 Valley fold.

11 Make cuts to front layers.

12 Valley fold cut parts.

13 Valley fold back up into position.

14 Trim ears, as shown.

15 Valley folds front and back.

16 Valley fold both sides.

17 Mountain fold both sides.

18 Valley and mountain fold each side.

Lion

LION

19 Inside reverse fold.

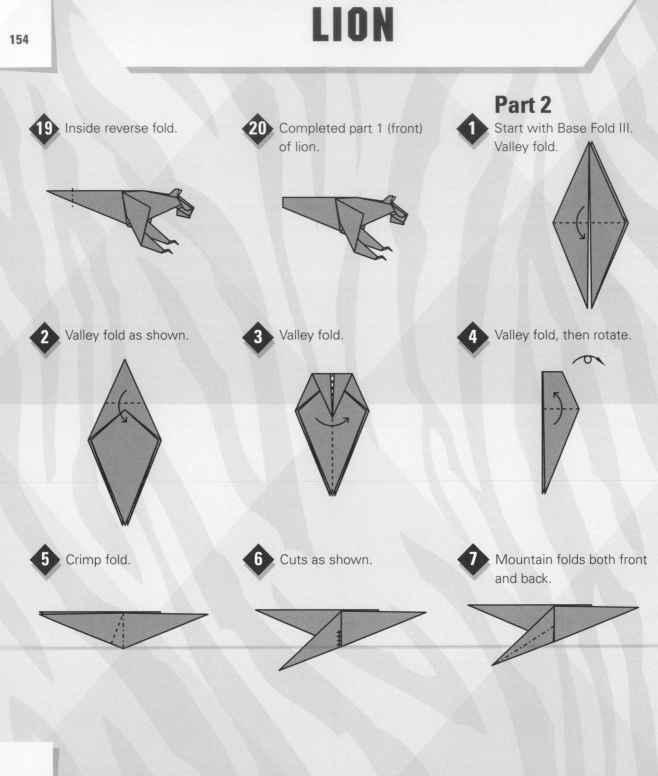

20 Completed part 1 (front) of lion.

Part 2

1 Start with Base Fold III. Valley fold.

2 Valley fold as shown.

3 Valley fold.

4 Valley fold, then rotate.

5 Crimp fold.

6 Cuts as shown.

7 Mountain folds both front and back.

LION

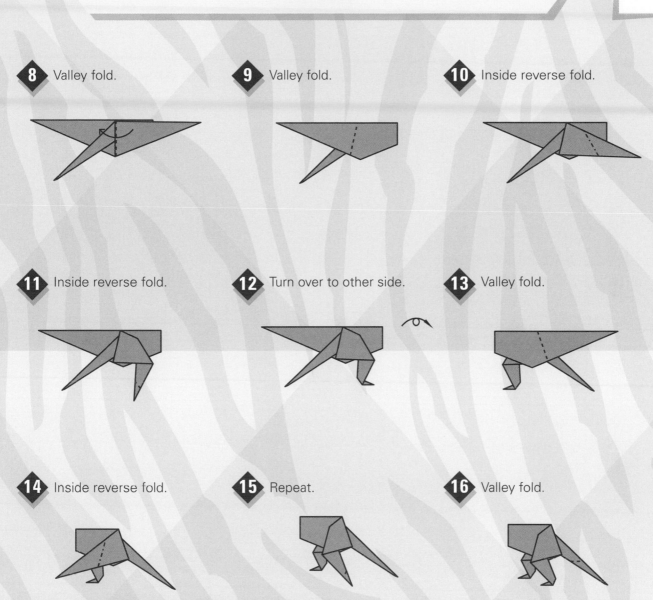

8 Valley fold.

9 Valley fold.

10 Inside reverse fold.

11 Inside reverse fold.

12 Turn over to other side.

13 Valley fold.

14 Inside reverse fold.

15 Repeat.

16 Valley fold.

Lion

17 Inside reverse fold.

18 Valley unfold tail tip.

19 Completed part 2 (rear) of lion.

To Attach

1 Join both parts together as shown and apply glue to hold.

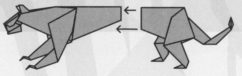

2 Completed Lion.

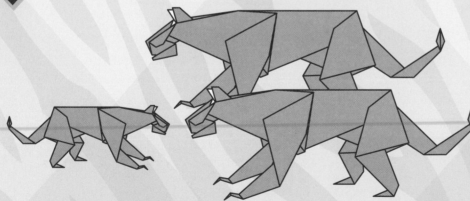

WATER BUFFALO

Part 1

1 Start with Base Fold III.
Valley fold.

2 Rotate.

3 Outside reverse fold.

4 Pleat fold.

5 Outside reverse fold.

6 Inside reverse fold.

7 Make cuts as shown.

8 Mountain folds both sides.

9 Make cuts as shown.

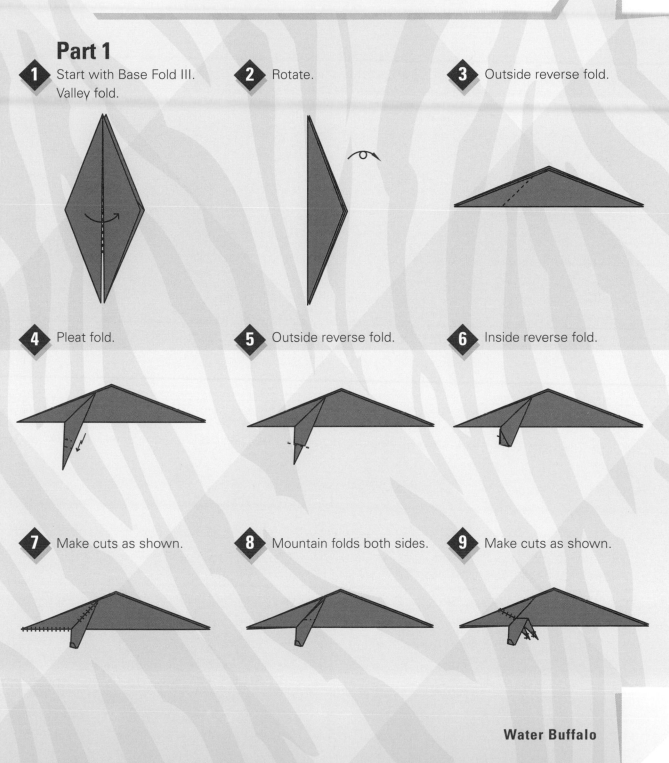

Water Buffalo

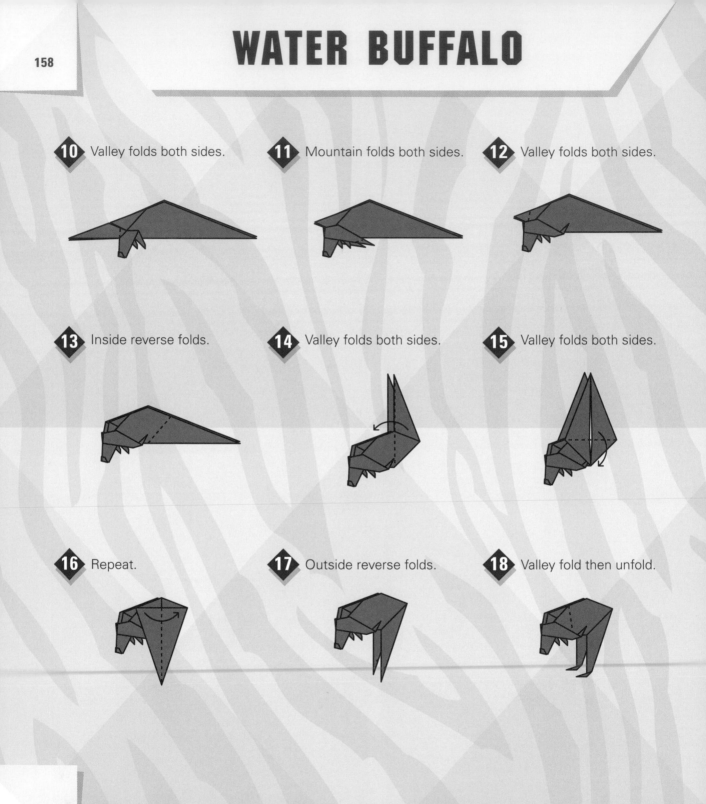

WATER BUFFALO

10 ▸ Valley folds both sides.

11 ▸ Mountain folds both sides.

12 ▸ Valley folds both sides.

13 ▸ Inside reverse folds.

14 ▸ Valley folds both sides.

15 ▸ Valley folds both sides.

16 ▸ Repeat.

17 ▸ Outside reverse folds.

18 ▸ Valley fold then unfold.

WATER BUFFALO

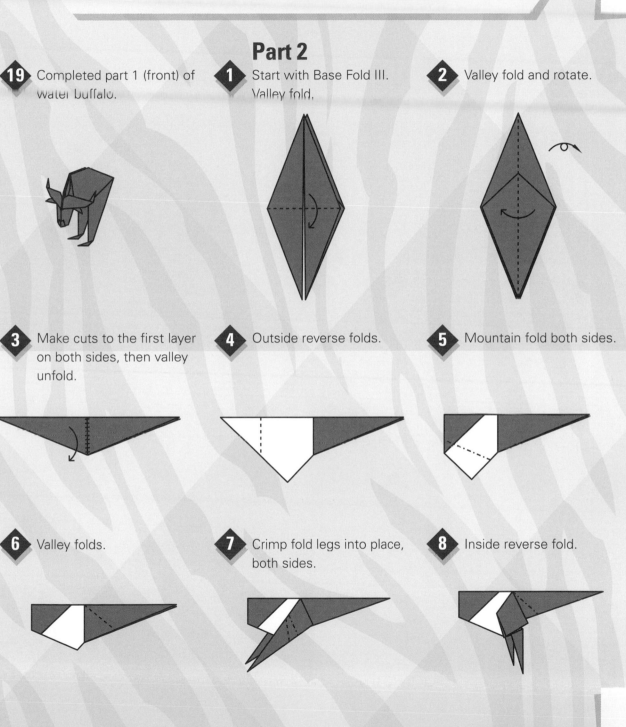

19 Completed part 1 (front) of water buffalo.

Part 2

1 Start with Base Fold III. Valley fold.

2 Valley fold and rotate.

3 Make cuts to the first layer on both sides, then valley unfold.

4 Outside reverse folds.

5 Mountain fold both sides.

6 Valley folds.

7 Crimp fold legs into place, both sides.

8 Inside reverse fold.

Water Buffalo

WATER BUFFALO

9 ▶ Valley folds to tail, mountain fold body inward.

10 ▶ Outside reverse folds.

11 ▶ Outside reverse fold.

12 ▶ Completed part 2 (rear) of water buffalo.

To Attach

1 ▶ Join both parts together and apply glue to hold.

2 ▶ Valley fold, then . . .

3 ▶ . . . mountain fold, to give tail "life."

4 ▶ Completed Water Buffalo.

WILDEBEEST

Part 1

1 Start with Base Fold III. Valley fold.

2 Rotate.

3 Crimp fold.

4 Outside reverse fold.

5 Cuts as shown.

6 Unfold to return to step 3 position.

7 Valley unfold.

8 Cut front layers and valley fold cut flaps.

9 Valley folds.

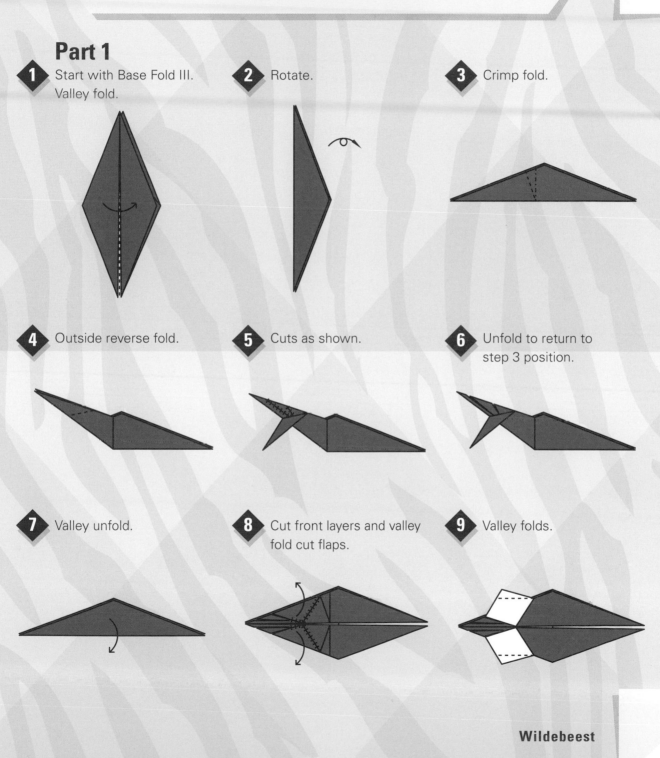

Wildebeest

10 Valley folds.

11 Repeat steps 3 and 4.

12 Valley fold both sides.

13 Cuts as shown.

14 Outside reverse folds.

15 Valley fold both sides.

16 Mountain folds both sides.

17 Inside reverse fold both sides.

18 Valley fold both sides.

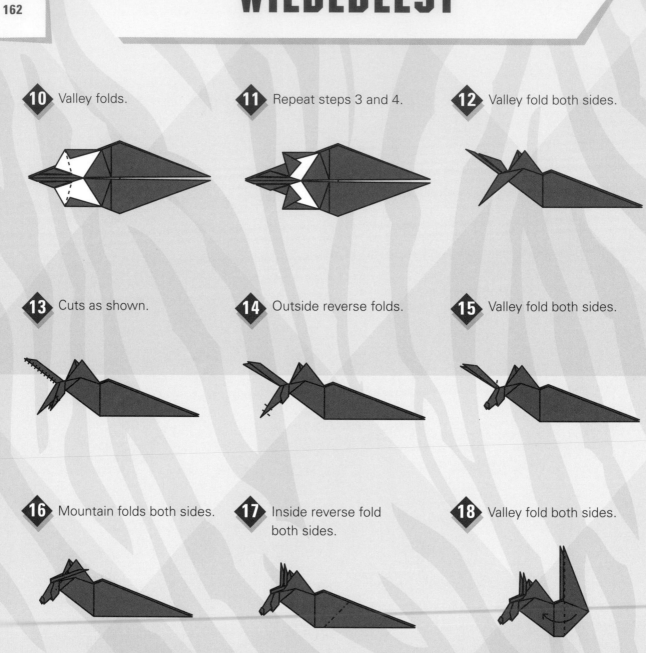

WILDEBEEST

19 Valley fold both sides.

20 Valley folds both front and back.

21 Valley folds both sides.

22 Pleat folds front and back.

23 Valley fold to turn head.

24 Pull and crimp into position.

25 Inside reverse fold.

26 Completed part 1 (front) of wildebeest.

Part 2

1 Start with Base Fold III. Valley fold.

Wildebeest

WILDEBEEST

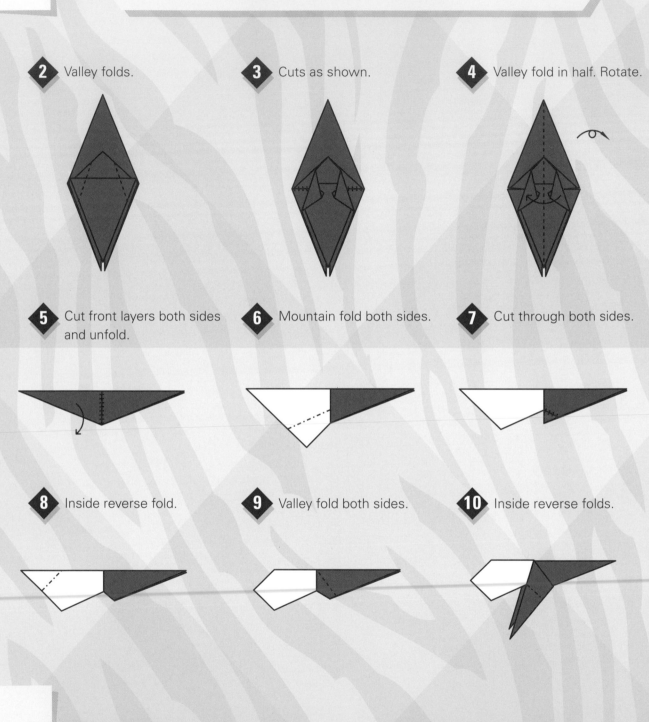

2 Valley folds.

3 Cuts as shown.

4 Valley fold in half. Rotate.

5 Cut front layers both sides and unfold.

6 Mountain fold both sides.

7 Cut through both sides.

8 Inside reverse fold.

9 Valley fold both sides.

10 Inside reverse folds.

11 All inside reverse folds.

12 Valley folds to both sides.

13 Squash fold tail.

14 Completed part 2 (rear) of wildebeest.

To Attach

1 Join both parts together and apply glue to hold.

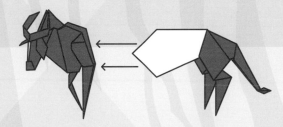

2 Completed Wildebeest.

ORANGUTAN

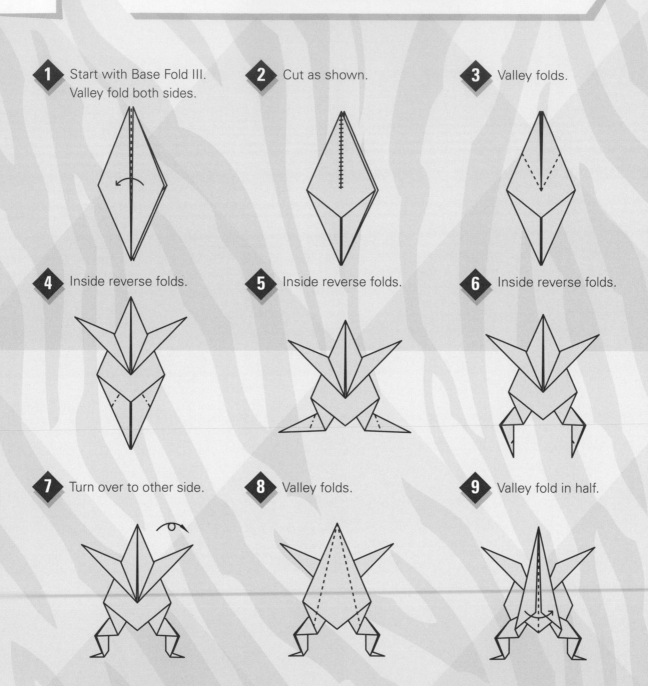

1 Start with Base Fold III. Valley fold both sides.

2 Cut as shown.

3 Valley folds.

4 Inside reverse folds.

5 Inside reverse folds.

6 Inside reverse folds.

7 Turn over to other side.

8 Valley folds.

9 Valley fold in half.

ORANGUTAN

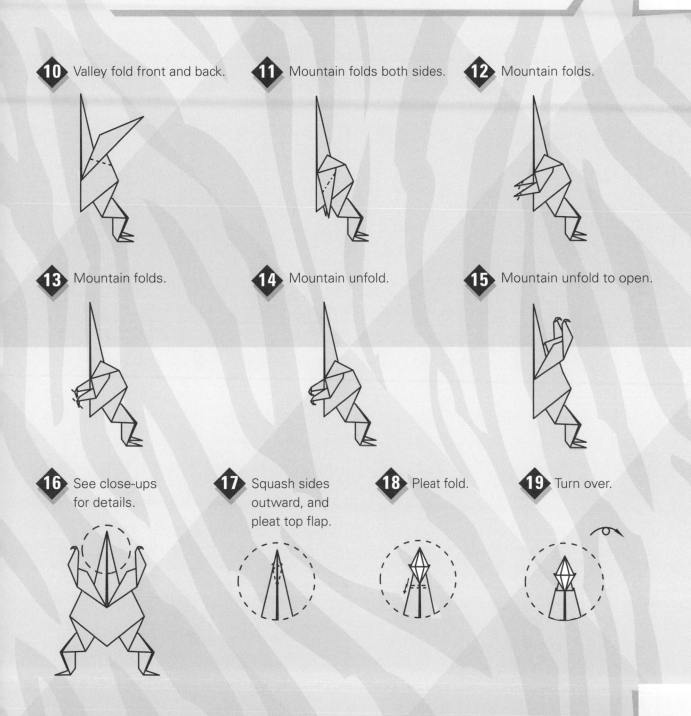

10 Valley fold front and back.

11 Mountain folds both sides.

12 Mountain folds.

13 Mountain folds.

14 Mountain unfold.

15 Mountain unfold to open.

16 See close-ups for details.

17 Squash sides outward, and pleat top flap.

18 Pleat fold.

19 Turn over.

ORANGUTAN

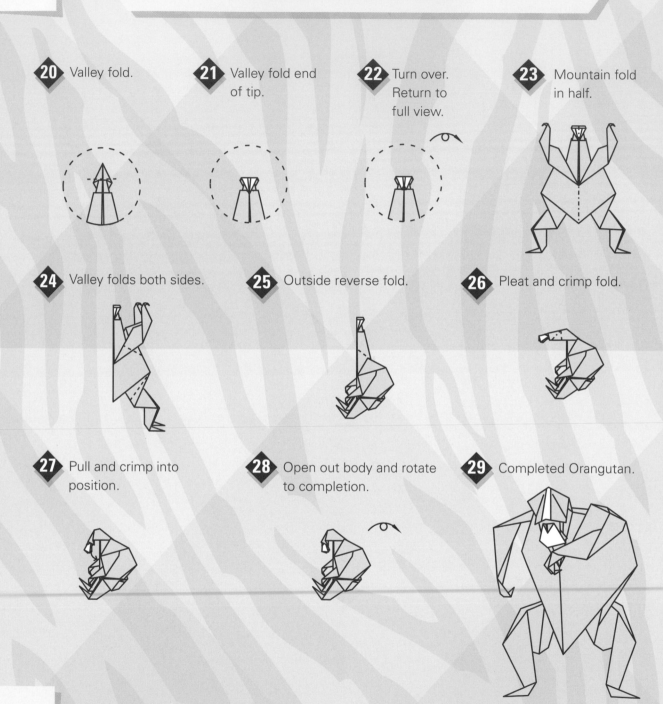

20 Valley fold.

21 Valley fold end of tip.

22 Turn over. Return to full view.

23 Mountain fold in half.

24 Valley folds both sides.

25 Outside reverse fold.

26 Pleat and crimp fold.

27 Pull and crimp into position.

28 Open out body and rotate to completion.

29 Completed Orangutan.

ZEBRA

Part 1

1 Start with Base Fold III. Pleat fold.

2 Valley fold.

3 Pull and crimp fold as shown, then rotate.

4 Inside reverse fold.

5 Valley fold.

6 Make cuts then valley unfold.

7 Valley fold.

8 Outside reverse fold.

9 Pull some paper out from inside.

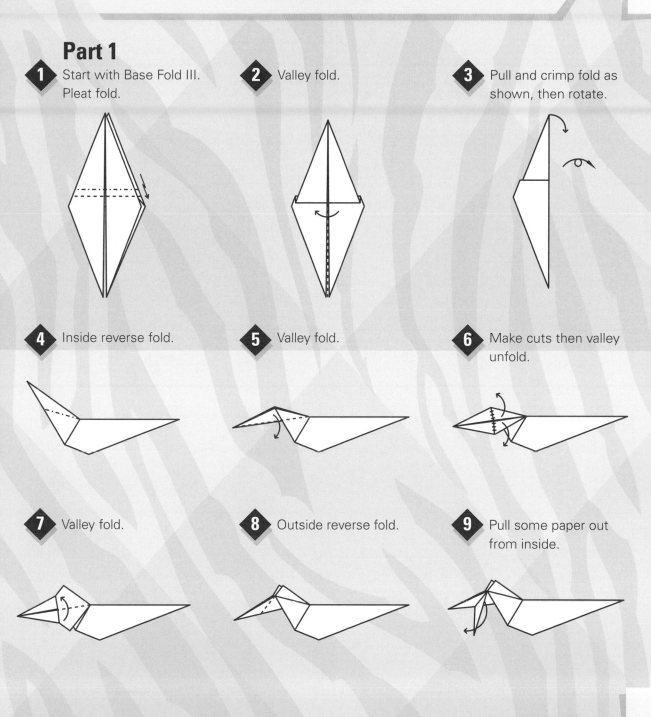

Zebra

ZEBRA

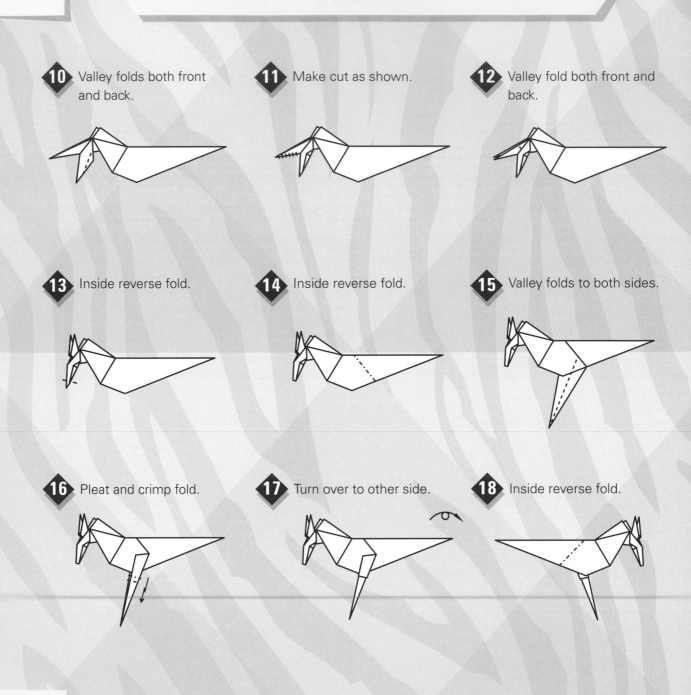

10 Valley folds both front and back.

11 Make cut as shown.

12 Valley fold both front and back.

13 Inside reverse fold.

14 Inside reverse fold.

15 Valley folds to both sides.

16 Pleat and crimp fold.

17 Turn over to other side.

18 Inside reverse fold.

ZEBRA

19 ▸ Valley folds to both sides.

20 ▸ Pleat and crimp fold.

21 ▸ Make cuts into mane, and add pattern.

22 ▸ Completed part 1 (front) of zebra.

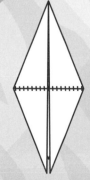

Part 2

1 ▸ Start with Base Fold III. Valley fold.

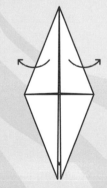

2 ▸ Turn over.

3 ▸ Cuts as shown.

4 ▸ Valley folds.

5 ▸ Cuts and mountain folds.

Zebra

ZEBRA

6 Turn over to other side.

7 Valley fold.

8 Valley fold in half and rotate.

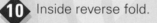

9 Valley fold, and mountain folds both sides.

10 Inside reverse fold.

11 Inside reverse fold.

12 Turn over to other side.

13 Valley fold.

14 Inside reverse folds.

15 Inside reverse fold.

16 Valley fold both sides.

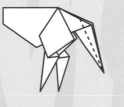

17 Squash fold tail, and add pattern.

To Attach

18 Completed part 2 (rear) of zebra.

1 Join both parts together and apply glue to hold.

2 Completed Zebra.

GAZELLE

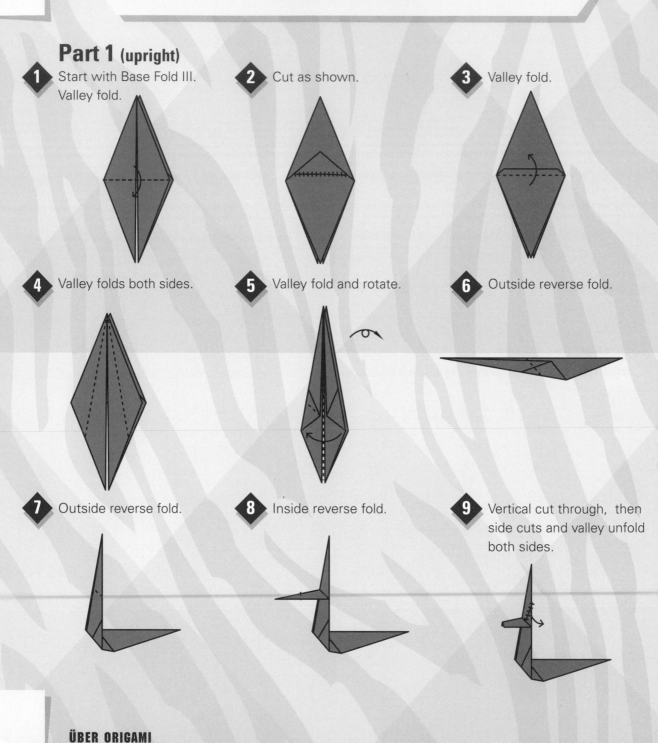

Part 1 (upright)

1 Start with Base Fold III. Valley fold.

2 Cut as shown.

3 Valley fold.

4 Valley folds both sides.

5 Valley fold and rotate.

6 Outside reverse fold.

7 Outside reverse fold.

8 Inside reverse fold.

9 Vertical cut through, then side cuts and valley unfold both sides.

GAZELLE

10 Cut as shown.

11 Valley fold.

12 Valley fold back.

13 Valley fold both sides.

14 Tuck "horns" in between head layers.

15 Inside reverse folds.

16 Valley fold.

17 Turn over to other side.

18 Inside reverse fold.

Gazelle

19 Valley fold.

20 Valley fold and crimp into position. Add coloring.

21 Completed part 1 (front) of upright gazelle.

Part 1 (grazing)

1 Start at step 6 of upright gazelle (page 174) and crimp fold.

7 Inside reverse fold both sides.

8 Outside reverse fold.

9 Inside reverse fold.

10 Valley fold both sides.

11 Cuts to front layer.

GAZELLE

12 Valley fold.

13 Cut as shown to separate. Add color if wanted.

14 Completed part 1 (front) of grazing gazelle.

Part 2

1 Start with Base Fold III. Valley folds.

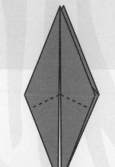

2 Turn over to other side.

3 Valley fold.

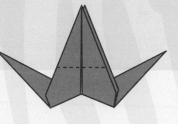

4 Valley fold.

5 Valley folds.

6 Valley fold in half.

GAZELLE

7 Rotate.

8 Outside reverse fold.

9 Inside reverse folds, both sides.

10 Repeat.

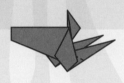

11 Completed part 2 (rear) of gazelle.

To Attach

1 Join part 1 (front) of either grazing or upright gazelle and part 2 (rear) together. Apply glue to hold, and add body coloring.

2 Completed Gazelles.

RATTLESNAKE

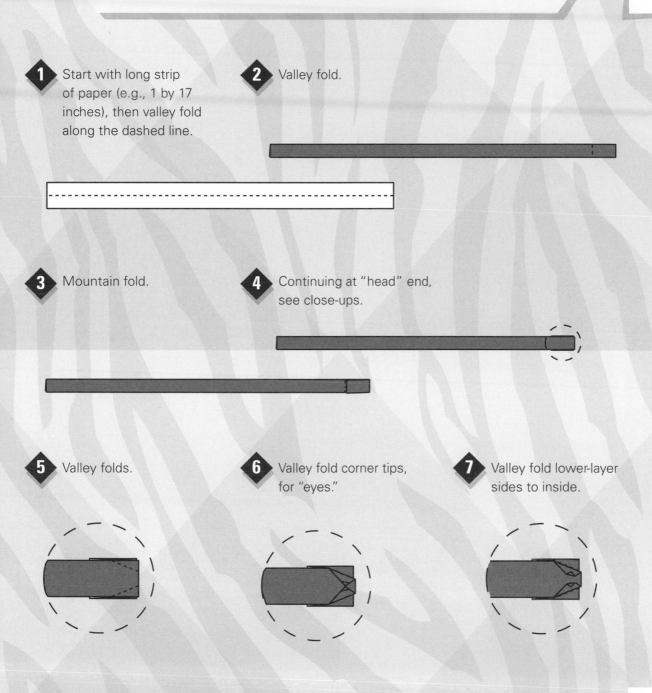

1 Start with long strip of paper (e.g., 1 by 17 inches), then valley fold along the dashed line.

2 Valley fold.

3 Mountain fold.

4 Continuing at "head" end, see close-ups.

5 Valley folds.

6 Valley fold corner tips, for "eyes."

7 Valley fold lower-layer sides to inside.

Rattlesnake

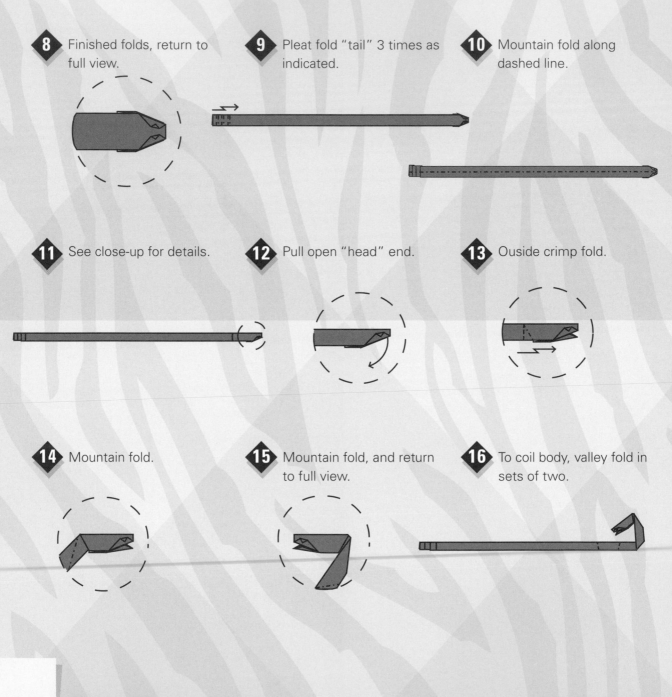

8 Finished folds, return to full view.

9 Pleat fold "tail" 3 times as indicated.

10 Mountain fold along dashed line.

11 See close-up for details.

12 Pull open "head" end.

13 Ouside crimp fold.

14 Mountain fold.

15 Mountain fold, and return to full view.

16 To coil body, valley fold in sets of two.

17 For ease in folding, turn snake form and do set of mountain folds.

18 Continue valley folds and/ or mountain folds down length of snake's "body."

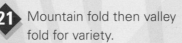

19 Continue coiling folds. Reverse a fold (valley/ mountain) to break coil for a more natural motion.

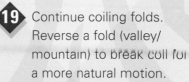
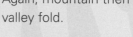

20 Approaching "tail," make folds closer together, and add variety to folds.

21 Mountain fold then valley fold for variety.

22 Again, mountain then valley fold.

23 Mountain fold "tail" front and back.

24 Adjust creased folds to give snake natural "body" movement.

25 Completed Rattlesnake.

RHINOCEROS

Part 1

1 Start with Base Fold III, inside reverse folds.

2 Valley fold.

3 Cut off corner as indicated.

4 Valley fold.

5 Pleat fold both layers together.

6 Valley fold in half, then rotate form.

7 Unfold pleat. Pull in direction of arrow.

8 Pleat fold at top, inside reverse folds at bottom.

9 Pleat fold at top, inside reverse folds for front "feet."

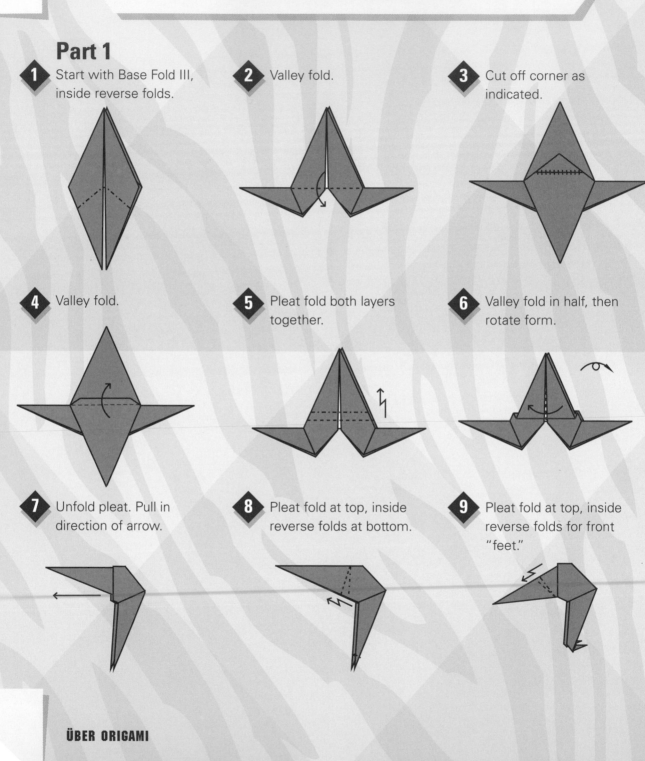

RHINOCEROS

10 Pleat fold top layer only.

11 Cut apart as shown, then valley fold top layer.

12 Inside reverse fold, then see close-ups.

13 Inside reverse fold to shape "horn," squash folds for "ears."

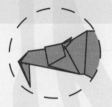

14 Completed head detail of rhinoceros.

15 Completed part 1 (front) of rhinoceros.

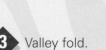

Part 2

1 Start with Base Fold III, valley fold each side.

2 Inside reverse fold.

3 Valley fold.

Rhinoceros

RHINOCEROS

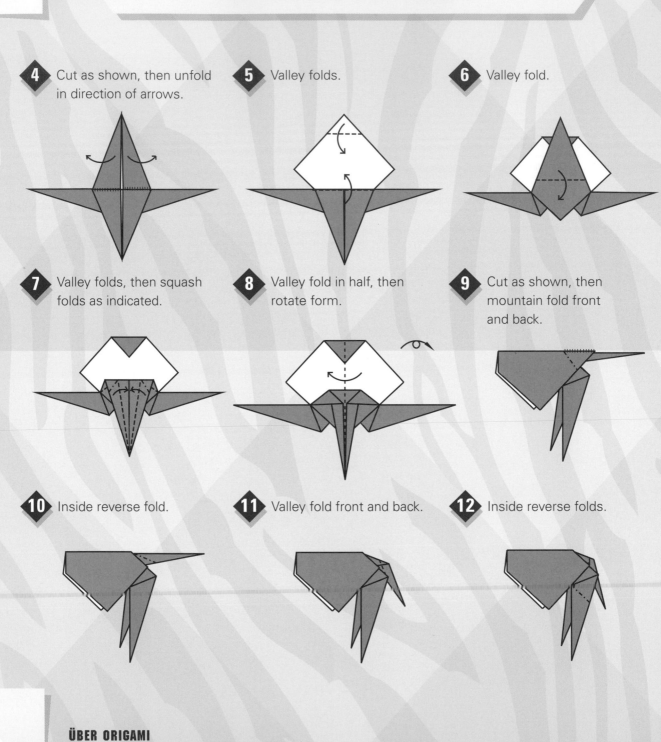

4 Cut as shown, then unfold in direction of arrows.

5 Valley folds.

6 Valley fold.

7 Valley folds, then squash folds as indicated.

8 Valley fold in half, then rotate form.

9 Cut as shown, then mountain fold front and back.

10 Inside reverse fold.

11 Valley fold front and back.

12 Inside reverse folds.

RHINOCEROS

13 Inside reverse fold "legs."

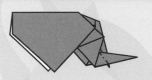

14 Inside reverse fold "tail."

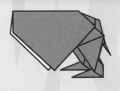

15 Outside reverse fold for "tail" tip.

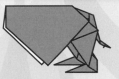

16 Valley fold layers together. Glue to secure.

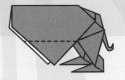

17 Inside reverse folds on "feet."

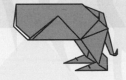

18 Completed part 2 (rear) of rhinoceros.

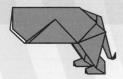

To Attach

1 Attach rhinoceros parts 1 and 2 as shown; apply glue to hold.

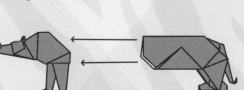

2 Completed Rhinoceros.

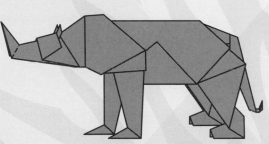

BUCKING BRONCO

Part 1

1 Start with Base Fold III.
Pleat fold layers together.

2 Unfold pleat and valley
fold in half.

3 Pleat fold in creases, and
rotate form.

4 Inside reverse fold.

5 Valley fold.

6 Make cuts, then unfold
upper portions.

7 Valley fold in half.

8 Outside reverse fold.

9 Cuts as shown.

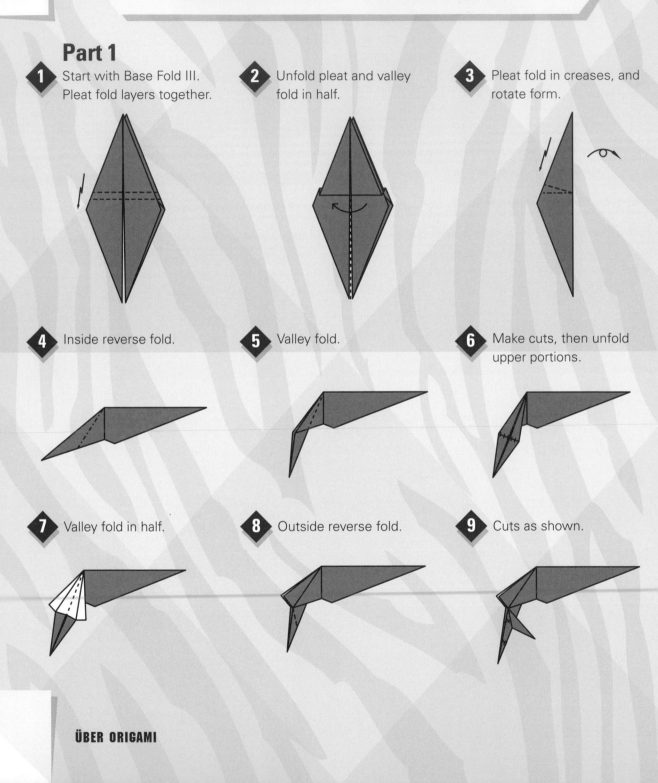

BUCKING BRONCO

10 Valley folds, then outside reverse fold.

11 Valley folds for "ears."

12 Pull some paper outward, both sides.

13 Valley folds.

14 Inside reverse fold.

15 Valley fold.

16 Valley fold and squash fold.

17 Mountain fold and turn over.

18 Valley fold and squash fold.

Bucking Bronco

BUCKING BRONCO

19 Outside reverse fold.

20 Inside reverse fold.

21 Turn over.

22 Outside reverse fold.

23 Inside reverse fold.

24 See next steps for close-up detail.

25 Reverse fold "ears" into "head" fold.

26 Back to full view.

27 Cuts on "mane" as shown.

BUCKING BRONCO

28 Completed part 1 (front) of bucking bronco.

Part 2

1 Start with Base Fold III, then valley fold.

2 Valley fold in half, and rotate.

3 Cut as shown both sides, single layer only.

4 Unfold both sides in direction of arrow.

5 Outside reverse fold.

6 Cuts as shown through all layers.

7 Valley fold both sides.

8 Valley fold each side to start "legs."

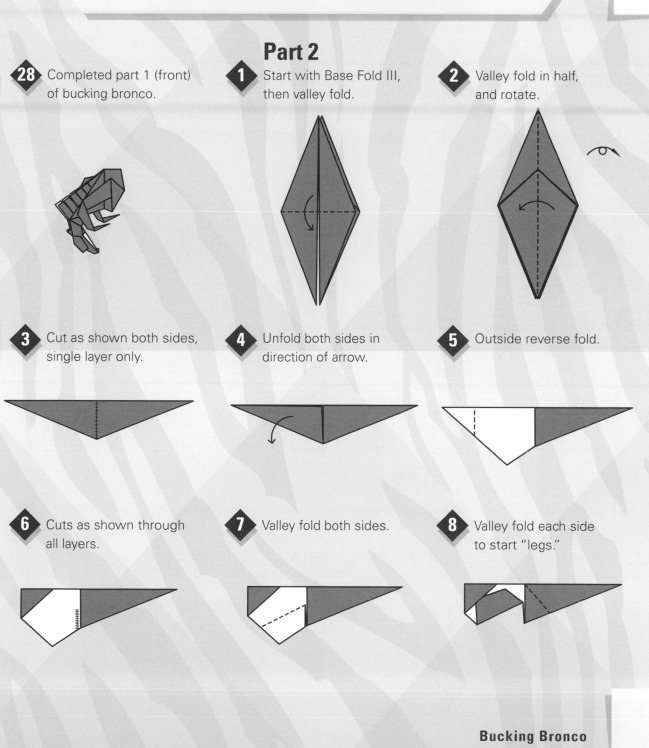

Bucking Bronco

BUCKING BRONCO

9 Inside reverse folds.

10 Inside reverse folds.

11 Outside reverse fold to start "tail."

12 Outside reverse fold.

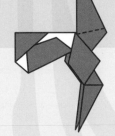

13 Outside reverse fold tip of "tail."

14 Pull "leg" forward and squash fold into place.

15 Completed part 2 (rear) of bucking bronco.

To Attach

1 Attach parts 1 and 2 together per arrows, and glue to hold.

2 Completed Bucking Bronco.

BRONTOSAUR

Part 1

1 Complete first five steps of Base Fold IV for diamond shape, then make valley folds.

2 Valley folds.

3 Valley fold in half.

4 Outside reverse fold.

5 Outside reverse fold.

6 Inside reverse fold.

7 Pleat fold under to form mouth.

8 Valley fold both front and back.

9 Pleat fold.

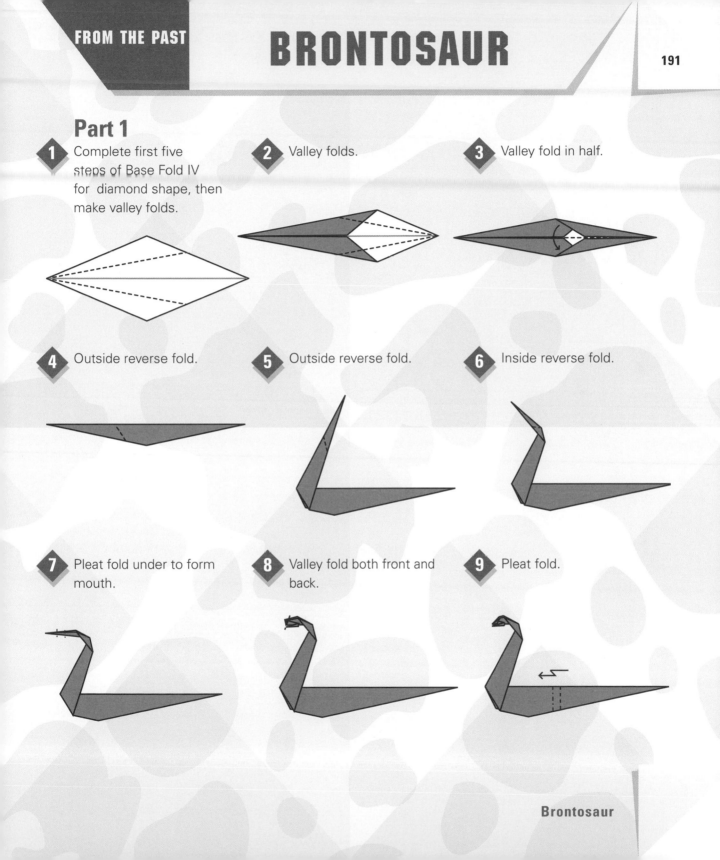

Brontosaur

BRONTOSAUR

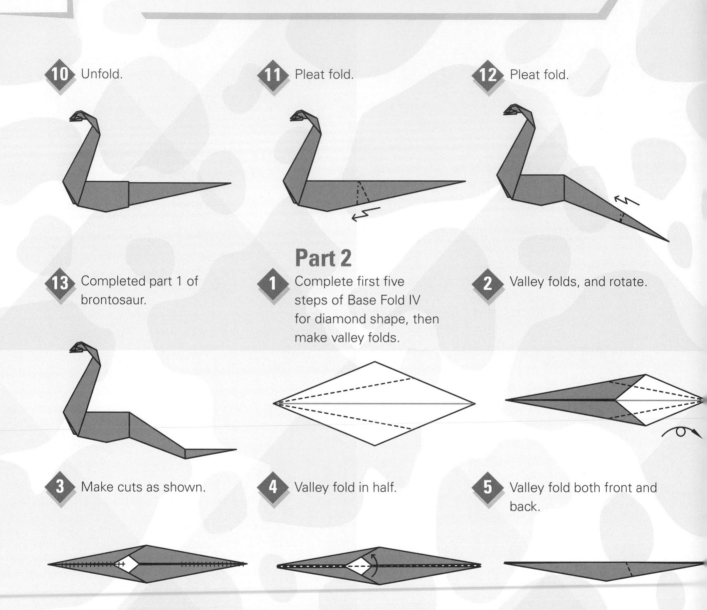

10 Unfold.

11 Pleat fold.

12 Pleat fold.

13 Completed part 1 of brontosaur.

Part 2

1 Complete first five steps of Base Fold IV for diamond shape, then make valley folds.

2 Valley folds, and rotate.

3 Make cuts as shown.

4 Valley fold in half.

5 Valley fold both front and back.

BRONTOSAUR

6 Inside reverse folds.

7 Valley fold front and back.

8 Valley fold both sides.

9 Valley fold both front and back.

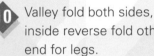

10 Valley fold both sides, inside reverse fold other end for legs.

11 Again, inside reverse fold both sides.

12 Then valley folds.

13 Valley folds again.

14 Valley folds.

BRONTOSAUR

15 Inside reverse folds.

16 Completed part 2 of brontosaur.

To Assemble

1 Join both parts together as indicated by the arrows, then apply glue to hold.

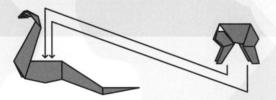

2 Completed Brontosaur.

PELYCOSAUR

Part 1

1 Start with Base Fold III, then valley fold.

2 Cut only the front.

3 Valley fold open the cut parts.

4 Valley fold in half.

5 Pleat fold.

6 Valley fold both sides.

7 Valley fold both sides.

8 Mountain fold front and back.

9 Valley fold both sides.

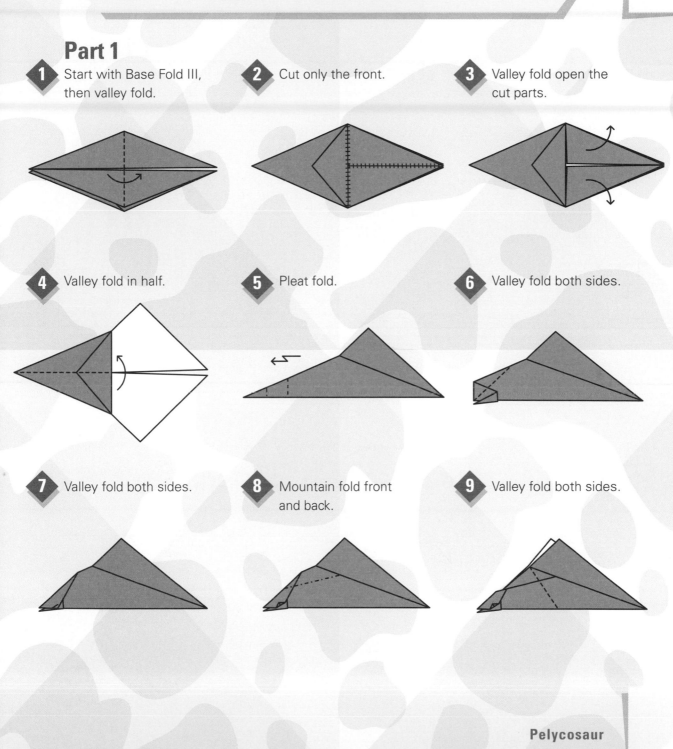

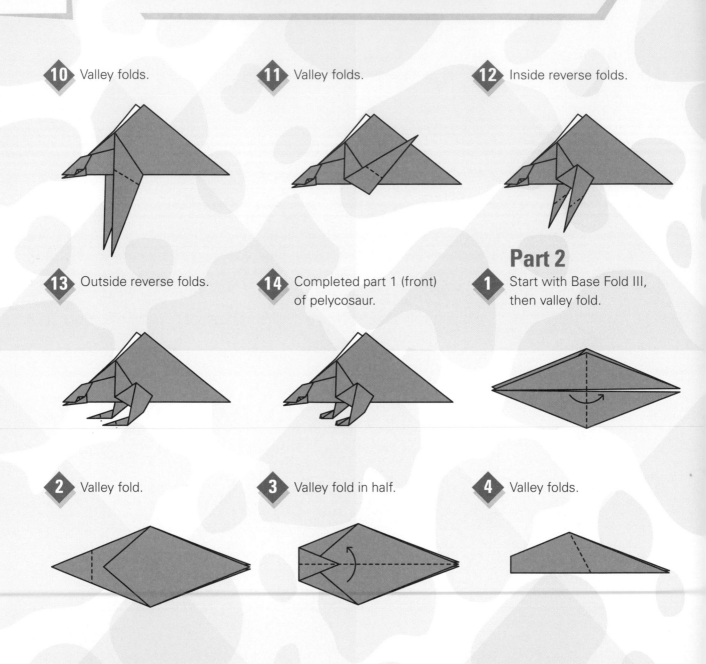

10 Valley folds.

11 Valley folds.

12 Inside reverse folds.

13 Outside reverse folds.

14 Completed part 1 (front) of pelycosaur.

Part 2

1 Start with Base Fold III, then valley fold.

2 Valley fold.

3 Valley fold in half.

4 Valley folds.

PELYCOSAUR

5 Mountain folds both sides.

6 Mountain folds both sides.

7 Pleat folds, both sides.

8 Inside reverse folds.

9 Completed part 2 (rear) of pelycosaur.

To Attach

1 Join both parts together as indicated by the arrows, then apply glue to hold.

2 Completed Pelycosaur.

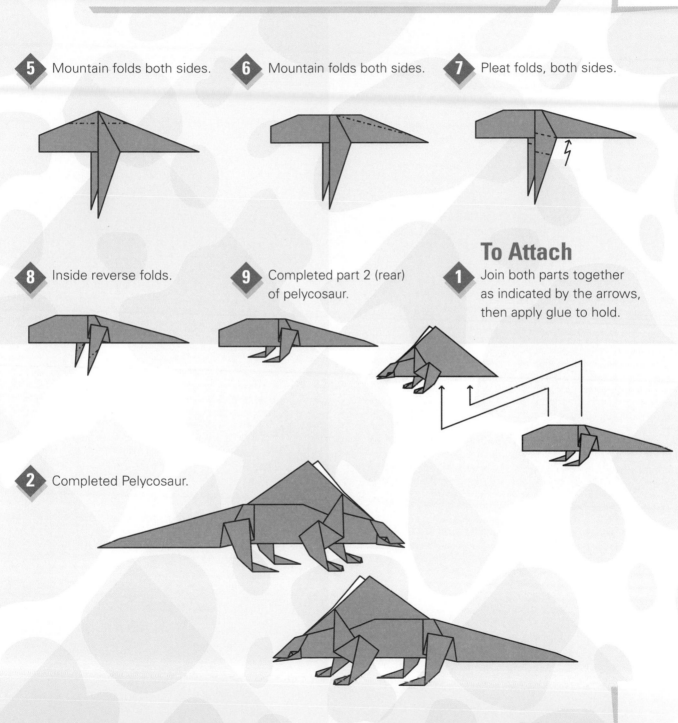

Pelycosaur

VELOCIRAPTOR

Part 1

1 Start with Base Fold III, then valley fold.

2 Cut as shown.

3 Valley fold.

4 Pleat fold both flaps together, and rotate.

5 Valley fold in half.

6 Inside reverse fold.

7 Inside reverse fold.

8 Pull in direction of arrow, and squash fold.

9 Valley fold front and back.

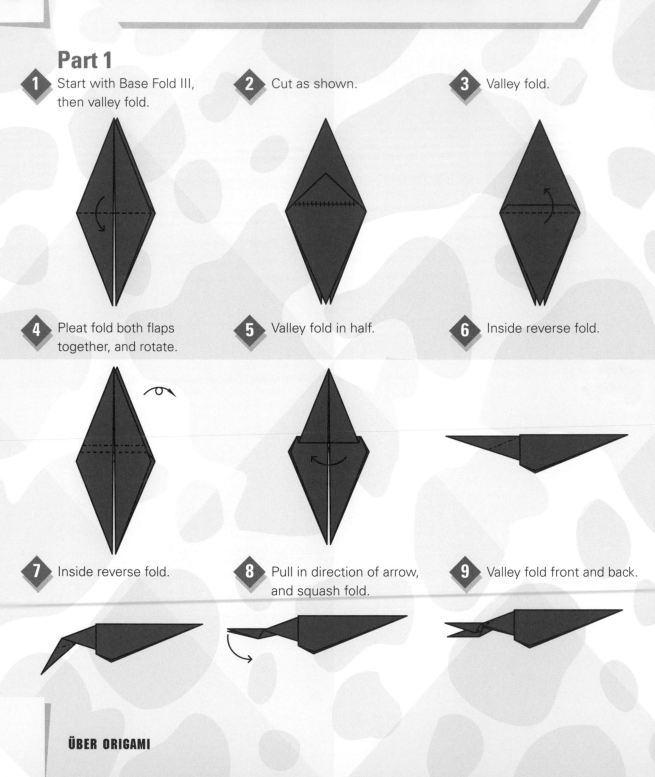

10 Outside reverse fold.

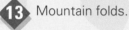

11 Inside reverse fold.

12 Make cuts to both front and back.

13 Mountain folds.

14 Inside reverse fold.

15 Valley fold front and back.

16 Inside reverse fold.

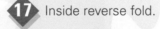

17 Inside reverse fold.

18 Inside reverse fold.

VELOCIRAPTOR

19 Outside reverse fold.

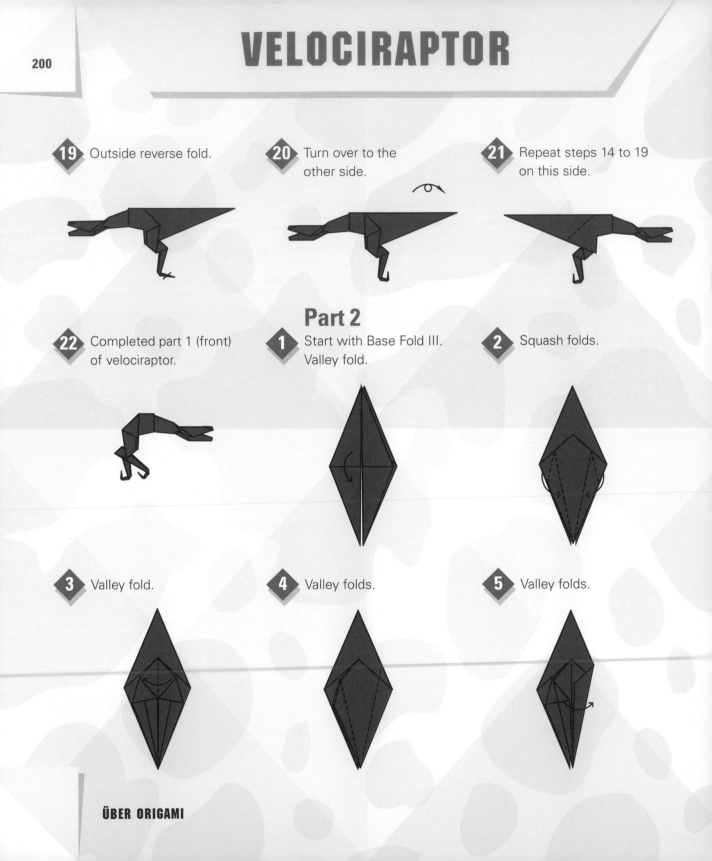

20 Turn over to the other side.

21 Repeat steps 14 to 19 on this side.

22 Completed part 1 (front) of velociraptor.

Part 2

1 Start with Base Fold III. Valley fold.

2 Squash folds.

3 Valley fold.

4 Valley folds.

5 Valley folds.

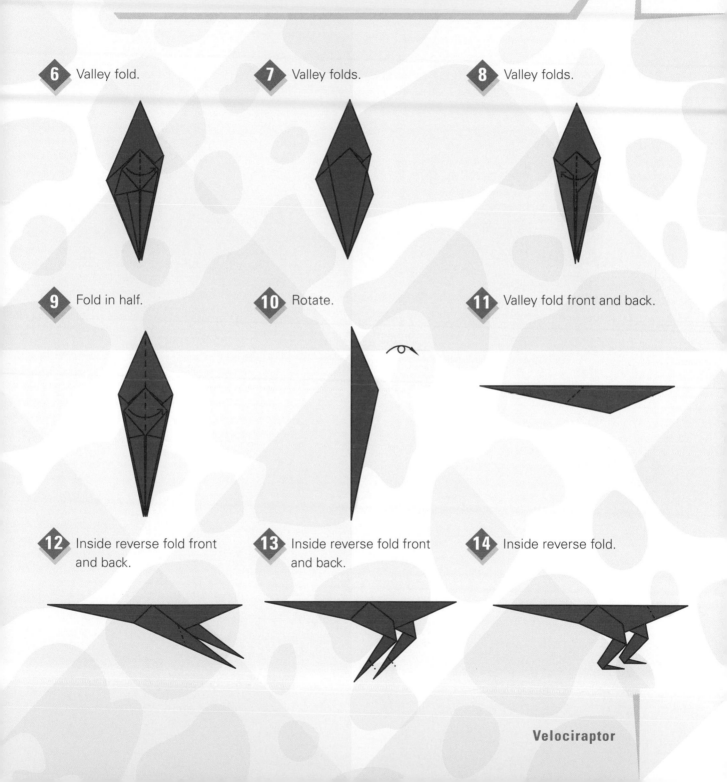

6 Valley fold.

7 Valley folds.

8 Valley folds.

9 Fold in half.

10 Rotate.

11 Valley fold front and back.

12 Inside reverse fold front and back.

13 Inside reverse fold front and back.

14 Inside reverse fold.

Velociraptor

VELOCIRAPTOR

15 Outside reverse fold.

16 Completed part 2 (rear) of velociraptor.

To Attach

1 Join both parts together as indicated by the arrows, then apply glue to hold.

2 Completed Velociraptor.

TRICERATOPS

Part 1

1 Start with Base Fold III. Valley folds front and back.

2 Cut both sides.

3 Valley folds front and back.

4 Mountain folds.

5 Mountain fold in half.

6 Valley fold both sides, then rotate.

7 Outside reverse folds.

8 Outside reverse folds front and back.

9 Inside reverse folds.

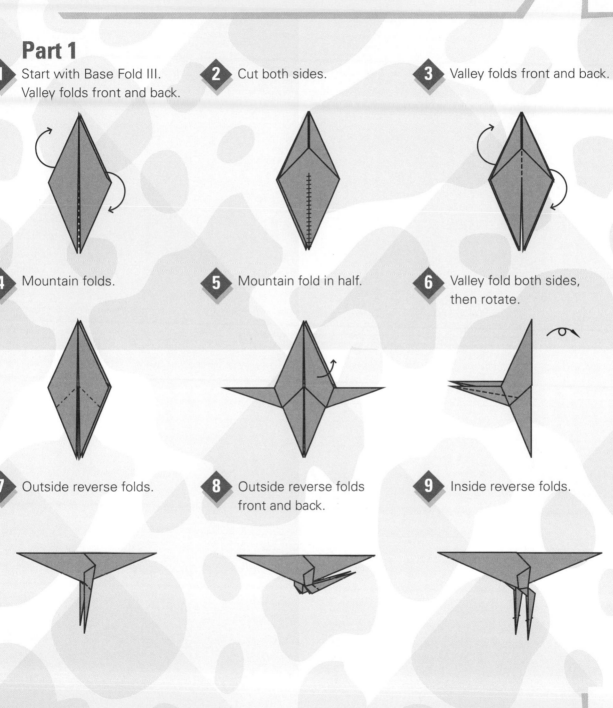

Triceratops

10 Outside reverse folds.

11 Valley fold open.

12 Valley folds.

13 Valley fold.

14 Valley folds front and back.

15 Valley fold in half.

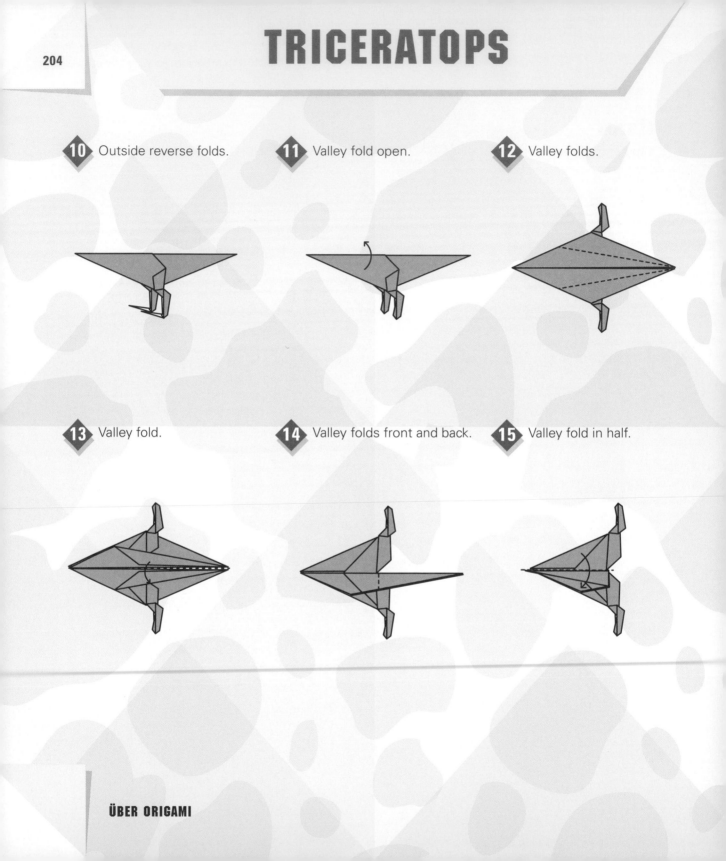

TRICERATOPS

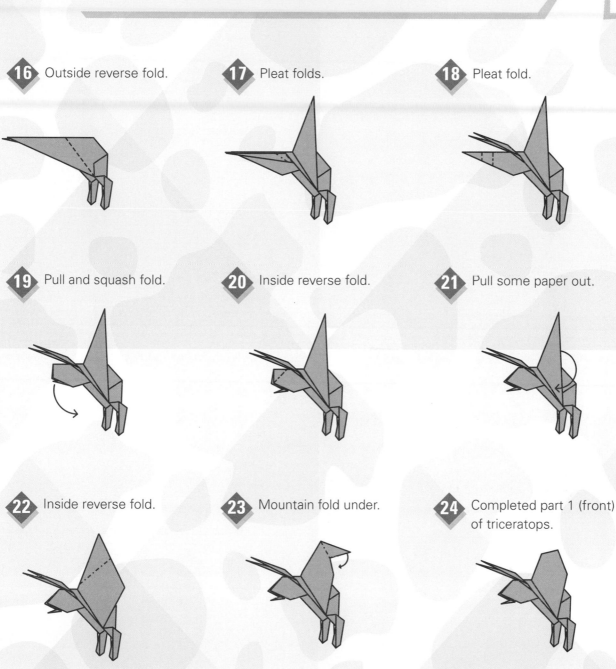

16 Outside reverse fold.

17 Pleat folds.

18 Pleat fold.

19 Pull and squash fold.

20 Inside reverse fold.

21 Pull some paper out.

22 Inside reverse fold.

23 Mountain fold under.

24 Completed part 1 (front) of triceratops.

TRICERATOPS

Part 2

1 Start with Base Fold III. Valley fold.

2 Valley fold in half.

3 Pull in direction of arrow. Squash fold.

4 Valley fold front and back, then rotate.

5 Inside reverse fold front and back.

6 Inside reverse fold both sides.

7 Outside reverse fold, front and back.

8 Inside reverse fold.

9 Outside reverse folds.

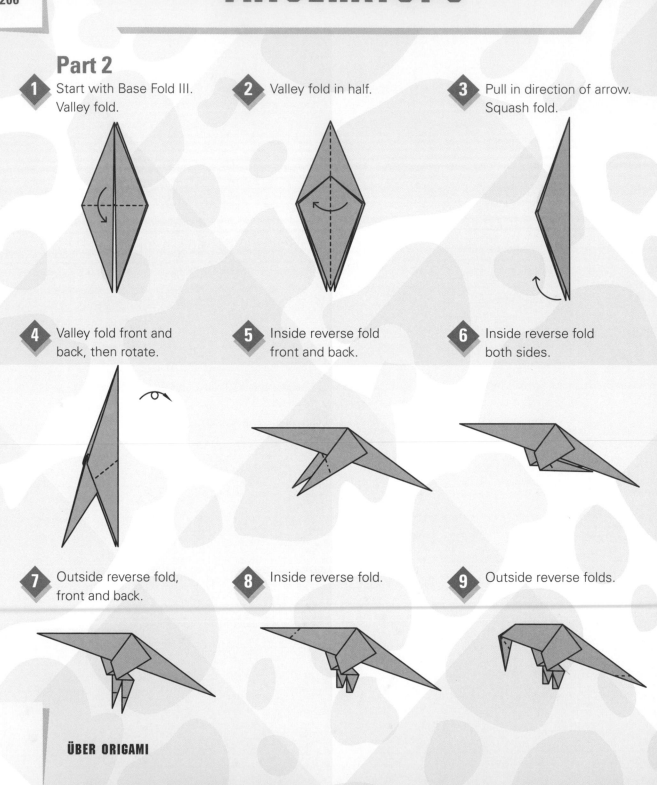

10 Completed part 2 (rear) of triceratops.

To Attach

1 Join both parts together as indicated, then apply glue to hold.

2 Completed Triceratops.

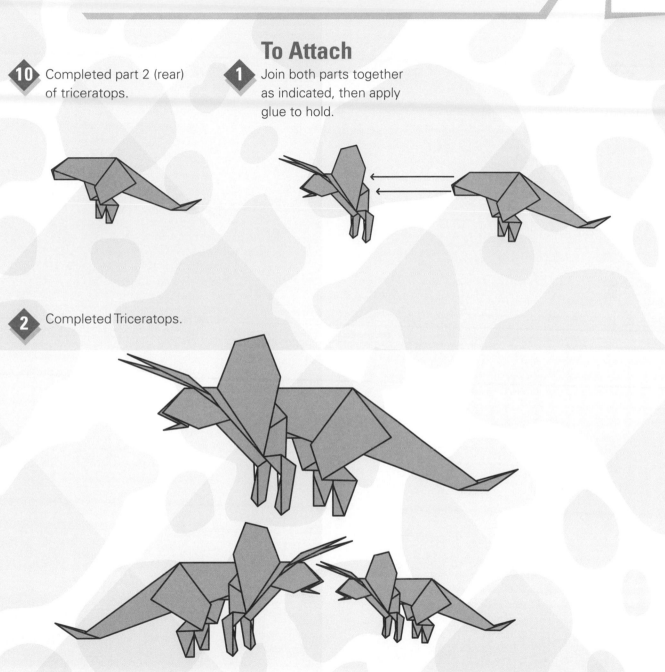

TYRANNOSAUR

Part 1

1 Start with Base Fold III. Inside reverse folds, and rotate.

2 Valley fold.

3 Cut, then valley fold.

4 Valley folds.

5 Pleat folds.

6 Valley fold in half.

7 Inside reverse fold.

8 Outside reverse fold.

9 Pull up and squash fold.

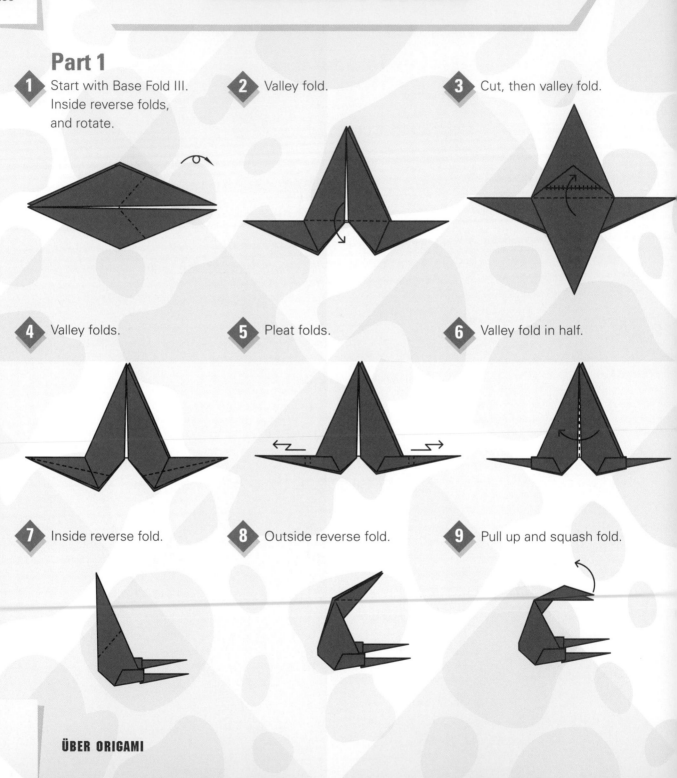

10 Outside reverse fold.

11 Inside reverse fold.

12 Pull up and squash fold.

13 Inside reverse folds.

14 Outside reverse folds.

15 Completed part 1 (front) of tyrannosaur.

Part 2

1 Start with Base Fold III. Valley fold.

2 Valley fold in half.

3 Valley fold front and back.

TYRANNOSAUR

4 Inside reverse fold front and back, then rotate.

5 Inside reverse fold front and back.

6 Inside reverse fold.

7 Outside reverse fold.

8 Mountain fold front and back.

9 Completed part 2 (rear) of tyrannosaur.

To Attach

1 Join both parts together as indicated and apply glue to hold. When dry, you can bend dinosaur into a lifelike pose for display.

2 Completed Tyrannosaur.

Part 1

1 Start with Base Fold I. Valley folds and squash folds (see next diagram).

2 Appearance just before completion.

3 Make cuts as shown, then valley fold out.

4 Valley fold in half.

5 Pleat folds.

6 Inside reverse folds.

7 Pleat fold, forming "mouth."

8 Cut and pleat fold both sides of "head," mountain fold down "body" as shown.

9 Completed part 1 (head and back) of stegosaur.

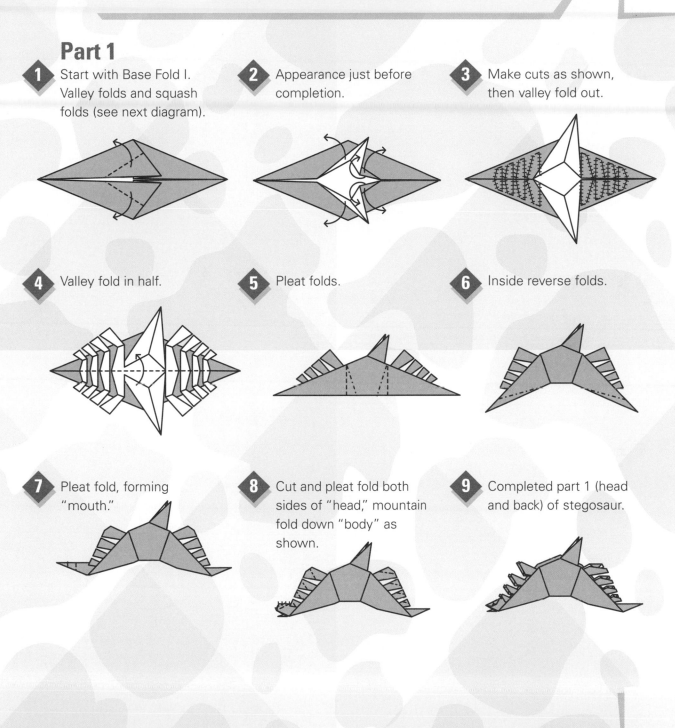

STEGOSAUR

Part 2

1 Start with Base Fold I. Make valley folds, then squash.

2 Appearance just before completion.

3 Make cuts as shown.

4 Valley fold in half.

5 Valley fold both front and back.

6 Mountain fold both sides.

7 Inside reverse fold both front and back.

8 Valley fold.

9 Mountain fold.

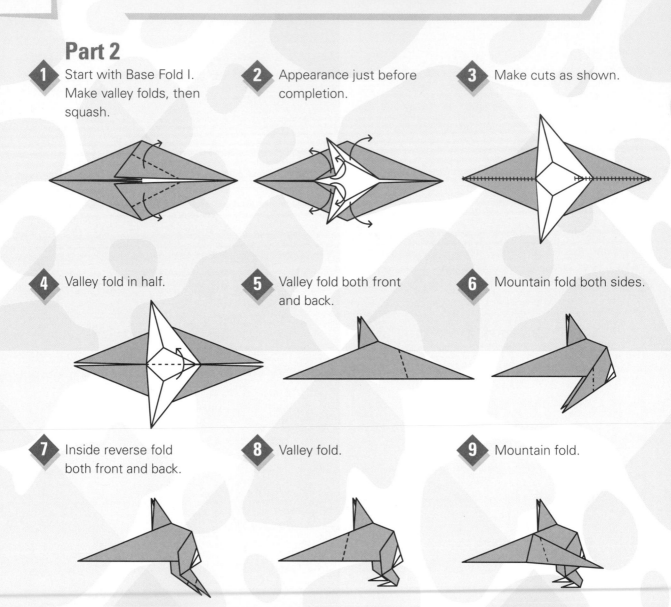

STEGOSAUR

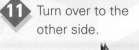

10 Outside reverse fold.

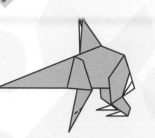

11 Turn over to the other side.

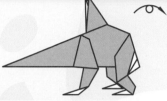

12 Valley fold.

13 Mountain fold.

14 Outside reverse fold.

15 Completed part 2 (body) of stegosaur.

1 **To Attach**

Lower part 1 into center of part 2 as shown, and apply glue to hold.

2 Completed Stegosaur.

PTERANODON

1 Start with Base Fold IV. Make cuts as shown on top layer only.

2 Valley fold cut parts.

3 Valley fold.

4 Valley fold.

5 Turn over to the other side.

6 Valley fold.

7 Valley fold.

8 Valley fold.

9 Valley fold. Mountain fold flap down.

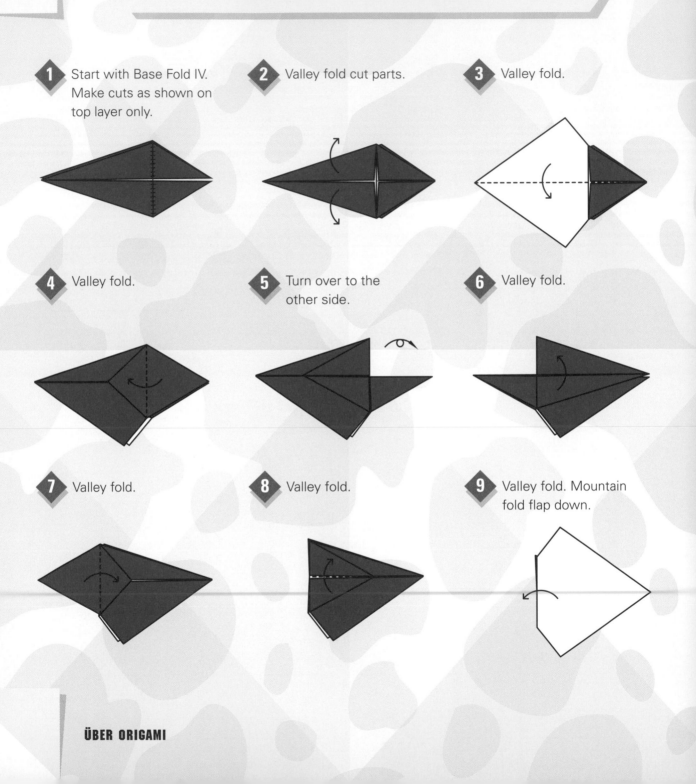

PTERANODON

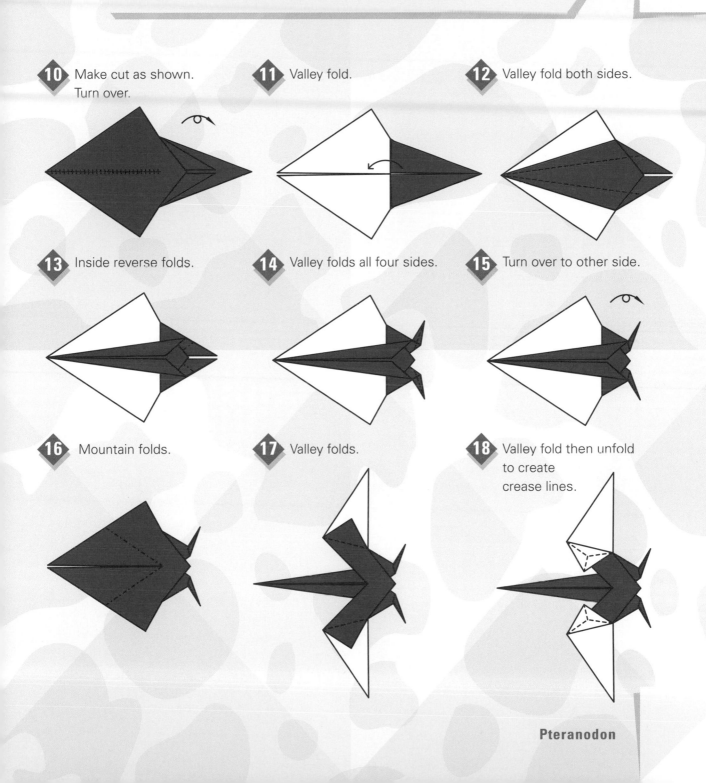

10 Make cut as shown. Turn over.

11 Valley fold.

12 Valley fold both sides.

13 Inside reverse folds.

14 Valley folds all four sides.

15 Turn over to other side.

16 Mountain folds.

17 Valley folds.

18 Valley fold then unfold to create crease lines.

Pteranodon

PTERANODON

19 Pinch together at the corner and fold inward.

20 Mountain folds.

21 Mountain fold in half. Turn over.

22 Inside reverse fold.

23 Inside reverse fold.

24 Inside reverse fold.

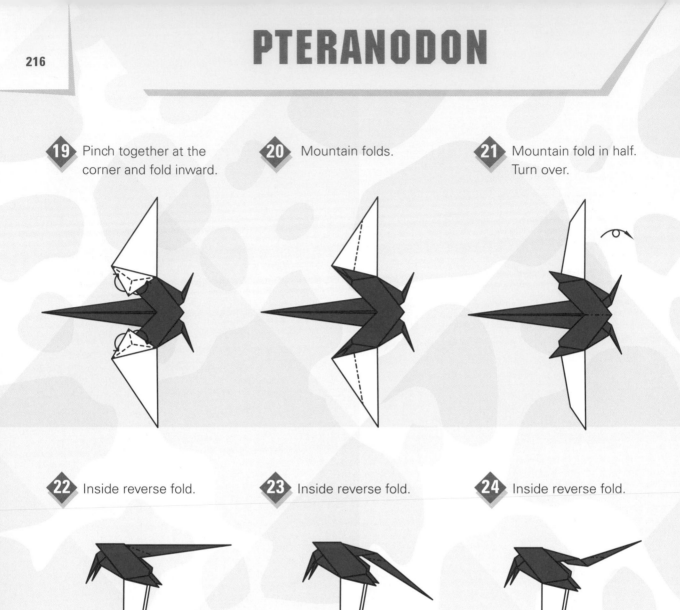

25 Inside reverse fold for head; valley fold both side wings.

26 Valley fold both sides.

27 Inside reverse folds.

28 Completed Pteranodon.

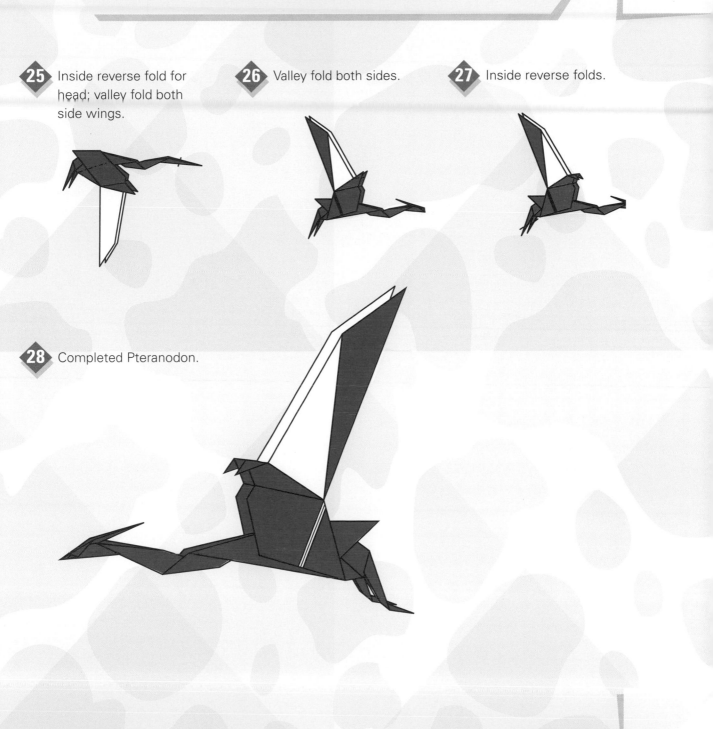

COMPSOGNATHUS

Part 1

1 Start with Base Fold IV. Valley fold front and back.

2 Cut as shown, then valley fold front and back.

3 Valley folds.

4 Turn over to other side.

5 Valley folds.

6 Inside reverse folds.

7 Valley fold both front and back.

8 Fold in half.

9 Inside reverse folds.

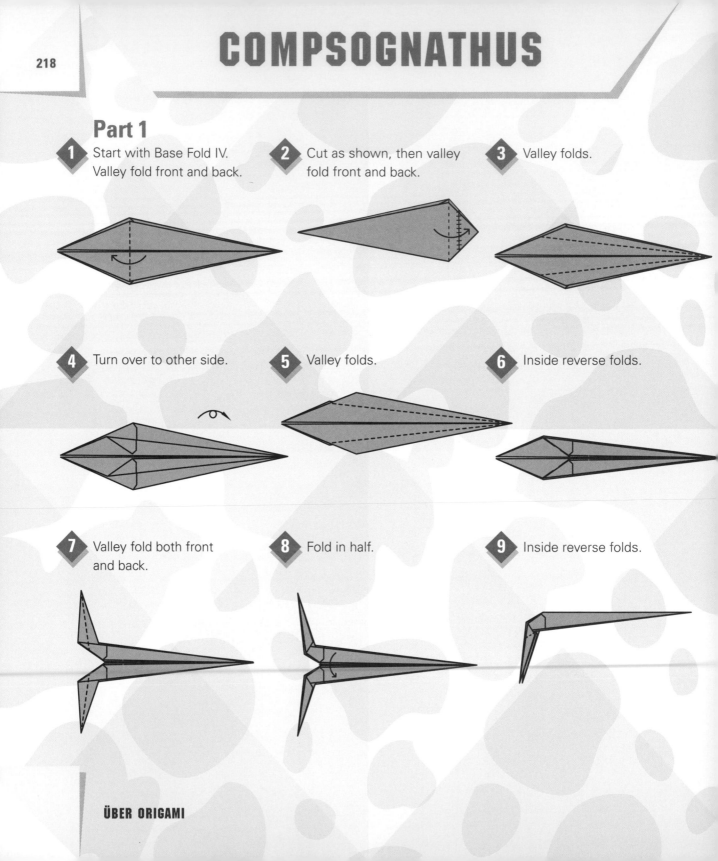

10 Inside reverse folds.

11 Inside reverse folds.

12 Outside reverse folds.

13 Outside reverse fold.

14 Inside reverse fold.

15 Outside reverse fold.

16 Pull and fold.

17 Cut, then open cut parts.

18 Outside reverse folds.

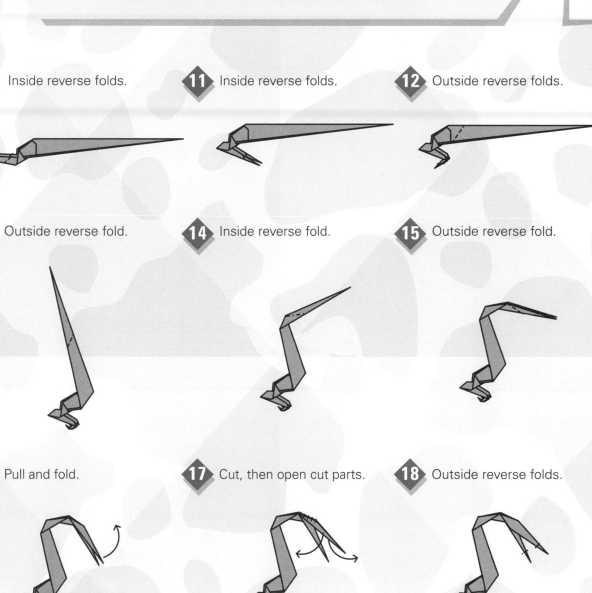

COMPSOGNATHUS

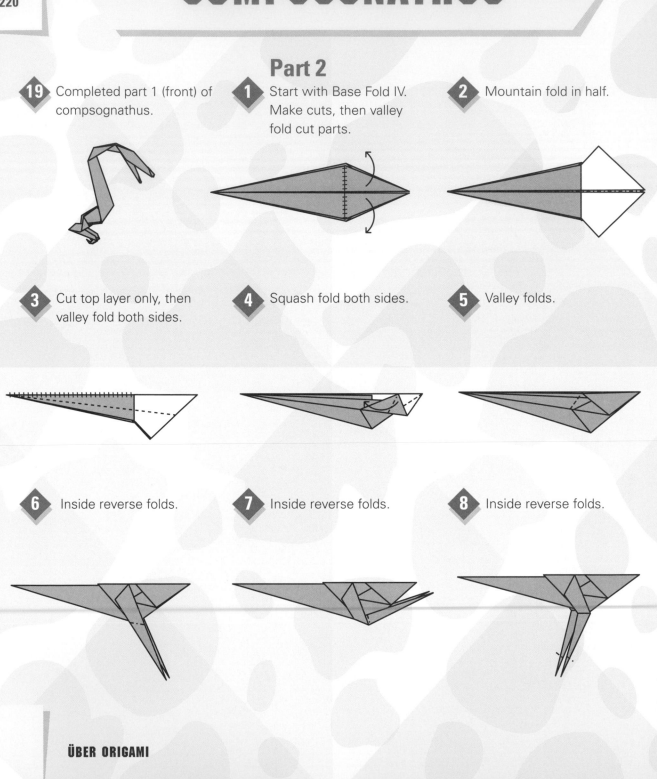

19 Completed part 1 (front) of compsognathus.

Part 2

1 Start with Base Fold IV. Make cuts, then valley fold cut parts.

2 Mountain fold in half.

3 Cut top layer only, then valley fold both sides.

4 Squash fold both sides.

5 Valley folds.

6 Inside reverse folds.

7 Inside reverse folds.

8 Inside reverse folds.

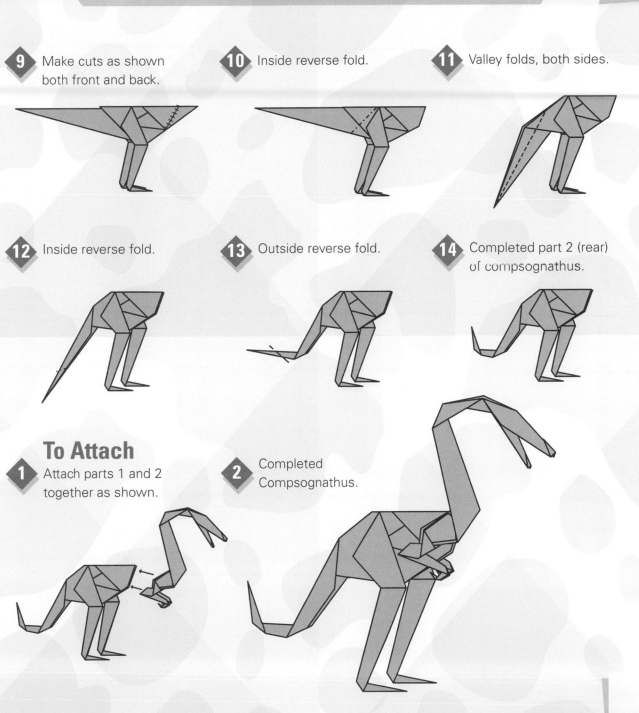

9 Make cuts as shown both front and back.

10 Inside reverse fold.

11 Valley folds, both sides.

12 Inside reverse fold.

13 Outside reverse fold.

14 Completed part 2 (rear) of compsognathus.

To Attach

1 Attach parts 1 and 2 together as shown.

2 Completed Compsognathus.

Compsognathus

MURAENOSAUR

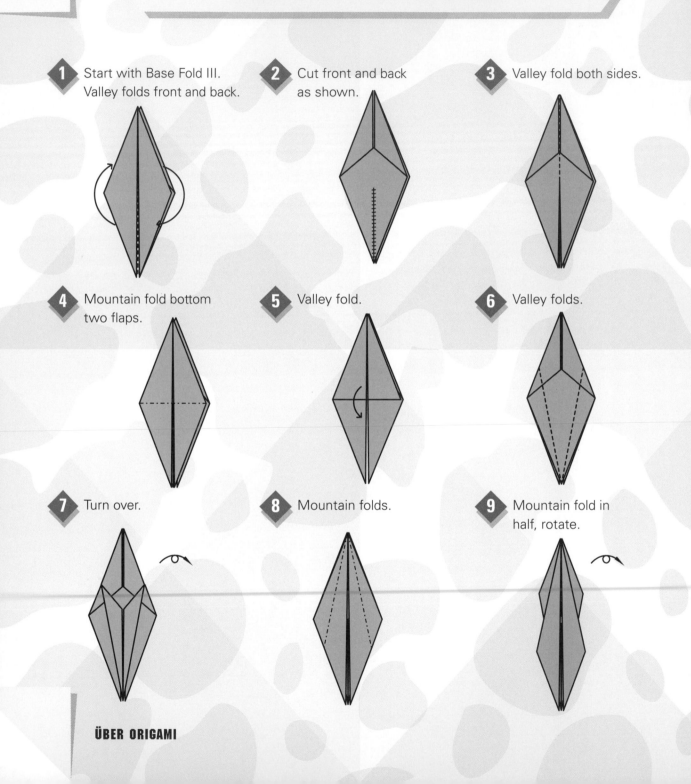

1 Start with Base Fold III. Valley folds front and back.

2 Cut front and back as shown.

3 Valley fold both sides.

4 Mountain fold bottom two flaps.

5 Valley fold.

6 Valley folds.

7 Turn over.

8 Mountain folds.

9 Mountain fold in half, rotate.

ÜBER ORIGAMI

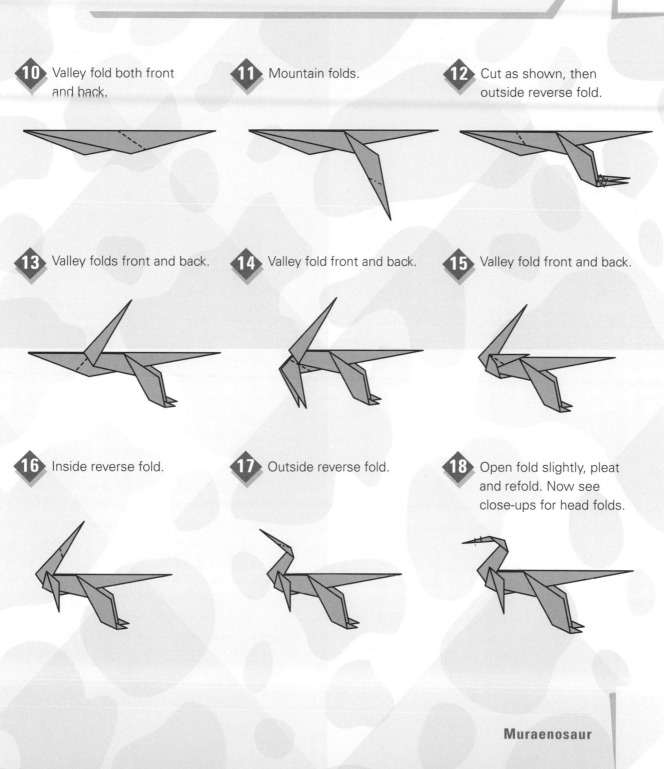

10 Valley fold both front and back.

11 Mountain folds.

12 Cut as shown, then outside reverse fold.

13 Valley folds front and back.

14 Valley fold front and back.

15 Valley fold front and back.

16 Inside reverse fold.

17 Outside reverse fold.

18 Open fold slightly, pleat and refold. Now see close-ups for head folds.

Muraenosaur

MURAENOSAUR

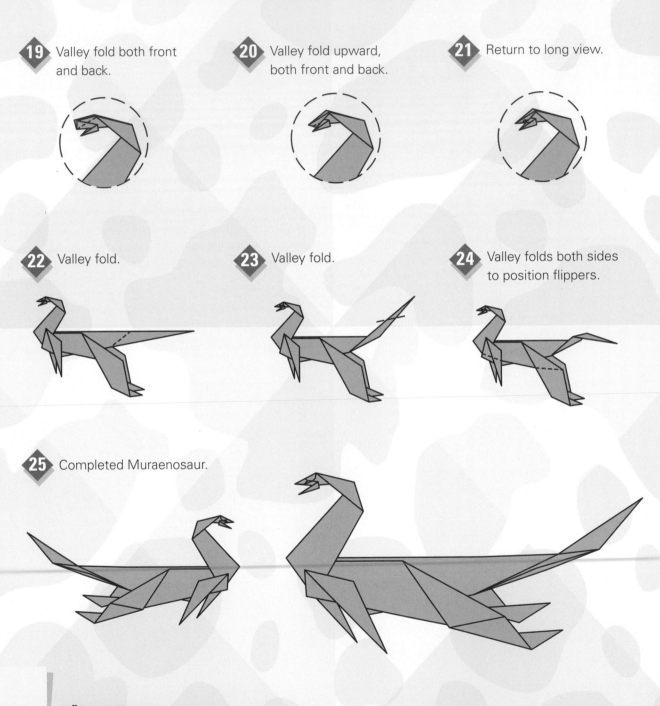

19 Valley fold both front and back.

20 Valley fold upward, both front and back.

21 Return to long view.

22 Valley fold.

23 Valley fold.

24 Valley folds both sides to position flippers.

25 Completed Muraenosaur.

PARASAUROLOPHUS

Part 1

1 Start with Base Fold III. Valley fold both sides.

2 Inside reverse folds.

3 Valley folds.

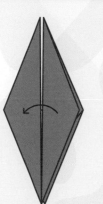

4 Make cut as shown, then valley fold in half.

5 Rotate.

6 Inside reverse fold both sides.

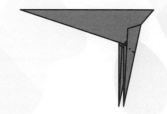

PARASAUROLOPHUS

7 Inside reverse fold both sides.

8 Inside reverse folds.

9 Inside reverse fold.

10 Inside reverse (hidden) for good angle.

11 Inside reverse fold.

12 Valley fold.

13 Valley fold.

14 Valley fold.

15 Valley fold.

PARASAUROLOPHUS

16 Outside reverse fold.

17 Outside reverse fold.

18 Mountain fold both sides.

19 Mountain fold both sides.

20 Completed part 1 (front) of parasaurolophus.

Part 2

1 Start with Base Fold III. Valley folds.

2 Turn over to the other side.

3 Valley fold.

4 Valley fold.

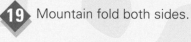

Parasaurolophus

PARASAUROLOPHUS

5 Fold in half then rotate.

6 Inside reverse fold.

7 Pleat fold.

8 Inside reverse fold.

9 Inside reverse fold upper leg, mountain fold tail.

10 Turn over.

11 Inside reverse fold.

12 Pleat fold.

13 Inside reverse fold upper leg and mountain fold tail. Inside reverse fold foot.

14 Completed part 2 (rear) of parasaurolophus.

To Attach

1 Join both parts together as indicated by the arrows, then apply glue to hold.

2 Completed Parasaurolophus.

Parasaurolophus

PACHYCEPHALOSAUR

Part 1

1 Start with Base Fold III. Inside reverse folds.

2 Valley folds.

3 Valley fold in half. Rotate form.

4 Inside reverse fold.

5 Inside reverse fold.

6 Inside reverse fold.

7 Partial inside reverse, crimping upwards.

8 Outside reverse fold.

9 Inside reverse fold.

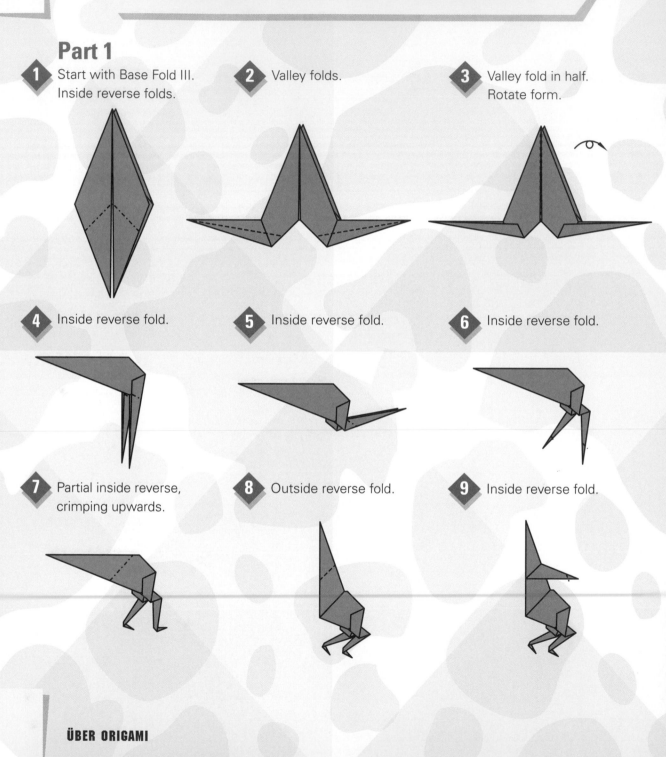

PACHYCEPHALOSAUR

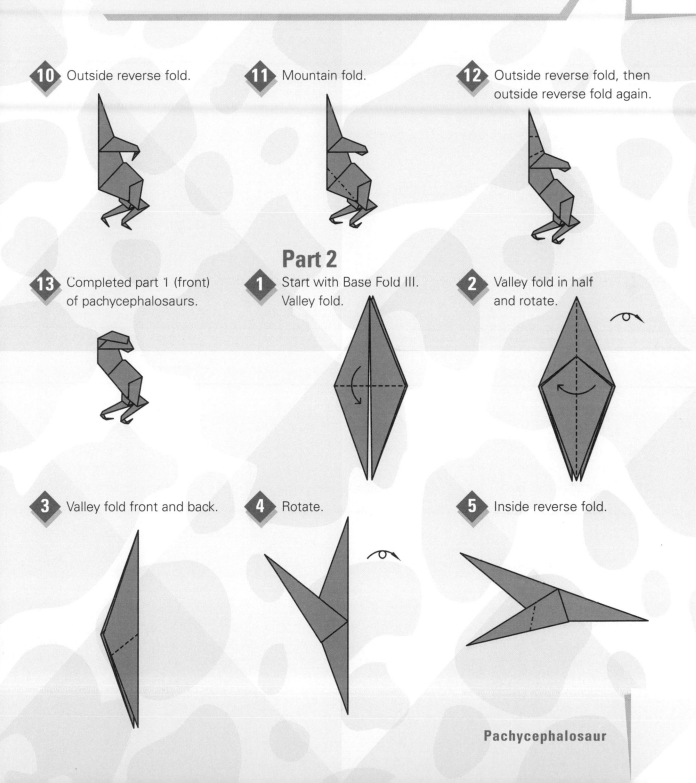

10 Outside reverse fold.

11 Mountain fold.

12 Outside reverse fold, then outside reverse fold again.

13 Completed part 1 (front) of pachycephalosaurs.

Part 2

1 Start with Base Fold III. Valley fold.

2 Valley fold in half and rotate.

3 Valley fold front and back.

4 Rotate.

5 Inside reverse fold.

Pachycephalosaur

PACHYCEPHALOSAUR

6 Inside reverse fold.

7 Inside reverse fold.

8 Outside reverse fold.

9 Inside reverse fold leg, then mountain fold tail.

10 Turn over to other side.

11 Valley fold.

12 Inside reverse fold.

13 Inside reverse folds.

14 Inside reverse fold upper leg, then mountain fold tail.

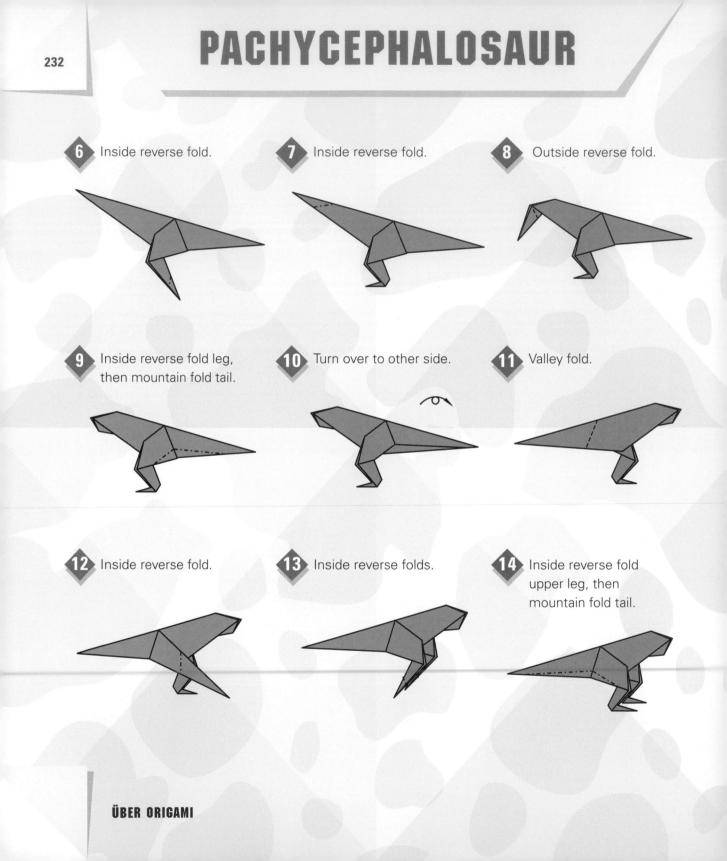

Pachycephalosaur

 15 Outside reverse fold.

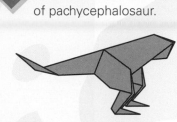 **16** Completed part 2 (rear) of pachycephalosaur.

To Attach

 1 Join both parts together as shown, and apply glue to hold.

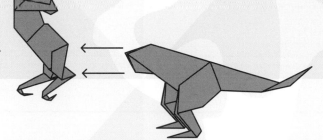

2 Completed Pachycephalosaur.

Pachycephalosaur

ANKYLOSAUR

Part 1

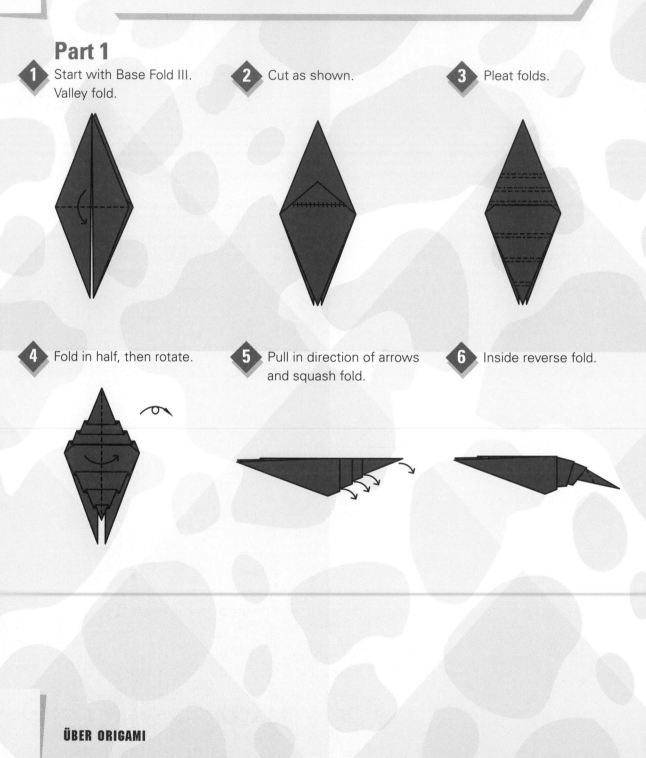

1 Start with Base Fold III. Valley fold.

2 Cut as shown.

3 Pleat folds.

4 Fold in half, then rotate.

5 Pull in direction of arrows and squash fold.

6 Inside reverse fold.

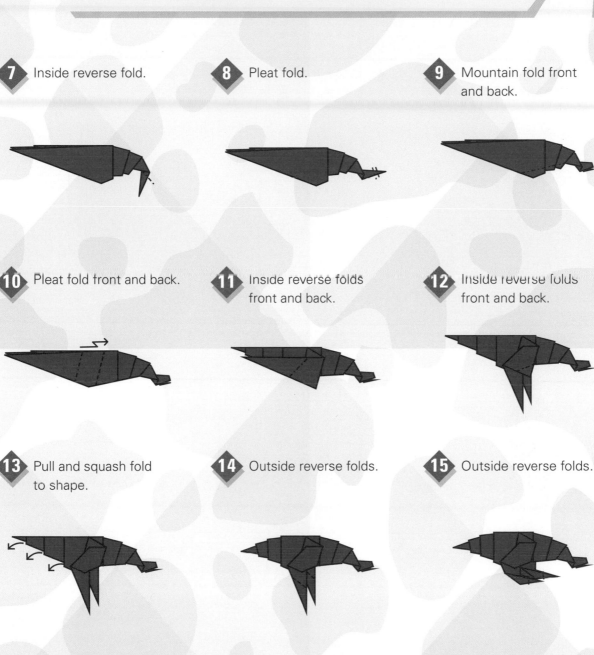

7 Inside reverse fold.

8 Pleat fold.

9 Mountain fold front and back.

10 Pleat fold front and back.

11 Inside reverse folds front and back.

12 Inside reverse folds front and back.

13 Pull and squash fold to shape.

14 Outside reverse folds.

15 Outside reverse folds.

ANKYLOSAUR

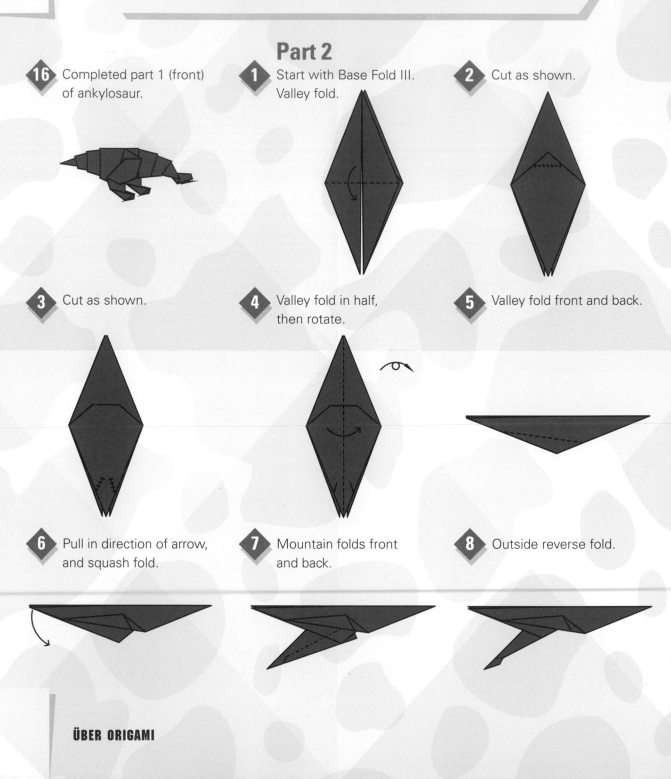

16 Completed part 1 (front) of ankylosaur.

Part 2

1 Start with Base Fold III. Valley fold.

2 Cut as shown.

3 Cut as shown.

4 Valley fold in half, then rotate.

5 Valley fold front and back.

6 Pull in direction of arrow, and squash fold.

7 Mountain folds front and back.

8 Outside reverse fold.

ANKYLOSAUR

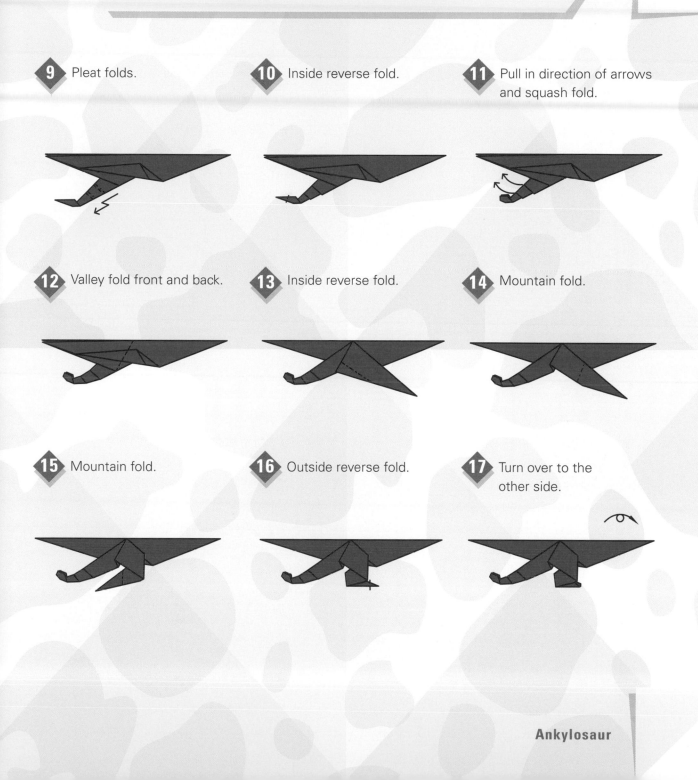

9 Pleat folds.

10 Inside reverse fold.

11 Pull in direction of arrows and squash fold.

12 Valley fold front and back.

13 Inside reverse fold.

14 Mountain fold.

15 Mountain fold.

16 Outside reverse fold.

17 Turn over to the other side.

Ankylosaur

ANKYLOSAUR

18 Inside reverse fold, then repeat steps 12 to 17.

19 Outside reverse fold.

20 Complete part 2 (rear) of ankylosaur.

To Attach

1 Join both parts together as indicated by the arrows and apply glue to hold.

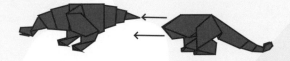

2 Completed Ankylosaur.

FANTASY DILOPHOSAUR

Part 1

1 Start with Base Fold III. Inside reverse folds.

2 Mountain folds.

3 Valley folds, then turn over to other side.

4 Valley folds left and right toward center.

5 Valley fold left and right side. Valley fold in half then rotate.

6 Inside reverse fold.

7 Inside reverse folds.

8 Valley fold.

9 Cut as shown then valley fold cut parts. Inside reverse fold legs.

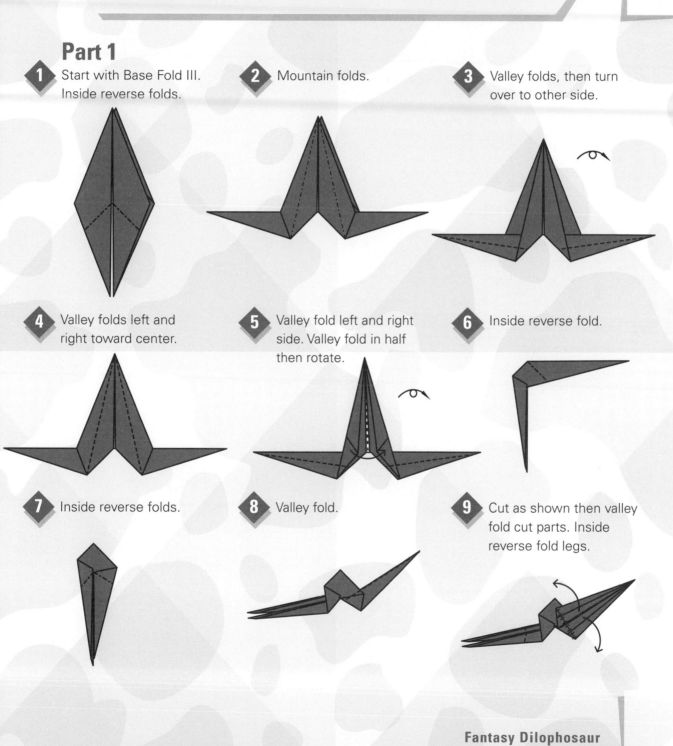

Fantasy Dilophosaur

FANTASY DILOPHOSAUR

10 Cut as shown.

11 Valley fold.

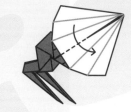

12 Mountain fold both sides.

13 Inside reverse fold.

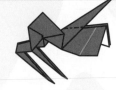

14 Pull down on flaps to loosen folds, then valley fold in the direction of arrows.

15 Outside reverse fold.

16 Pleat fold.

17 Outside reverse fold.

18 Now mountain fold.

FANTASY DILOPHOSAUR

19 Inside reverse folds.

20 Outside reverse folds.

21 Pull frill into position, as shown.

22 Completed part 1 (front) of fantasy dilophosaur.

Part 2

1 Start with Base Fold III. Valley fold.

2 Turn over.

3 Valley fold.

4 Mountain fold in half, then rotate.

5 Inside reverse folds front and back.

Fantasy Dilophosaur

FANTASY DILOPHOSAUR

6 Mountain fold both front and back.

7 Outside reverse fold both sides.

8 Inside reverse fold.

9 Outside reverse folds.

10 Completed part 2 (rear) of fantasy dilophosaur.

To Attach

1 Join both parts together as shown, and apply glue to hold.

2 Completed Fantasy Dilophosaur.

BAROSAUR

1 Start with Base Fold IV and valley fold front and back.

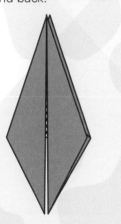

2 Cut as shown front and back.

3 Valley fold front and back.

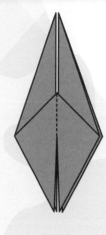

4 Mountain fold left and right, and rotate.

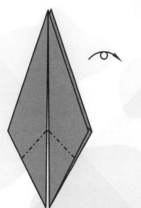

5 Mountain folds.

6 Valley fold in direction of the arrow.

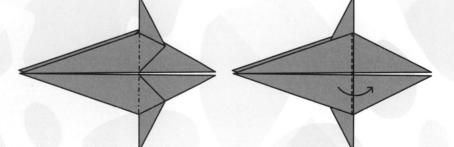

BAROSAUR

7 Mountain fold in half.

8 Valley fold both sides.

9 Outside reverse fold.

10 Outside reverse fold.

11 Valley fold both sides.

12 Outside reverse folds.

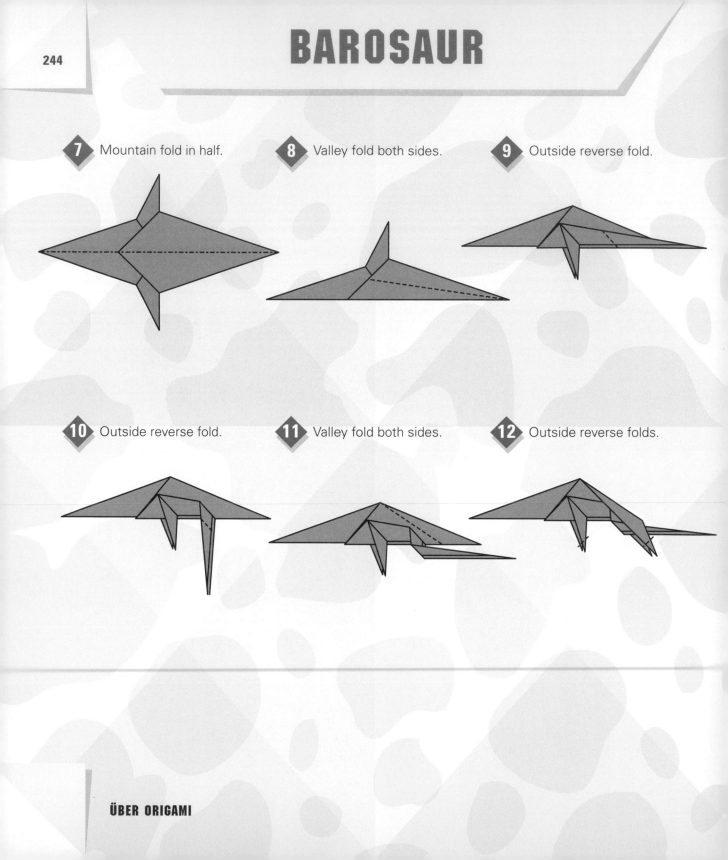

13 Mountain fold both sides.

14 Inside reverse folds.

15 Inside reverse fold, then see close-up for head details.

16 Outside reverse fold.

17 Pleat fold.

18 Head completed, return to full view.

19 Completed Barosaur.

MYTHS AND MONSTERS

Now you can be Dr. Frankenstein
and bring your own monsters to life!

PEGASUS

Part 1

1 Start with Base Fold III and valley fold front and back.

2 Cut through layers, valley fold front and back again.

3 Valley fold top layer.

4 Cut off corner, as shown, then valley fold layer back.

5 Valley fold form in half.

6 Mountain fold front and back layers; inside reverse fold. Rotate.

7 Valley folds front and back.

8 Pleat folds front and back.

9 Pull front "leg" outward and in direction of arrow, squash into position.

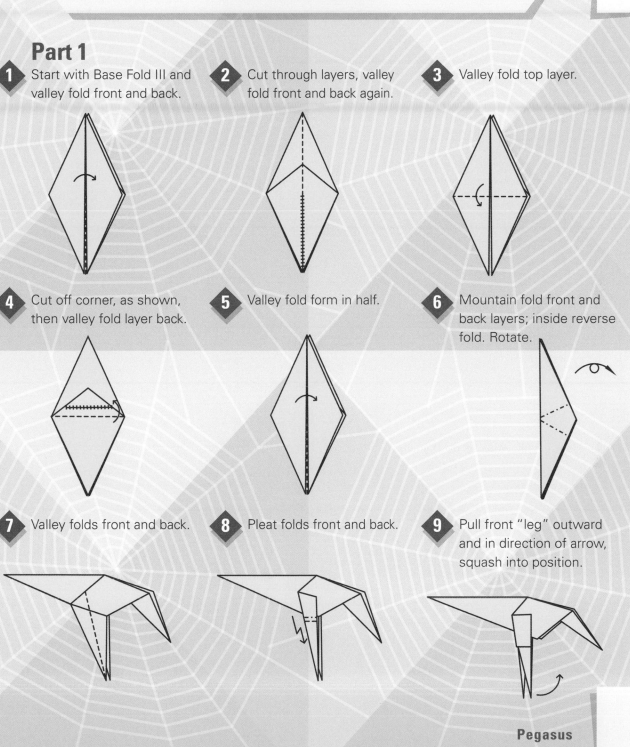

Pegasus

10 Outside reverse fold.

11 Valley fold.

12 Make cuts in layer as indicated.

13 Open cut layers in direction of arrows. Valley fold in half.

14 Valley fold to crease, then outside reverse fold lower layer only.

15 Pull paper out from inside of reversed layer and flatten to form "head."

16 Valley fold and cut tip. See close-ups on next page for "head" detail.

17 Cut off other tip.

18 Partially cut through both sides as shown.

PEGASUS

 19 Open upper folds in direction of arrows, and outside reverse fold tip to form "mask."

20 Valley fold both sides.

21 Mountain fold both "ears" into head section.

 22 Completed "head," return to full view.

23 Valley fold "mane" to one side.

24 Make cuts through layers as indicated.

 25 Valley fold "wings" front and back.

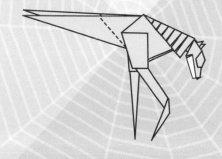

26 Completed part 1 (front) of Pegasus.

1 **Part 2**

Start with Base Fold III, then inside reverse folds.

Pegasus

PEGASUS

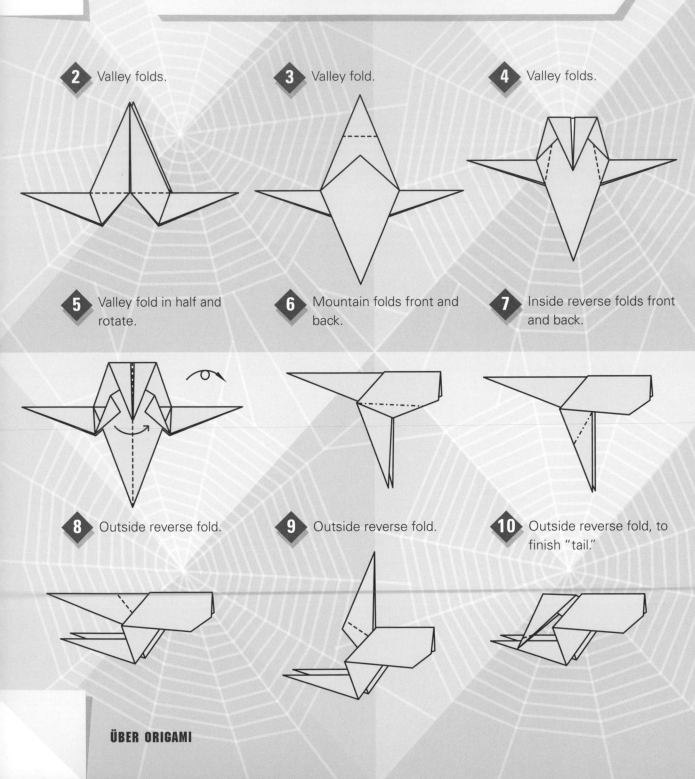

2 Valley folds.

3 Valley fold.

4 Valley folds.

5 Valley fold in half and rotate.

6 Mountain folds front and back.

7 Inside reverse folds front and back.

8 Outside reverse fold.

9 Outside reverse fold.

10 Outside reverse fold, to finish "tail."

PEGASUS

11 In side reverse folds front and back.

12 Completed part 2 (rear) of Pegasus.

1 ## To Attach

Attach parts 1 and 2 of Pegasus, and glue to hold.

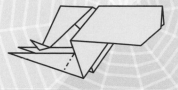

2 Completed Pegasus.

Pegasus

PHOENIX

Part 1

1 Start with a square sheet cut diagonally; valley folds and crease, then unfold.

2 Valley folds again and crease, then unfold.

3 Pinch corners together, folding inward along dashed lines.

4 Valley folds.

5 Valley folds.

6 Mountain folds.

7 Pleat fold.

8 Pleat fold.

9 Mountain fold in half, and rotate form.

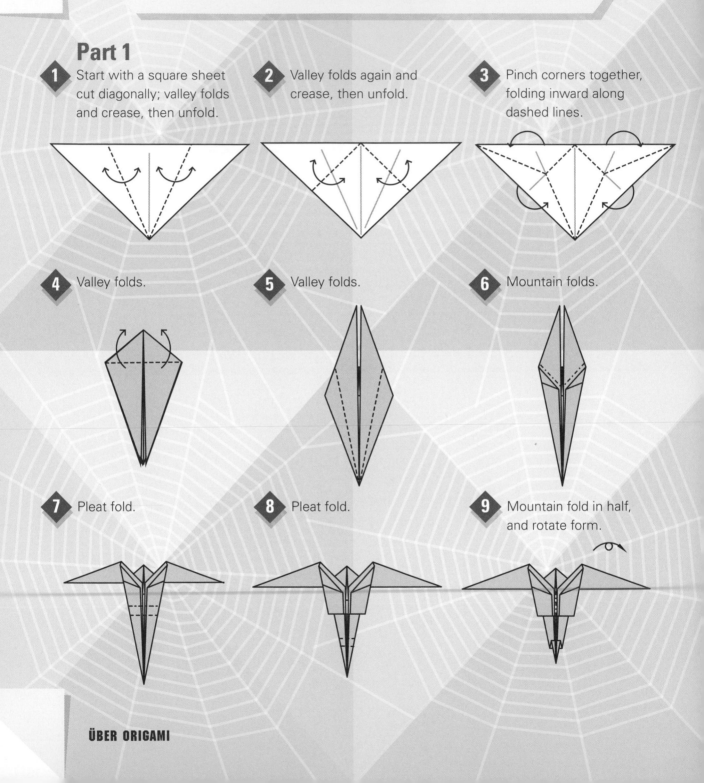

PHOENIX

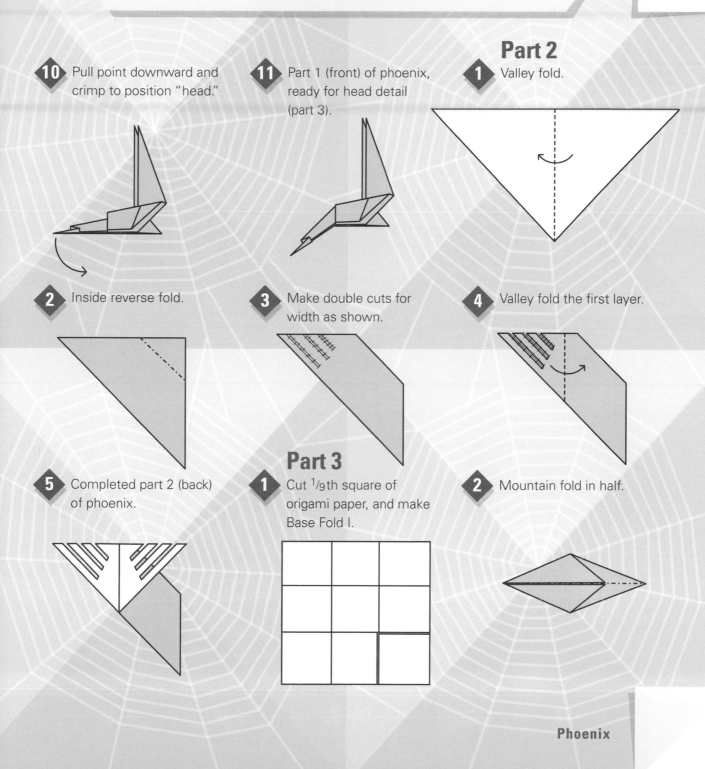

10 Pull point downward and crimp to position "head."

11 Part 1 (front) of phoenix, ready for head detail (part 3).

Part 2

1 Valley fold.

2 Inside reverse fold.

3 Make double cuts for width as shown.

4 Valley fold the first layer.

5 Completed part 2 (back) of phoenix.

Part 3

1 Cut 1/9th square of origami paper, and make Base Fold I.

2 Mountain fold in half.

Phoenix

3 Squash fold both sides, outside reverse fold tip.

4 Valley fold both sides.

5 Completed part 3 ("head" section) of phoenix.

To Attach

1 Join parts 1 and 3 together, apply glue.

2 Cut off flap as shown.

3 Join combined parts 1 and 3 with part 2 as shown, and apply glue to secure.

4 Completed Phoenix.

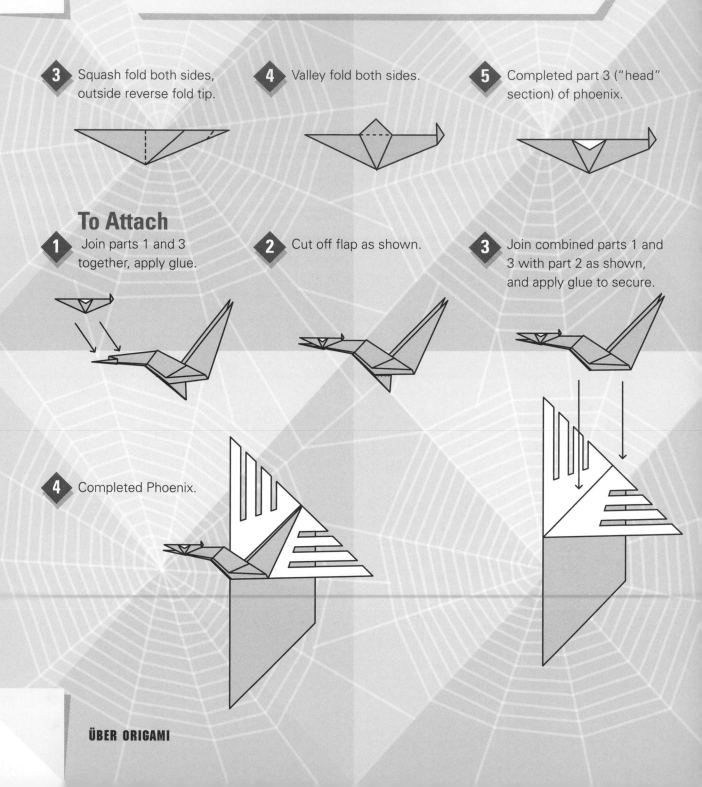

FLYING DRAGON

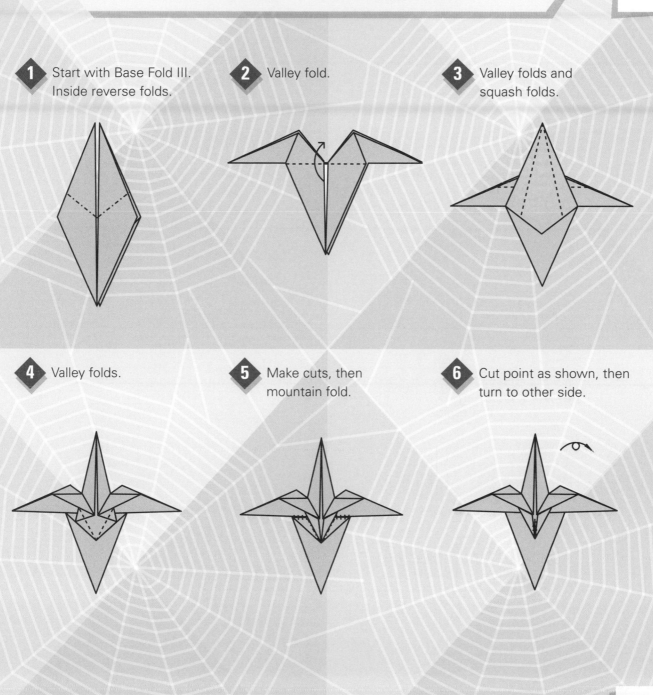

1 Start with Base Fold III. Inside reverse folds.

2 Valley fold.

3 Valley folds and squash folds.

4 Valley folds.

5 Make cuts, then mountain fold.

6 Cut point as shown, then turn to other side.

Flying Dragon

FLYING DRAGON

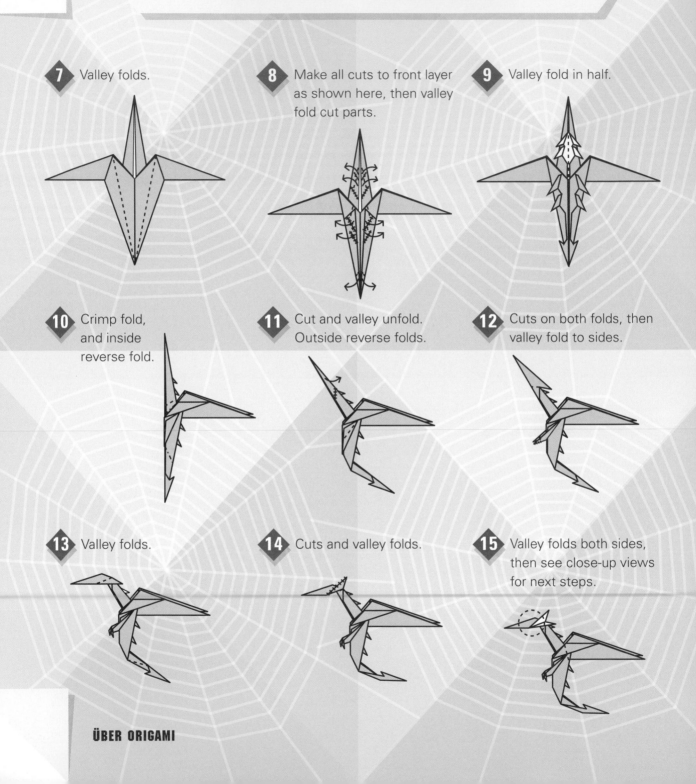

7 Valley folds.

8 Make all cuts to front layer as shown here, then valley fold cut parts.

9 Valley fold in half.

10 Crimp fold, and inside reverse fold.

11 Cut and valley unfold. Outside reverse folds.

12 Cuts on both folds, then valley fold to sides.

13 Valley folds.

14 Cuts and valley folds.

15 Valley folds both sides, then see close-up views for next steps.

FLYING DRAGON

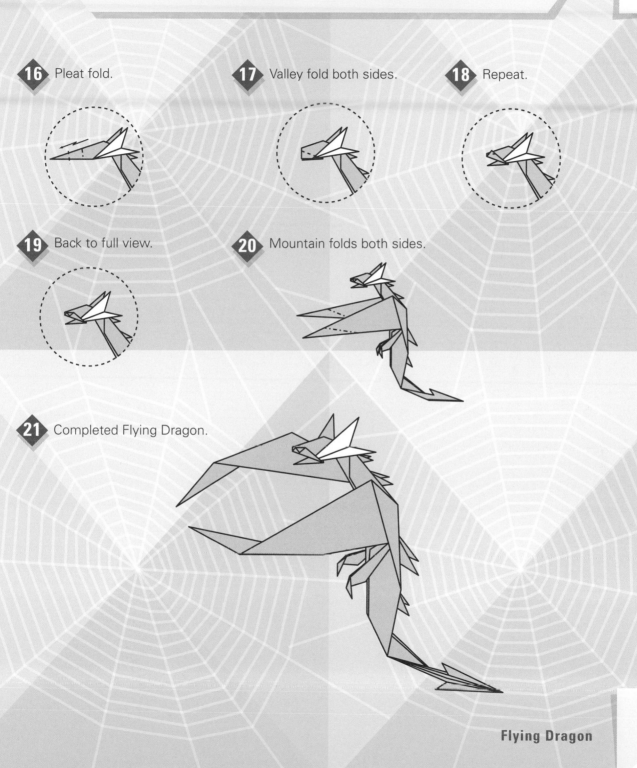

16 Pleat fold.

17 Valley fold both sides.

18 Repeat.

19 Back to full view.

20 Mountain folds both sides.

21 Completed Flying Dragon.

Flying Dragon

CYCLOPS

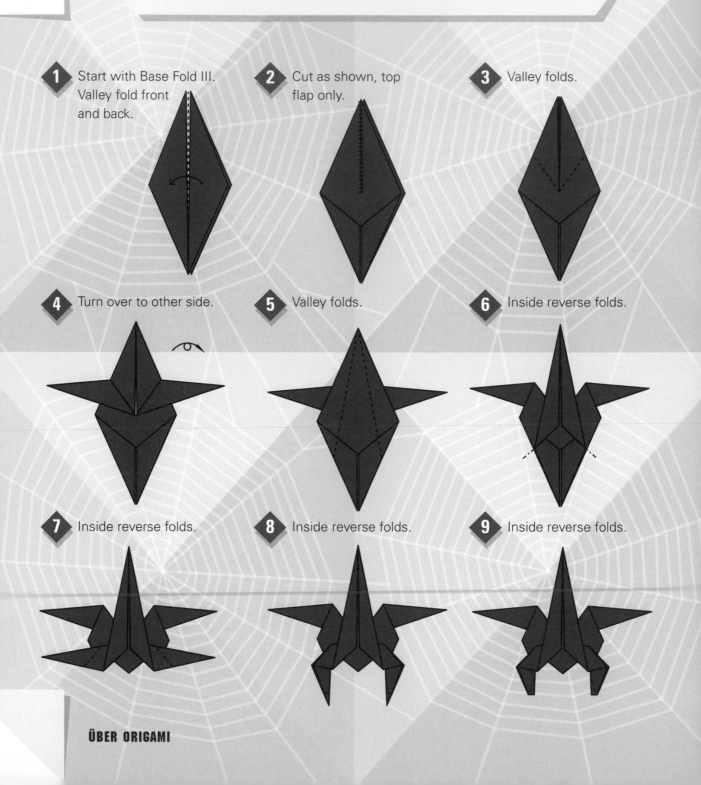

1 Start with Base Fold III. Valley fold front and back.

2 Cut as shown, top flap only.

3 Valley folds.

4 Turn over to other side.

5 Valley folds.

6 Inside reverse folds.

7 Inside reverse folds.

8 Inside reverse folds.

9 Inside reverse folds.

ÜBER ORIGAMI

CYCLOPS

10 Cut front layers only.

11 Valley folds.

12 Turn over to other side.

13 Pleat fold.

14 Valley fold in half.

15 Crimp fold.

16 Outside reverse fold.

17 Cut as shown.

18 Valley and squash folds.

Cyclops

CYCLOPS

19 Inside reverse folds.

20 Outside reverse folds, both sides.

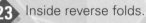

21 Crimp fold.

22 Outside reverse folds.

23 Inside reverse folds.

24 Outside reverse folds.

25 Completed Cyclops.

MERMAID

Part 1

1 Start with Base Fold III. Valley fold both sides.

2 Inside reverse folds.

3 Valley folds.

4 Make cut as shown.

5 Turn over to other side.

6 Valley fold.

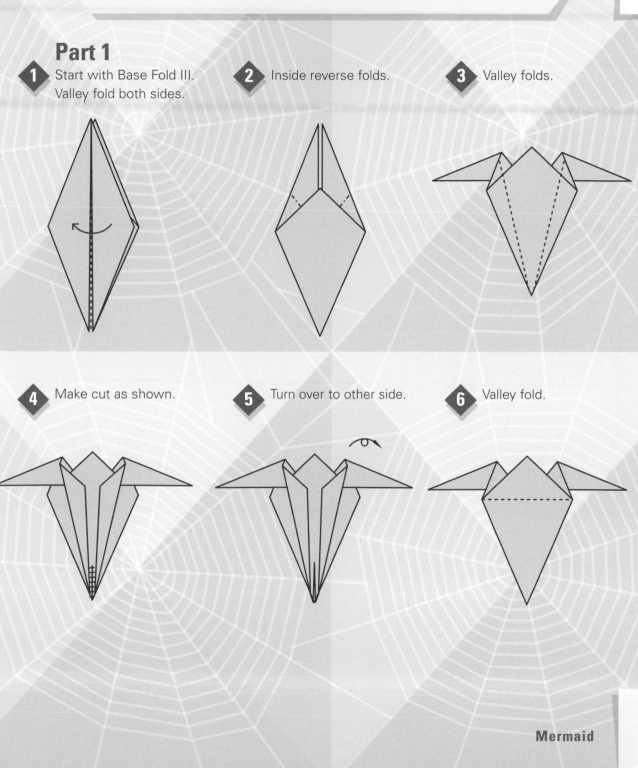

Mermaid

MERMAID

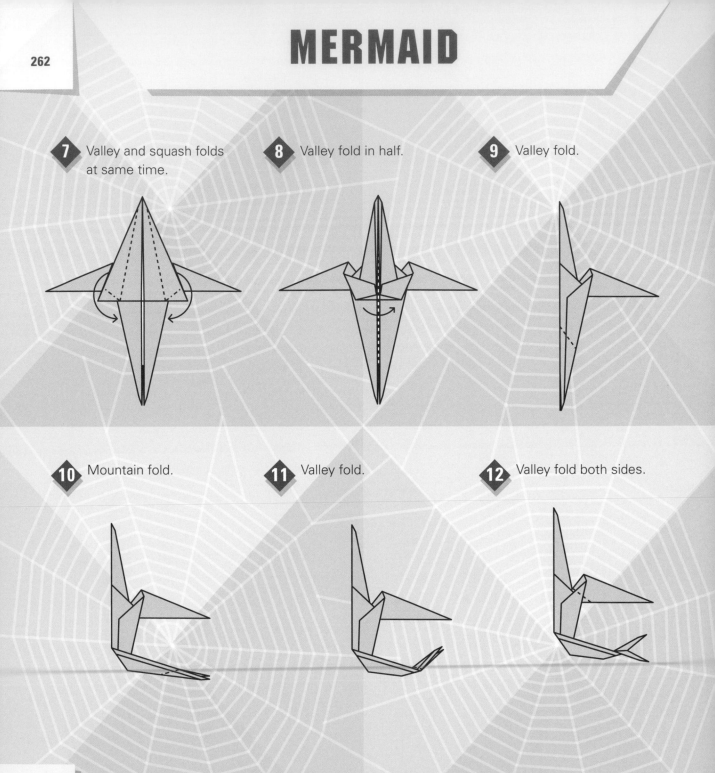

7 Valley and squash folds at same time.

8 Valley fold in half.

9 Valley fold.

10 Mountain fold.

11 Valley fold.

12 Valley fold both sides.

MERMAID

13 Valley fold.

14 Inside reverse fold.

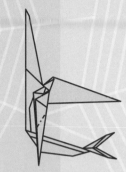

15 Crimp fold.

16 Outside reverse fold.

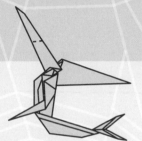

17 Outside reverse fold.

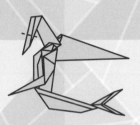

18 Turn over to other side.

19 Valley fold.

20 Valley fold.

21 Inside reverse fold.

Mermaid

MERMAID

22 Inside reverse folds.

23 Outside reverse folds.

24 Completed part 1 of mermaid.

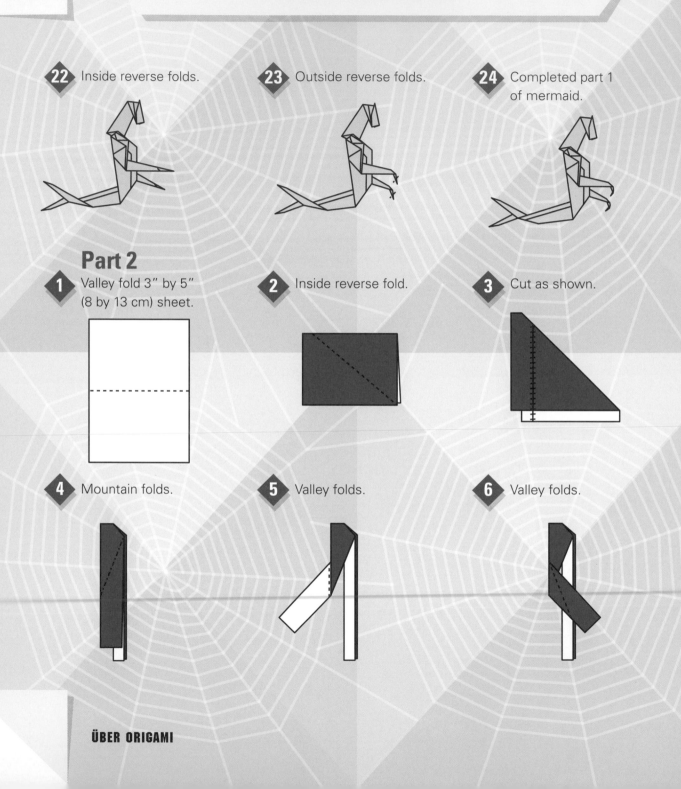

Part 2

1 Valley fold 3" by 5" (8 by 13 cm) sheet.

2 Inside reverse fold.

3 Cut as shown.

4 Mountain folds.

5 Valley folds.

6 Valley folds.

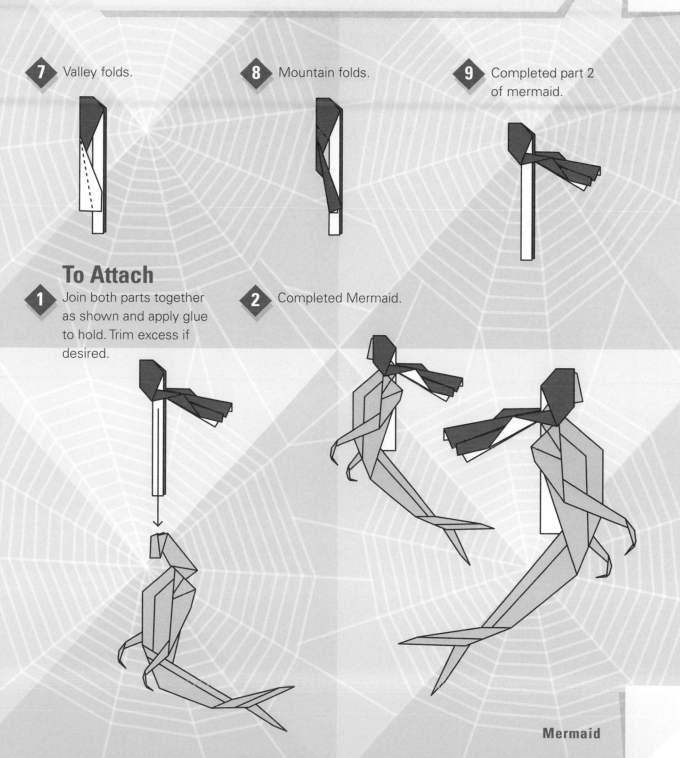

7 Valley folds.

8 Mountain folds.

9 Completed part 2 of mermaid.

To Attach

1 Join both parts together as shown and apply glue to hold. Trim excess if desired.

2 Completed Mermaid.

Mermaid

UNICORN

Part 1

1 Start with Base Fold III. Valley fold in half.

2 Valley fold. Repeat behind.

3 Inside reverse fold.

4 Outside reverse fold.

5 Valley fold.

6 Cuts and valley unfolds.

7 Valley fold.

8 Unfolds and valley fold.

9 Cuts as shown.

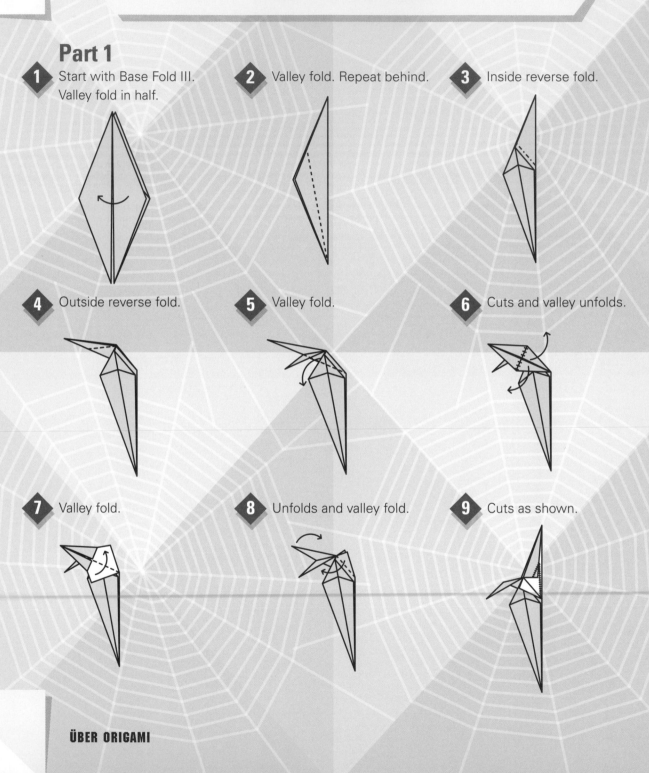

UNICORN

10 Unfold to return to step 8 position.

11 Pull a single layer to each side.

12 Valley folds.

13 Inside reverse fold.

14 Outside reverse fold.

15 Cuts as shown.

16 Mountain folds.

17 Outside reverse folds.

18 Pleat folds.

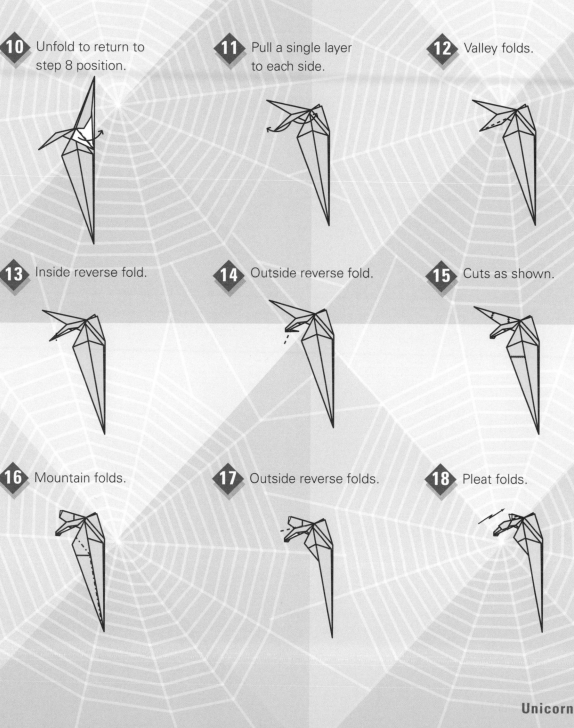

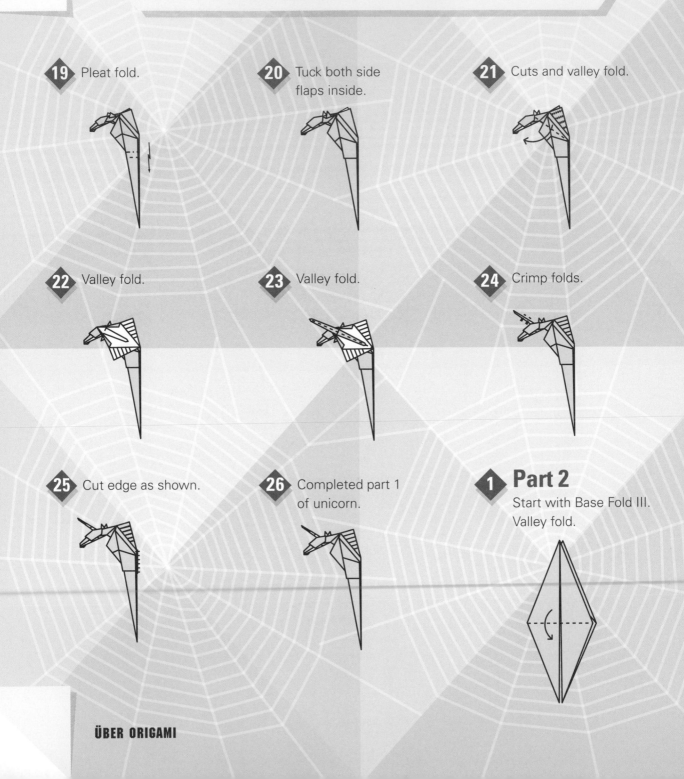

UNICORN

19 Pleat fold.

20 Tuck both side flaps inside.

21 Cuts and valley fold.

22 Valley fold.

23 Valley fold.

24 Crimp folds.

25 Cut edge as shown.

26 Completed part 1 of unicorn.

1 **Part 2**
Start with Base Fold III. Valley fold.

UNICORN

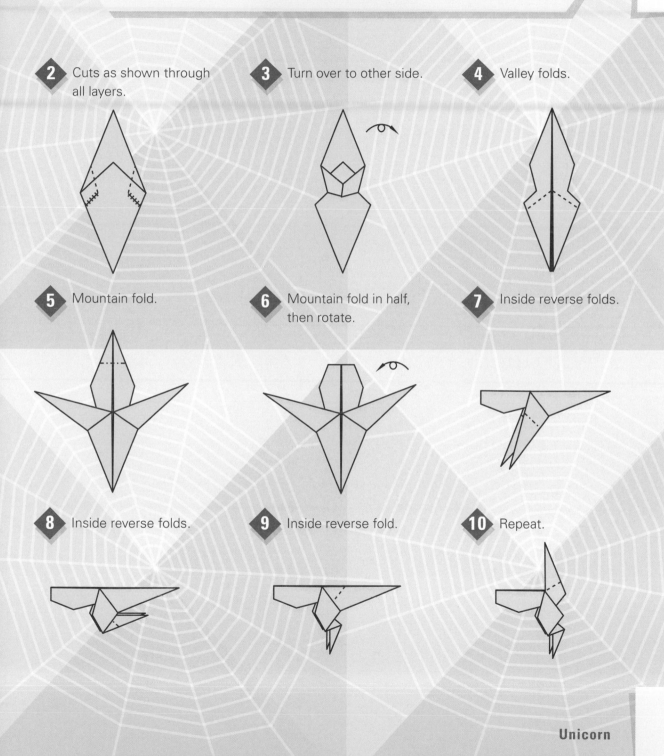

2 Cuts as shown through all layers.

3 Turn over to other side.

4 Valley folds.

5 Mountain fold.

6 Mountain fold in half, then rotate.

7 Inside reverse folds.

8 Inside reverse folds.

9 Inside reverse fold.

10 Repeat.

Unicorn

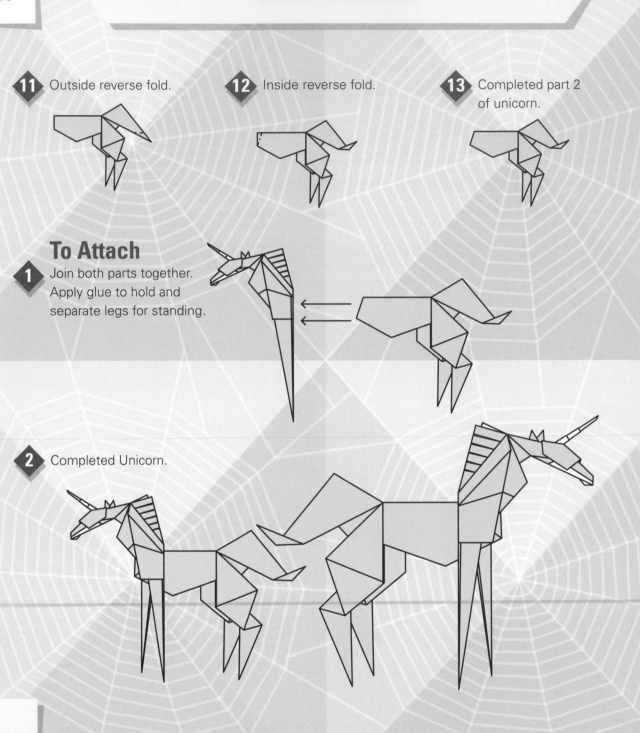

11 Outside reverse fold.

12 Inside reverse fold.

13 Completed part 2 of unicorn.

To Attach

1 Join both parts together. Apply glue to hold and separate legs for standing.

2 Completed Unicorn.

MEDUSA

Part 1

1 Start with Base Fold III.
Inside reverse folds.

2 Valley fold.

3 Valley folds and squash fold.

4 Valley fold.

5 Turn over to other side.

6 Valley folds.

7 Valley folds.

8 Pleat folds.

9 Turn over to other side.

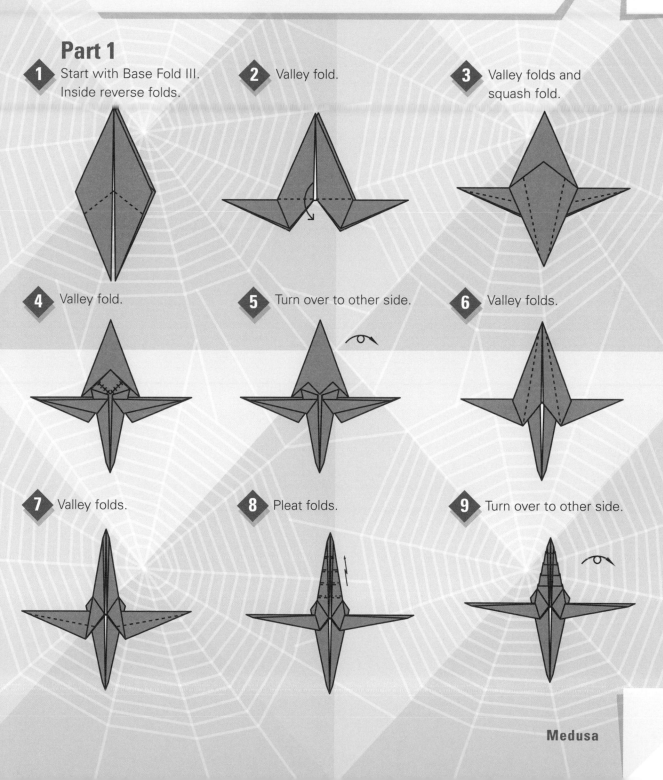

Medusa

MEDUSA

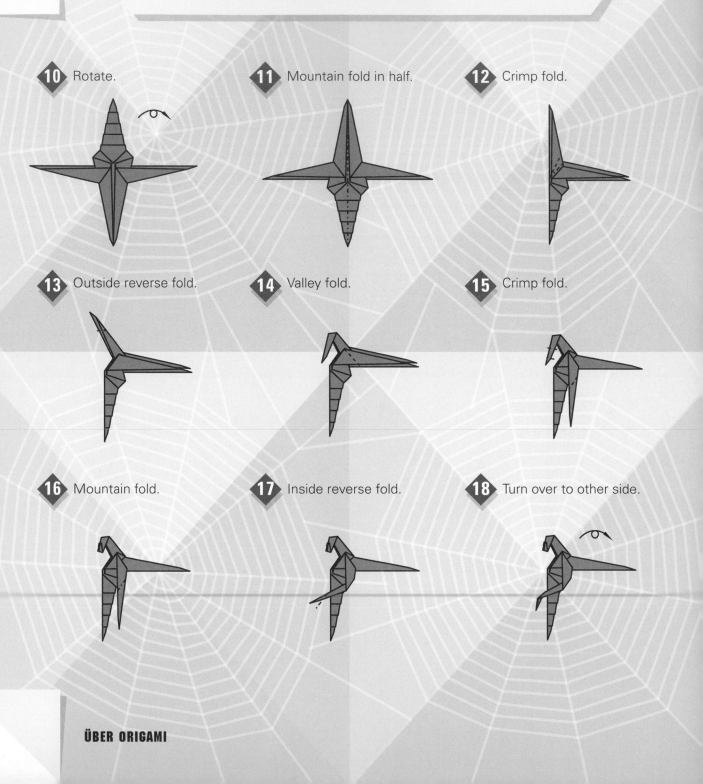

10 Rotate.

11 Mountain fold in half.

12 Crimp fold.

13 Outside reverse fold.

14 Valley fold.

15 Crimp fold.

16 Mountain fold.

17 Inside reverse fold.

18 Turn over to other side.

MEDUSA

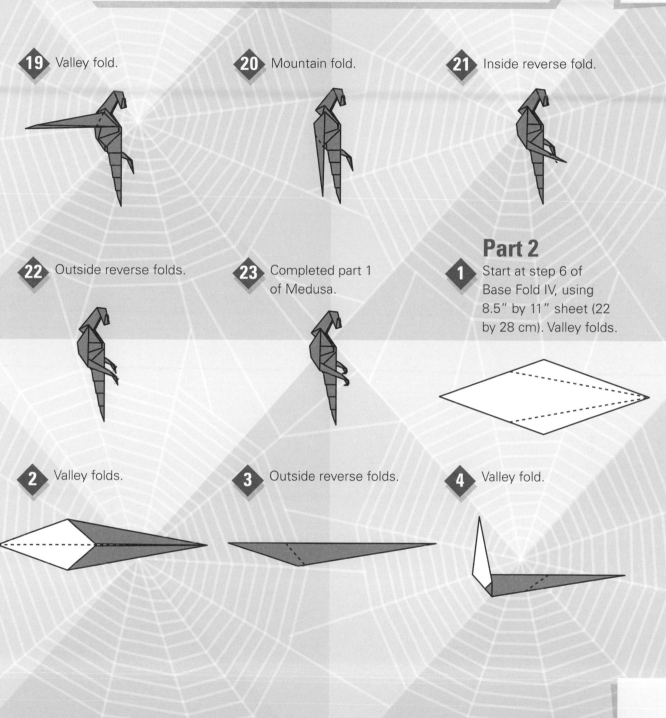

19 Valley fold.

20 Mountain fold.

21 Inside reverse fold.

22 Outside reverse folds.

23 Completed part 1 of Medusa.

Part 2

1 Start at step 6 of Base Fold IV, using 8.5" by 11" sheet (22 by 28 cm). Valley folds.

2 Valley folds.

3 Outside reverse folds.

4 Valley fold.

Medusa

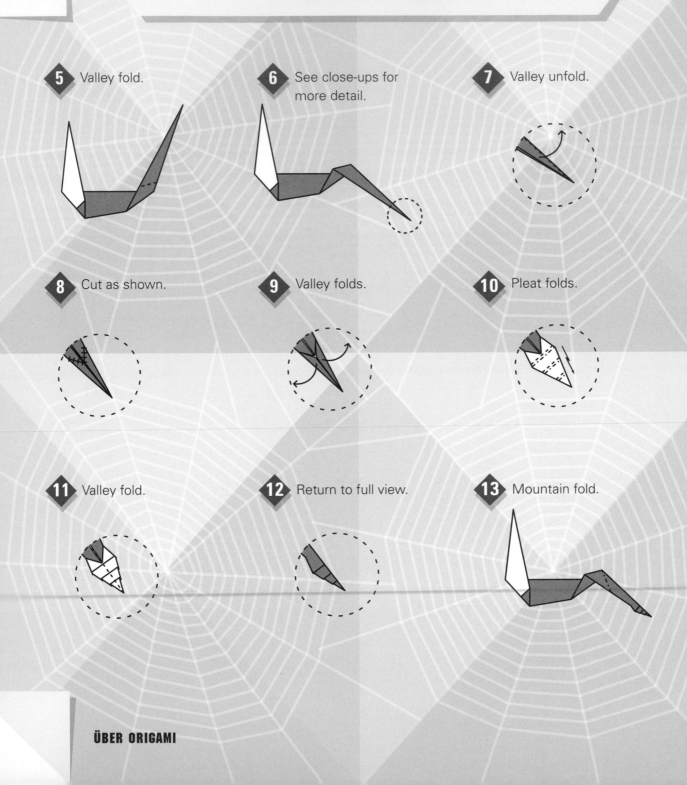

5 Valley fold.

6 See close-ups for more detail.

7 Valley unfold.

8 Cut as shown.

9 Valley folds.

10 Pleat folds.

11 Valley fold.

12 Return to full view.

13 Mountain fold.

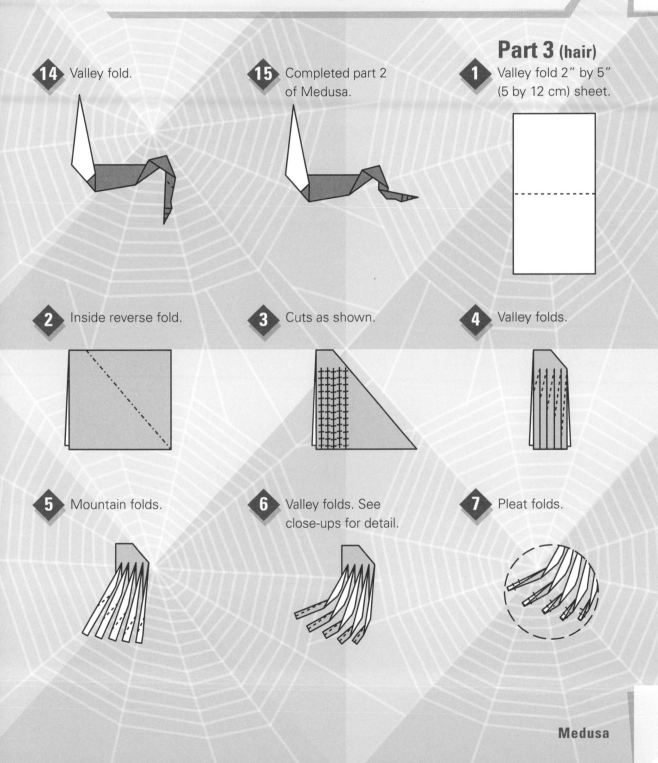

14 Valley fold.

15 Completed part 2 of Medusa.

Part 3 (hair)

1 Valley fold 2″ by 5″ (5 by 12 cm) sheet.

2 Inside reverse fold.

3 Cuts as shown.

4 Valley folds.

5 Mountain folds.

6 Valley folds. See close-ups for detail.

7 Pleat folds.

Medusa

MEDUSA

8 Trim "mouths." Back to full-view.

9 Completed part 3 of Medusa.

To Attach

1 Join all parts together and apply glue to hold.

2 Inside reverse fold.

3 Open out body and tail slightly for standing.

4 Completed Medusa.

VAMPIRE BAT

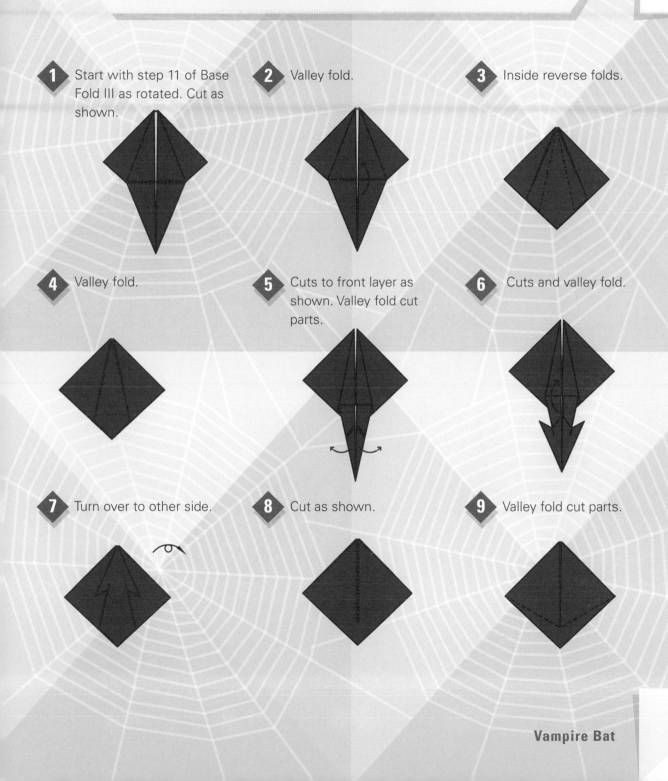

1 Start with step 11 of Base Fold III as rotated. Cut as shown.

2 Valley fold.

3 Inside reverse folds.

4 Valley fold.

5 Cuts to front layer as shown. Valley fold cut parts.

6 Cuts and valley fold.

7 Turn over to other side.

8 Cut as shown.

9 Valley fold cut parts.

Vampire Bat

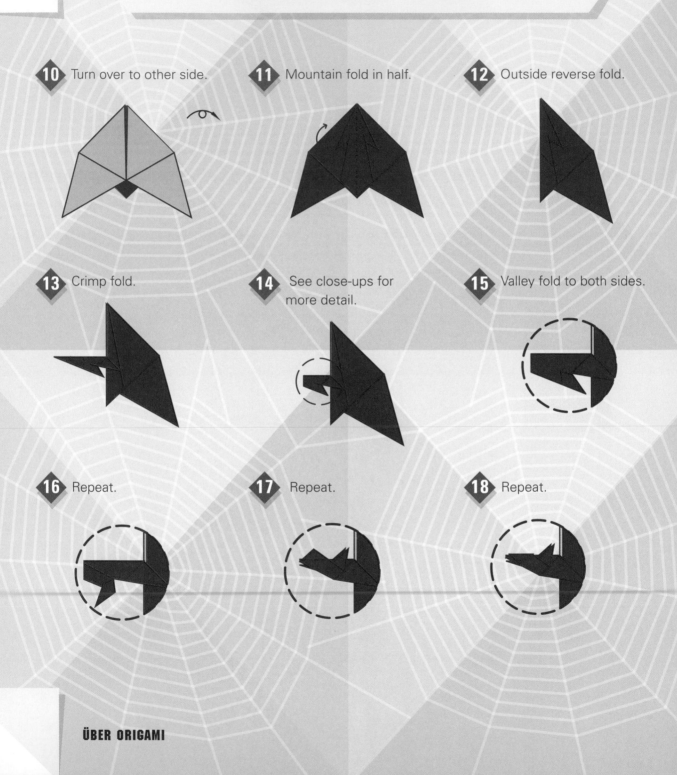

10 Turn over to other side.

11 Mountain fold in half.

12 Outside reverse fold.

13 Crimp fold.

14 See close-ups for more detail.

15 Valley fold to both sides.

16 Repeat.

17 Repeat.

18 Repeat.

VAMPIRE BAT

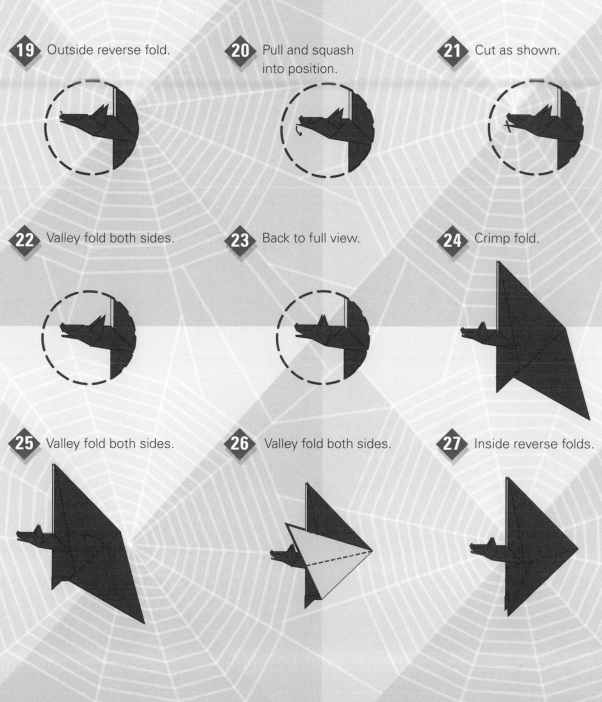

19 Outside reverse fold.

20 Pull and squash into position.

21 Cut as shown.

22 Valley fold both sides.

23 Back to full view.

24 Crimp fold.

25 Valley fold both sides.

26 Valley fold both sides.

27 Inside reverse folds.

Vampire Bat

VAMPIRE BAT

28 Mountain fold both sides.

29 Mountain fold both sides.

30 Valley fold both sides.

31 Valley fold both sides.

32 Valley fold both sides.

33 Completed Vampire Bat.

FRANKENSTEIN'S MONSTER

Part 1

1 Start with Base Fold III. Inside reverse folds.

2 Valley fold.

3 Turn over to other side.

4 Valley folds.

5 Valley fold.

6 Valley and squash folds at same time.

7 Valley fold.

8 Turn over to other side.

9 Valley folds.

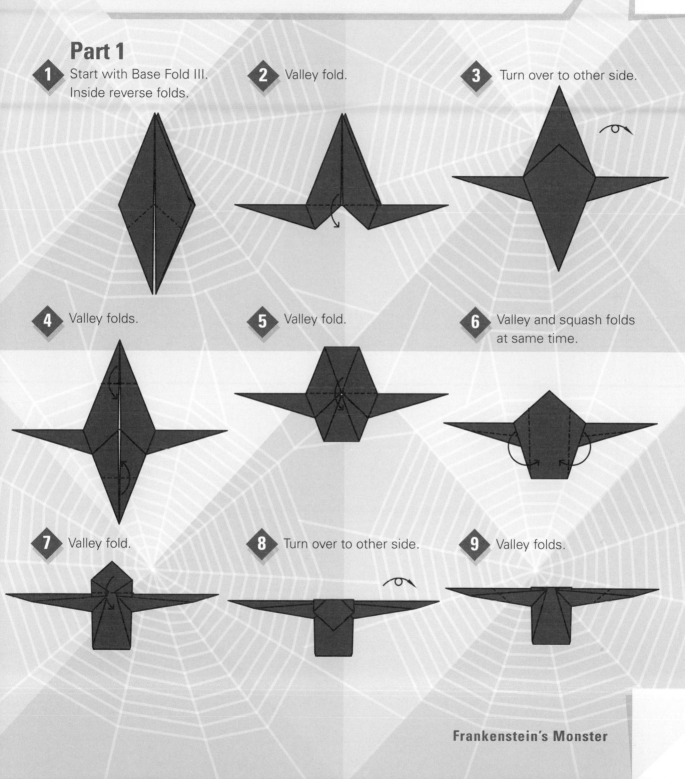

Frankenstein's Monster

FRANKENSTEIN'S MONSTER

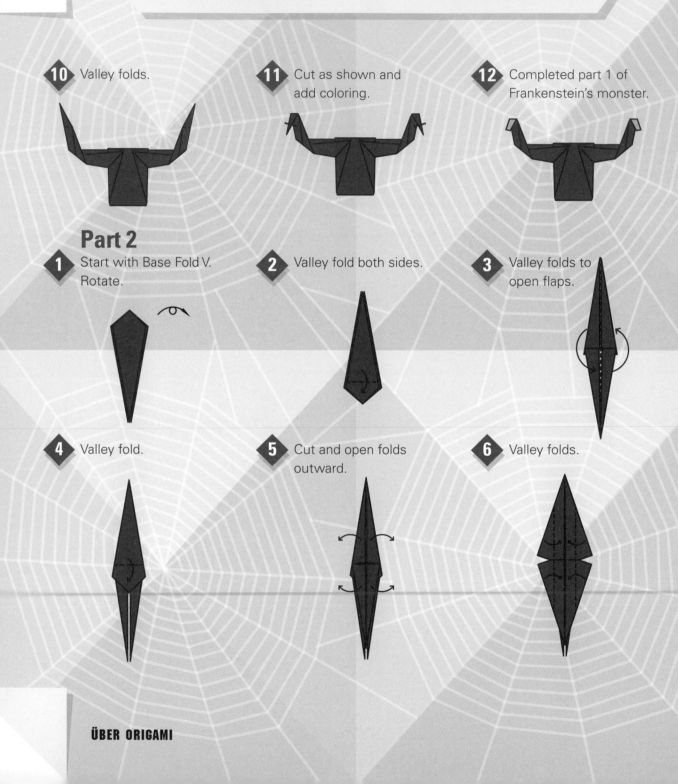

10 Valley folds.

11 Cut as shown and add coloring.

12 Completed part 1 of Frankenstein's monster.

Part 2

1 Start with Base Fold V. Rotate.

2 Valley fold both sides.

3 Valley folds to open flaps.

4 Valley fold.

5 Cut and open folds outward.

6 Valley folds.

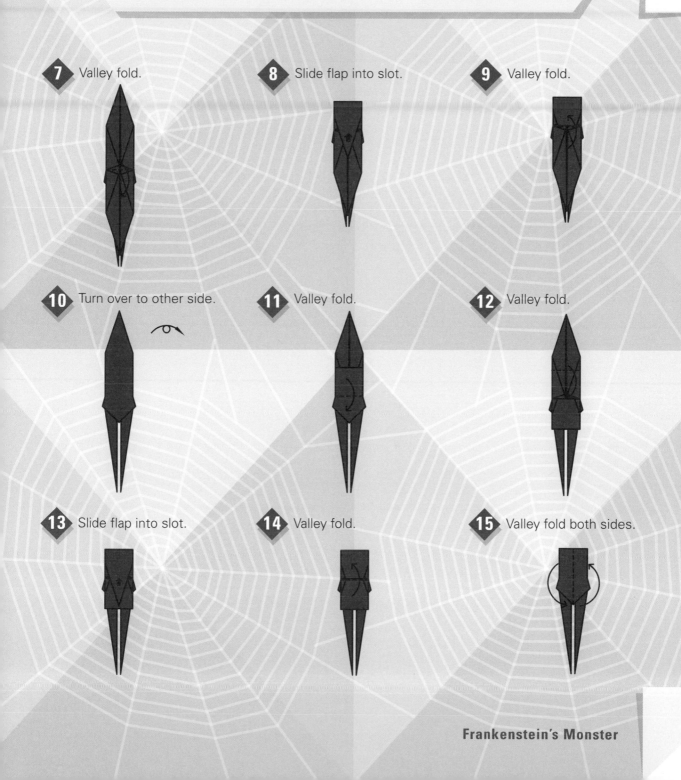

7 Valley fold.

8 Slide flap into slot.

9 Valley fold.

10 Turn over to other side.

11 Valley fold.

12 Valley fold.

13 Slide flap into slot.

14 Valley fold.

15 Valley fold both sides.

Frankenstein's Monster

FRANKENSTEIN'S MONSTER

16 Cut top layers, front and back.

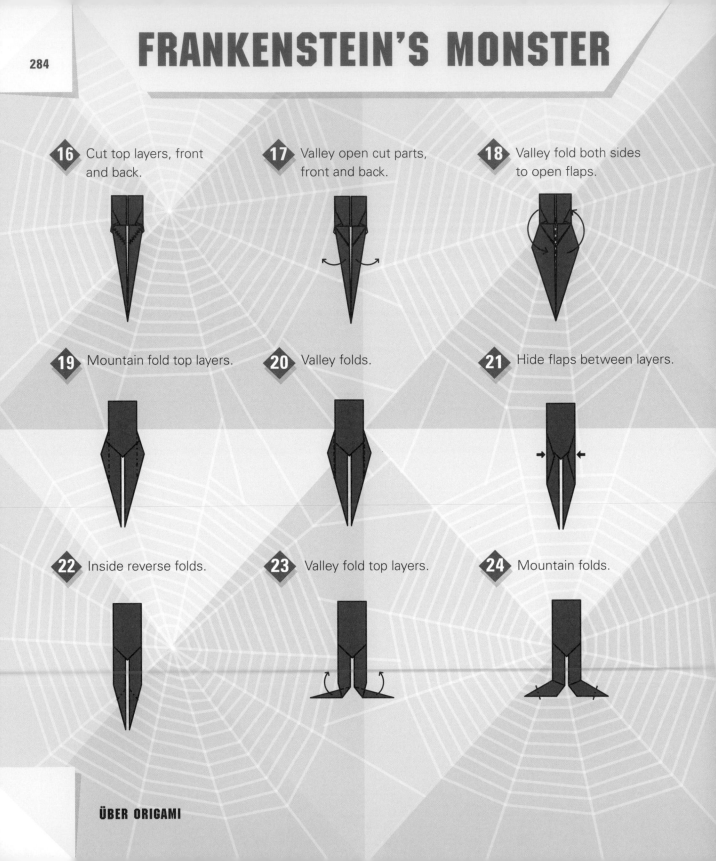

17 Valley open cut parts, front and back.

18 Valley fold both sides to open flaps.

19 Mountain fold top layers.

20 Valley folds.

21 Hide flaps between layers.

22 Inside reverse folds.

23 Valley fold top layers.

24 Mountain folds.

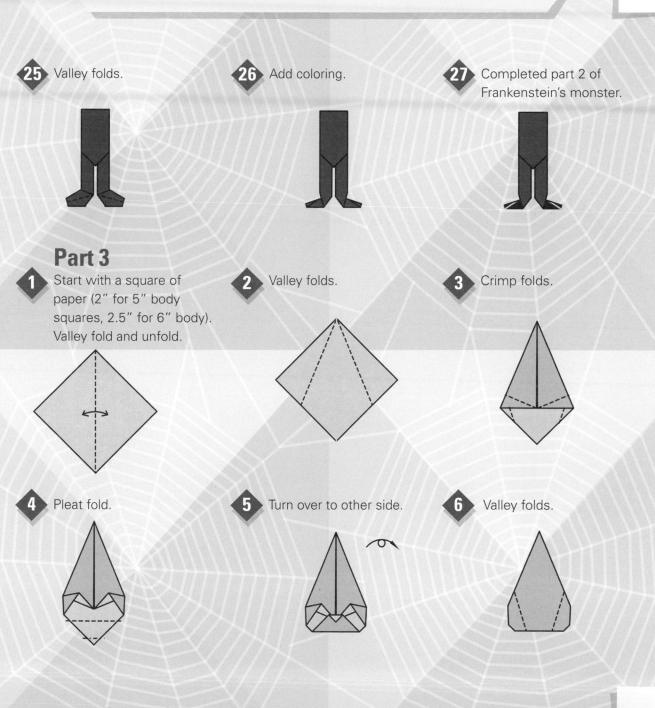

25 Valley folds.

26 Add coloring.

27 Completed part 2 of Frankenstein's monster.

Part 3

1 Start with a square of paper (2" for 5" body squares, 2.5" for 6" body). Valley fold and unfold.

2 Valley folds.

3 Crimp folds.

4 Pleat fold.

5 Turn over to other side.

6 Valley folds.

FRANKENSTEIN'S MONSTER

7 Valley fold in half.

8 Inside reverse fold.

9 Outside reverse fold.

10 Add color to both sides.

11 Open out forward.

12 Completed part 3 of Frankenstein's monster.

To Attach

1 Insert part 2 into part 1 as shown, and apply glue to hold.

2 Position part 3 (head) onto body. Open folds to stand.

3 Completed Frankenstein's Monster.

WEREWOLF

Part 1

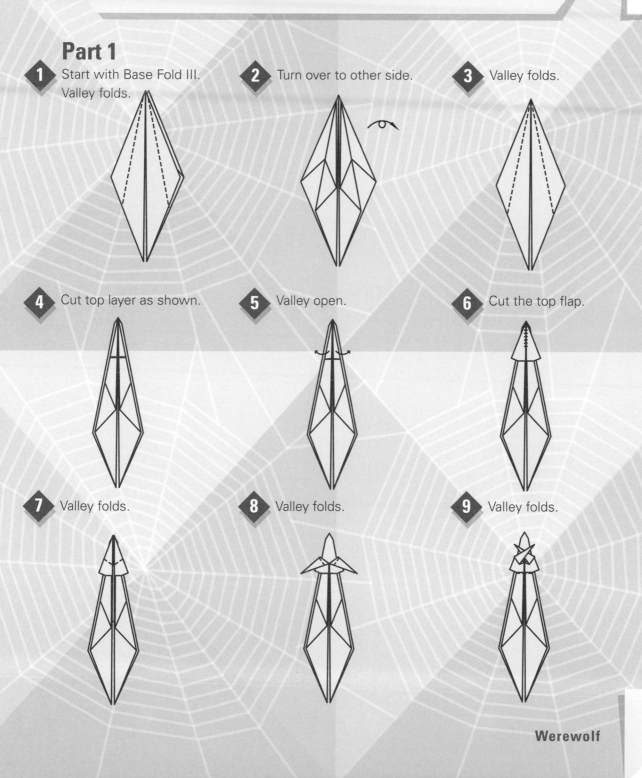

1 Start with Base Fold III.
Valley folds.

2 Turn over to other side.

3 Valley folds.

4 Cut top layer as shown.

5 Valley open.

6 Cut the top flap.

7 Valley folds.

8 Valley folds.

9 Valley folds.

Werewolf

WEREWOLF

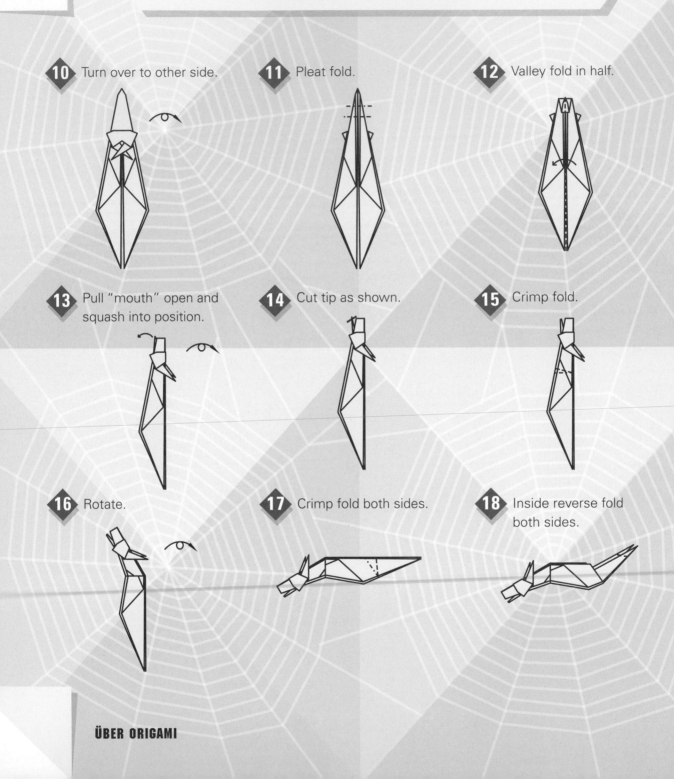

10 Turn over to other side.

11 Pleat fold.

12 Valley fold in half.

13 Pull "mouth" open and squash into position.

14 Cut tip as shown.

15 Crimp fold.

16 Rotate.

17 Crimp fold both sides.

18 Inside reverse fold both sides.

WEREWOLF

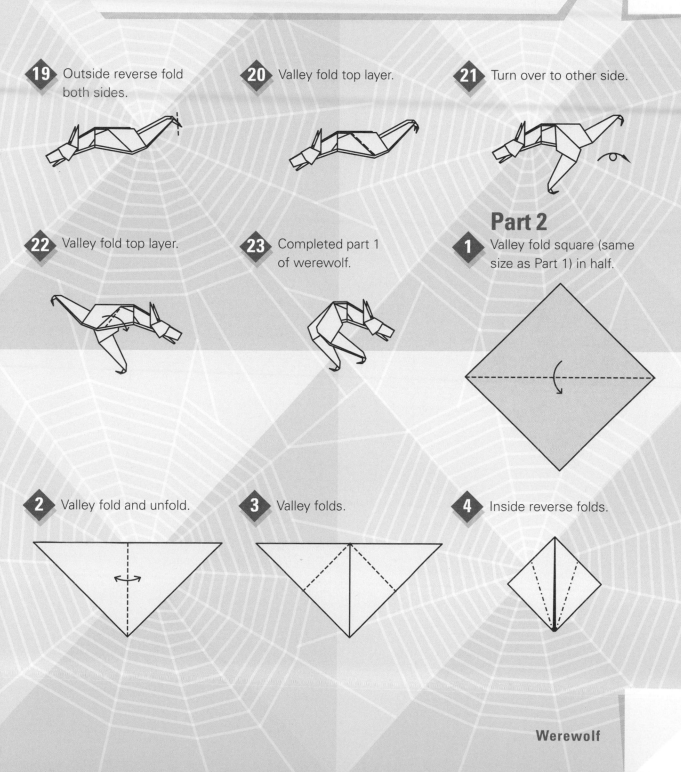

19 Outside reverse fold both sides.

20 Valley fold top layer.

21 Turn over to other side.

22 Valley fold top layer.

23 Completed part 1 of werewolf.

Part 2

1 Valley fold square (same size as Part 1) in half.

2 Valley fold and unfold.

3 Valley folds.

4 Inside reverse folds.

Werewolf

WEREWOLF

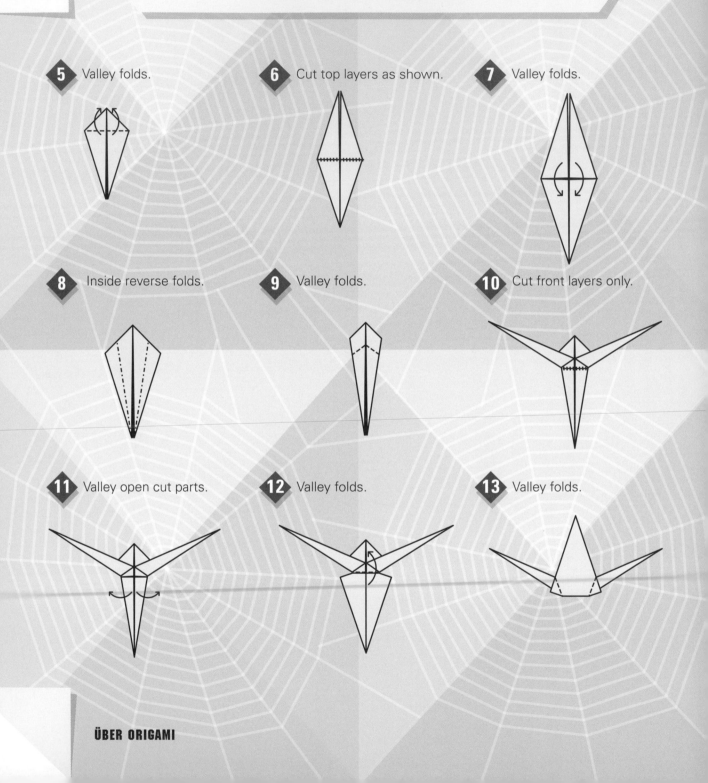

5 ▸ Valley folds.

6 ▸ Cut top layers as shown.

7 ▸ Valley folds.

8 ▸ Inside reverse folds.

9 ▸ Valley folds.

10 ▸ Cut front layers only.

11 ▸ Valley open cut parts.

12 ▸ Valley folds.

13 ▸ Valley folds.

14 Valley fold in half.

15 Inside reverse fold.

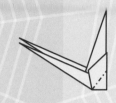

16 Valley fold.

17 Outside reverse fold.

18 Outside reverse fold.

19 Turn over to other side.

20 Valley fold.

21 Outside reverse fold.

22 Outside reverse fold.

Werewolf

WEREWOLF

23 Inside reverse fold.

24 Completed part 2 of werewolf.

To Attach

1 Join both parts together as shown and apply glue to hold.

2 Completed Werewolf.

ALIEN

Part 1

1 Start with Base Fold V. Rotate.

2 Valley fold.

3 Inside reverse folds.

4 Cuts and valley open.

5 See close-ups for detail.

6 Pleat folds.

7 Back to full view.

8 Valley fold.

9 Cut as shown.

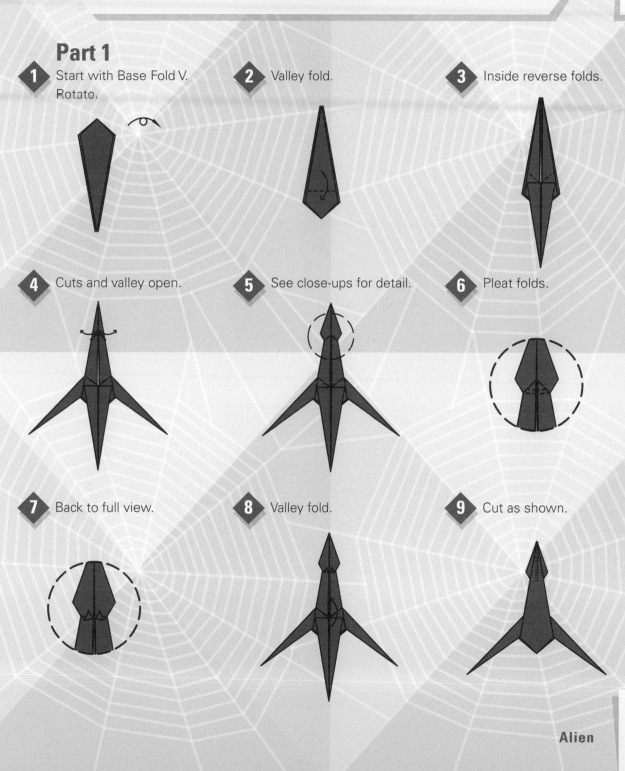

Alien

ALIEN

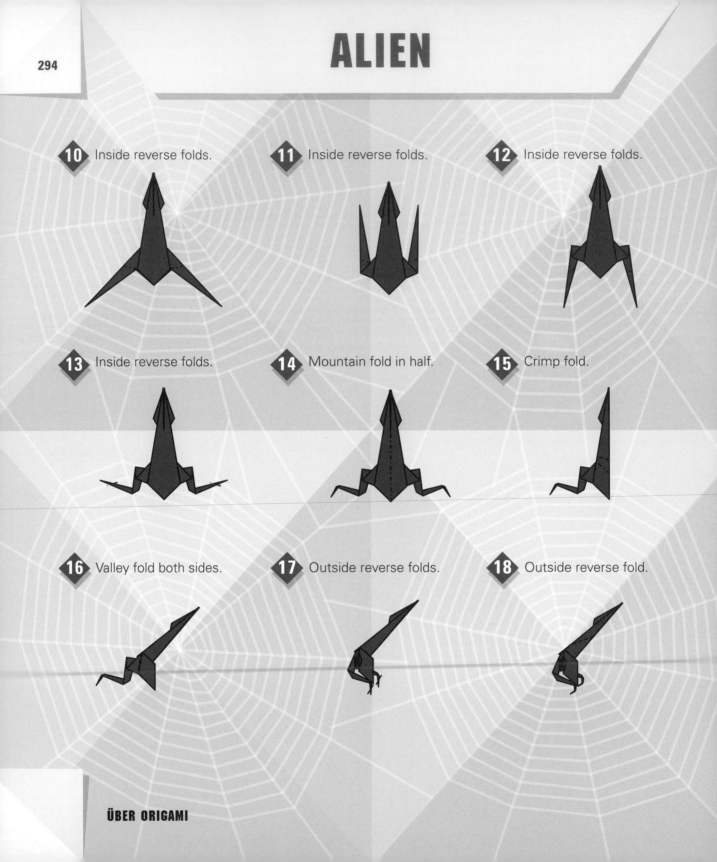

10 Inside reverse folds.

11 Inside reverse folds.

12 Inside reverse folds.

13 Inside reverse folds.

14 Mountain fold in half.

15 Crimp fold.

16 Valley fold both sides.

17 Outside reverse folds.

18 Outside reverse fold.

ALIN

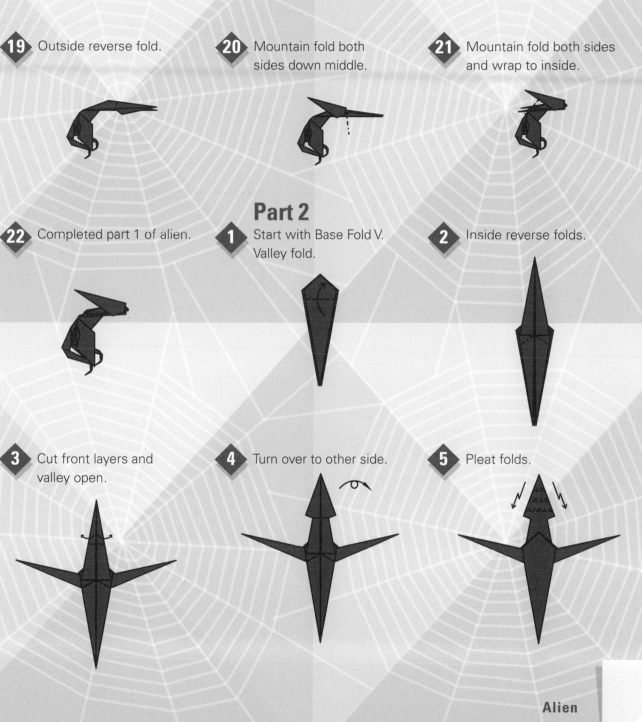

19 Outside reverse fold.

20 Mountain fold both sides down middle.

21 Mountain fold both sides and wrap to inside.

22 Completed part 1 of alien.

Part 2

1 Start with Base Fold V. Valley fold.

2 Inside reverse folds.

3 Cut front layers and valley open.

4 Turn over to other side.

5 Pleat folds.

Alien

ALIEN

6 Valley fold.

7 Inside reverse folds.

8 Inside reverse folds.

9 Mountain fold in half.

10 Inside reverse folds.

11 Valley fold both sides.

12 Crimp fold.

13 Crimp fold.

14 Crimp fold.

ALIEN

15 Valley fold.

16 Turn over to other side.

17 Valley fold.

18 Completed part 2 of alien.

To Attach

1 Join both parts together as shown and apply glue to hold.

2 Completed Alien.

Alien

MAN AND MACHINE

Add famous figures and heavy machines
to your growing origami world.

RODEO COWBOY

Part 1

1 Start with a square sheet cut diagonally; valley folds to crease, then unfold.

2 Valley folds again to crease, then unfold.

3 Pinch corners together and fold inward along dashed lines.

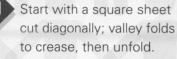
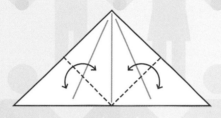
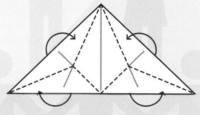

4 Valley folds.

5 Make cuts and valley fold both sides back.

6 Inside reverse fold cut parts.

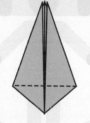
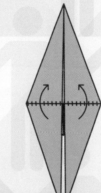

7 Mountain folds.

8 Valley fold in half.

9 Valley fold at left, and inside reverse fold.

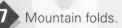
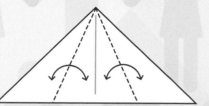

Rodeo Cowboy

RODEO COWBOY

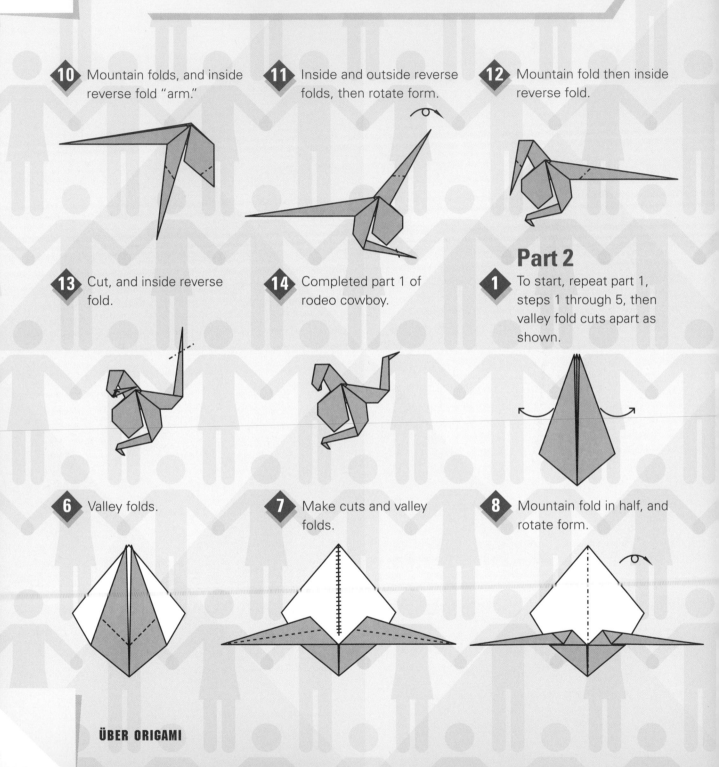

10 Mountain folds, and inside reverse fold "arm."

11 Inside and outside reverse folds, then rotate form.

12 Mountain fold then inside reverse fold.

13 Cut, and inside reverse fold.

14 Completed part 1 of rodeo cowboy.

Part 2

1 To start, repeat part 1, steps 1 through 5, then valley fold cuts apart as shown.

6 Valley folds.

7 Make cuts and valley folds.

8 Mountain fold in half, and rotate form.

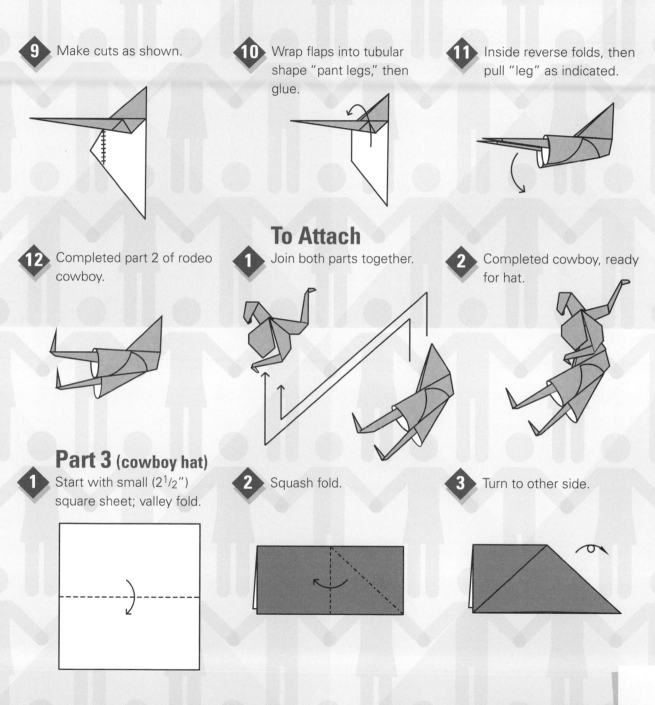

9 Make cuts as shown.

10 Wrap flaps into tubular shape "pant legs," then glue.

11 Inside reverse folds, then pull "leg" as indicated.

12 Completed part 2 of rodeo cowboy.

To Attach

1 Join both parts together.

2 Completed cowboy, ready for hat.

Part 3 (cowboy hat)

1 Start with small (2$\frac{1}{2}$") square sheet; valley fold.

2 Squash fold.

3 Turn to other side.

Rodeo Cowboy

RODEO COWBOY

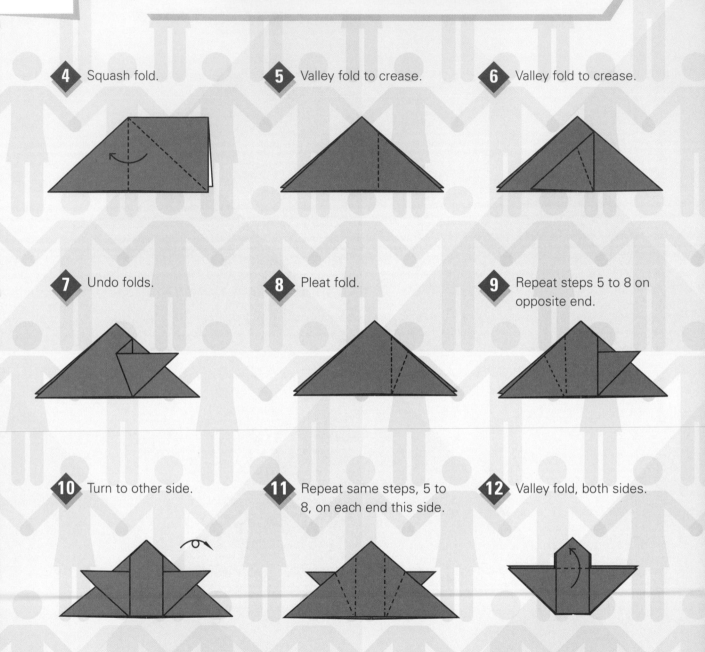

4 Squash fold.

5 Valley fold to crease.

6 Valley fold to crease.

7 Undo folds.

8 Pleat fold.

9 Repeat steps 5 to 8 on opposite end.

10 Turn to other side.

11 Repeat same steps, 5 to 8, on each end this side.

12 Valley fold, both sides.

RODEO COWBOY

13 Pleat fold sides, front and back, squashing underfolds.

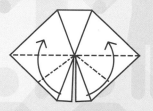

14 Unfold, then valley folds, bringing corners together, and glue.

15 Valley folds to add shape to "brim." Rotate.

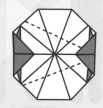

16 View of shaped "hat." Rotate to front.

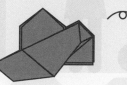

17 Open out, loosen, folds as shown.

18 Completed cowboy hat.

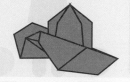

To Assemble

1 Place hat on cowboy, place cowboy on bronco's back (page 186).

2 Completed Rodeo Cowboy on Bucking Bronco.

Rodeo Cowboy

GEORGE WASHINGTON

Part 1

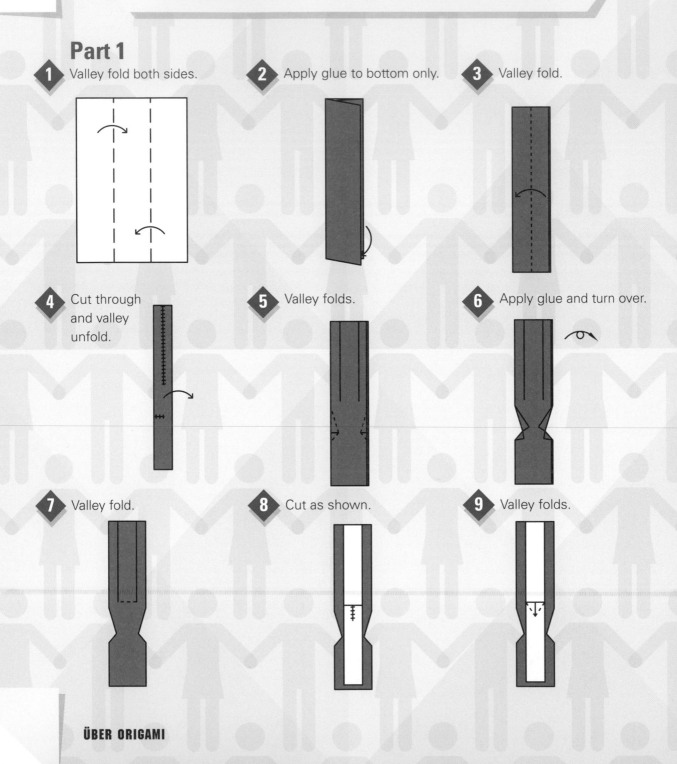

1 Valley fold both sides.

2 Apply glue to bottom only.

3 Valley fold.

4 Cut through and valley unfold.

5 Valley folds.

6 Apply glue and turn over.

7 Valley fold.

8 Cut as shown.

9 Valley folds.

10 Pleat folds.

11 Mountain folds.

12 Apply glue to hold.

13 Cut through layers as shown.

14 Valley fold outward.

15 Mountain folds.

16 Valley open right arm loosely (see next step).

17 See close-ups for detail.

18 Pleat fold.

19 Valley folds and squash corners.

20 Mountain fold.

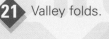

21 Valley folds.

22 Valley fold.

23 Completed hand.

24 Repeat steps 18 through 23 on other side. Then return to full view.

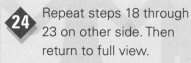

25 Mountain fold in half.

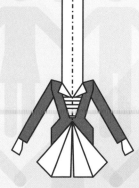

26 Pull and crimp fold.

27 Outside reverse fold.

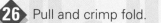

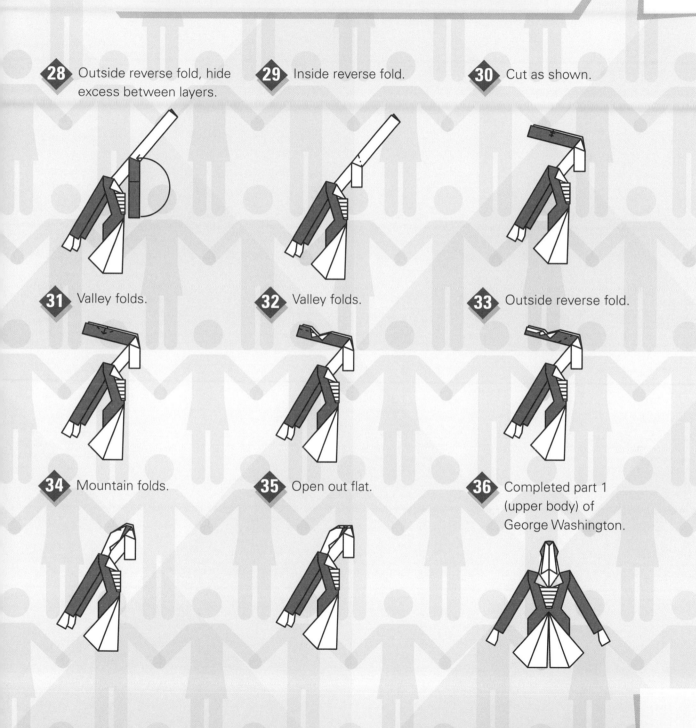

28 Outside reverse fold, hide excess between layers.

29 Inside reverse fold.

30 Cut as shown.

31 Valley folds.

32 Valley folds.

33 Outside reverse fold.

34 Mountain folds.

35 Open out flat.

36 Completed part 1 (upper body) of George Washington.

GEORGE WASHINGTON

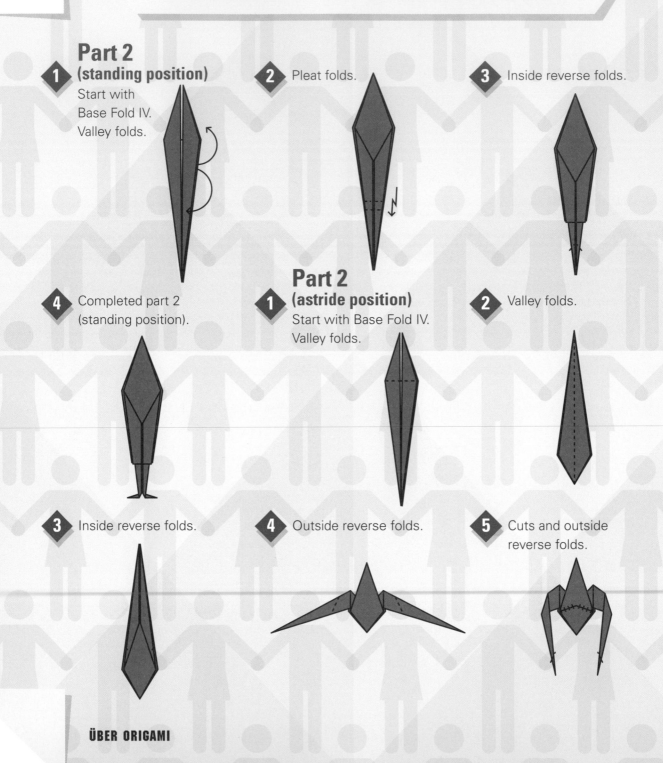

Part 2
1 **(standing position)**
Start with
Base Fold IV.
Valley folds.

2 Pleat folds.

3 Inside reverse folds.

4 Completed part 2
(standing position).

Part 2
1 **(astride position)**
Start with Base Fold IV.
Valley folds.

2 Valley folds.

3 Inside reverse folds.

4 Outside reverse folds.

5 Cuts and outside
reverse folds.

ÜBER ORIGAMI

6 Completed part 2 (astride position for horseback).

2 Mountain fold figure in half. Add coloring if wanted.

4 Completed George Washington.

Part 3 (hat)

1 Make tri-cornered hat for George Washington (see Minuteman, page 316).

3 Add hat. If astride, fold arms for "riding."

To Attach

1 Join parts 1 and 2 (astride or standing) together and glue.

BETSY ROSS

Part 1

1 Valley fold both sides inward.

2 Apply glue at bottom only.

3 Valley fold.

4 Cut layers, then open out.

5 Valley fold and glue.

6 Turn over.

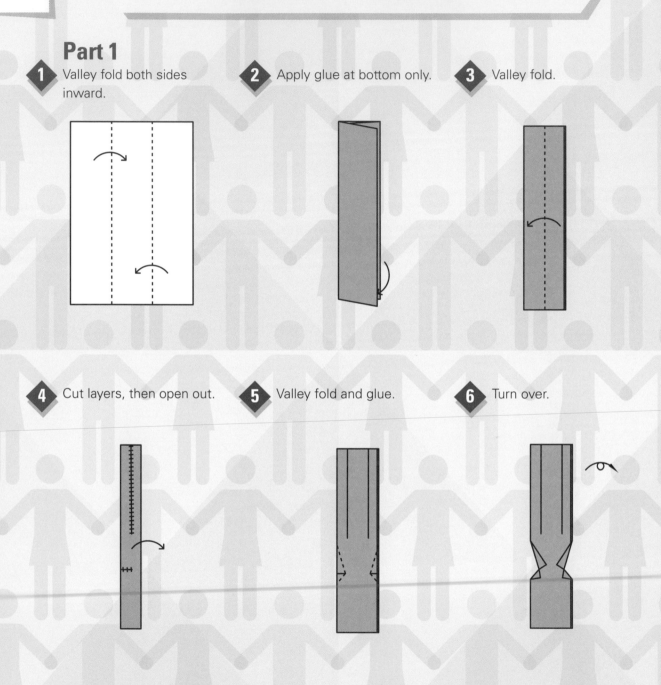

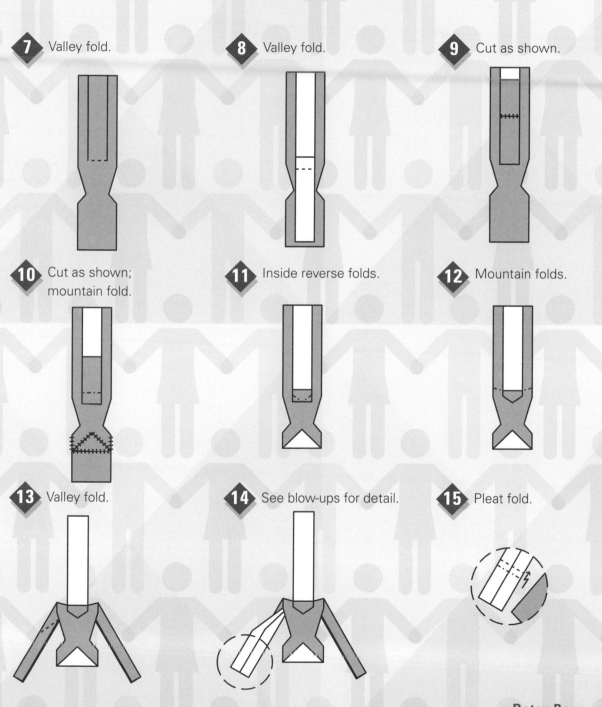

7 Valley fold.

8 Valley fold.

9 Cut as shown.

10 Cut as shown; mountain fold.

11 Inside reverse folds.

12 Mountain folds.

13 Valley fold.

14 See blow-ups for detail.

15 Pleat fold.

Betsy Ross

BETSY ROSS

16 Valley folds and squash corners.

17 Mountain fold.

18 Valley fold.

19 Valley fold.

20 Return to full view.

21 Mirror steps 13 to 20 for other hand.

22 Mountain fold in half.

23 Pull and crimp fold.

24 Outside reverse fold.

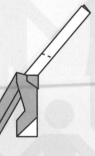

25 Outside reverse fold; slip excess inside.

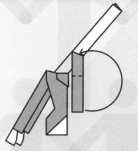

26 Inside reverse fold.

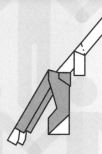

27 Cut as shown.

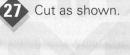

28 Valley folds.

29 Outside reverse fold.

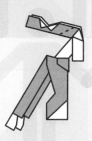

30 Mountain folds.

31 Open out figure.

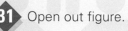

32 Valley folds.

33 Completed part 1 (upper body) of Betsy Ross.

BETSY ROSS

Part 2

1 Roll into cone shape and glue to hold.

2 Cut as shown.

3 Completed part 2 (lower body) of Betsy Ross.

Part 3 (hat)

1 Cut paper circle as shown.

2 Pull and apply glue to hold.

3 Completed brim.

4 On square sheet, valley folds.

5 Valley fold sides upward to stand at 90 degrees.

6 Valley fold and tuck flap into box-like shape.

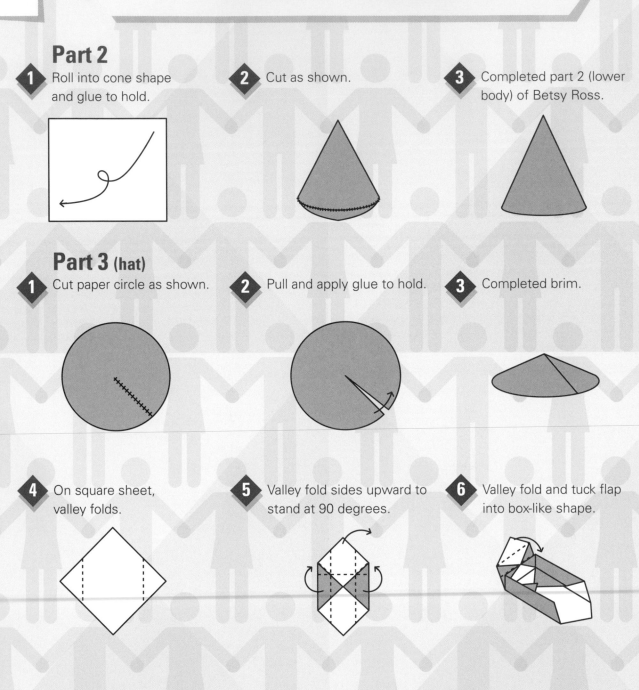

BETSY ROSS

7 Cut as shown to shorten form, turn over.

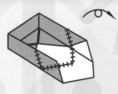

8 Glue shortened box form to brim.

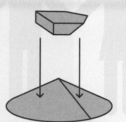

9 Completed Betsy Ross's hat.

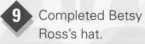

To Attach

1 Join parts together as shown, apply glue to hold. If wanted, add color to face, hands, hair, inner hat; American flag suggested.

2 Completed Betsy Ross.

MINUTEMAN

Parts 1 and 2

1 Use parts 1 (upper body) and 2 (lower body, standing) of George Washington (pages 304–309).

3 Valley fold sides to center sides again, and then in half.

Part 3 (rifle)

1 Valley fold a length of dark paper in half.

2 Valley fold a second sheet to center.

4 Valley fold.

5 Valley fold first length through center between layers as shown.

6 Valley fold as shown.

7 Mountain fold.

8 Mountain fold both sides into middle.

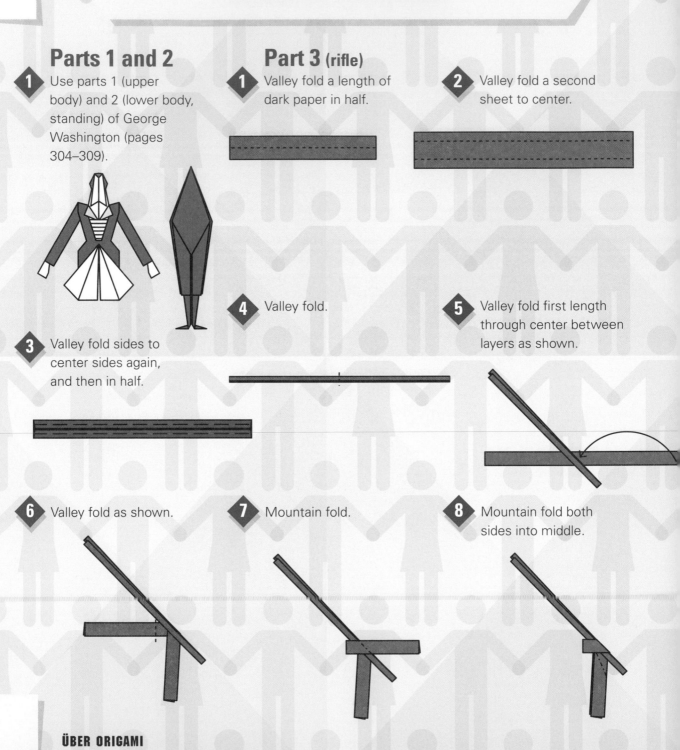

9 Pull barrel in direction of arrow.

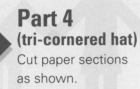

10 Valley fold and apply glue to hold.

11 Completed part 3 (pioneer rifle).

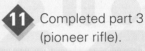

Part 4
(tri-cornered hat)

1 Cut paper sections as shown.

2 Roll rectangular length into a tube.

3 Join and apply glue to hold.

4 Mountain fold opposite sides inward to touch. Rotate.

5 Repeat mountain folds inward.

6 Rotate.

7 Valley fold brim upward at angles, as shown.

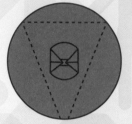

8 Completed tri-cornered hat.

Overhead View

Front View

To Attach

1 Join parts 1 (upper body) and 2 (lower body) as shown. Apply glue to hold.

2 Position and valley fold arms to hold rifle. Add hat, and glue all to secure.

3 Completed Minuteman.

PIONEER GIRL

Part 1

1 Start with Base Fold VI; valley folds.

2 Make cuts, then valley fold back.

3 Reverse fold sides.

4 Mountain folds.

5 Cut top two layers. Valley unfold cut parts.

6 Valley fold in half.

7 Valley folds both sides.

8 Pleat fold.

9 Outside reverse fold.

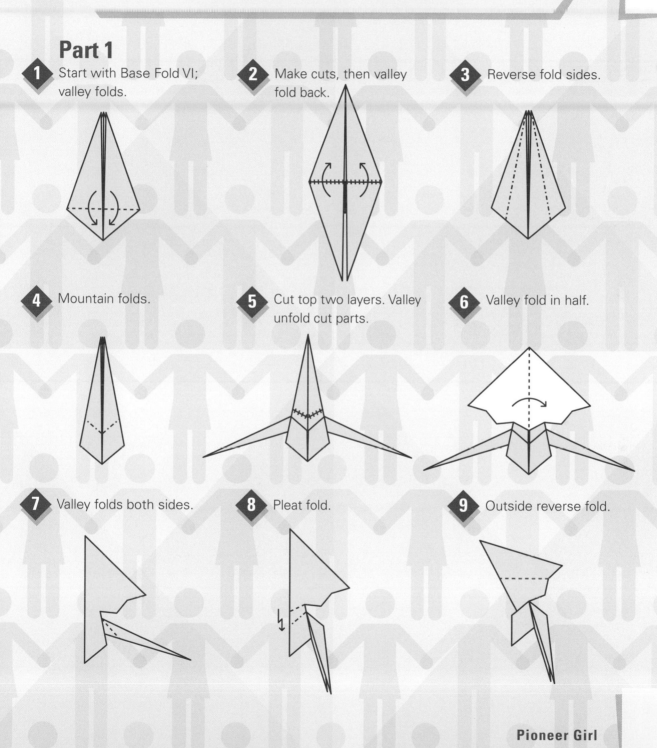

Pioneer Girl

PIONEER GIRL

10 Cut as shown.

11 Mountain folds.

12 Inside reverse fold.

13 Cut as shown.

14 Cut as shown.

15 Valley fold both sides.

16 Mountain folds.

17 Repeat.

18 Completed part 1 of pioneer girl.

Part 2

1 Start with Base Fold VI, valley fold.

2 Cuts and valley folds.

3 Valley fold cut parts.

4 Valley folds.

5 Cut along center and valley fold side flaps.

6 Rotate.

7 Mountain fold in half.

8 Make cuts as shown.

9 Wrap flap around both legs; apply glue.

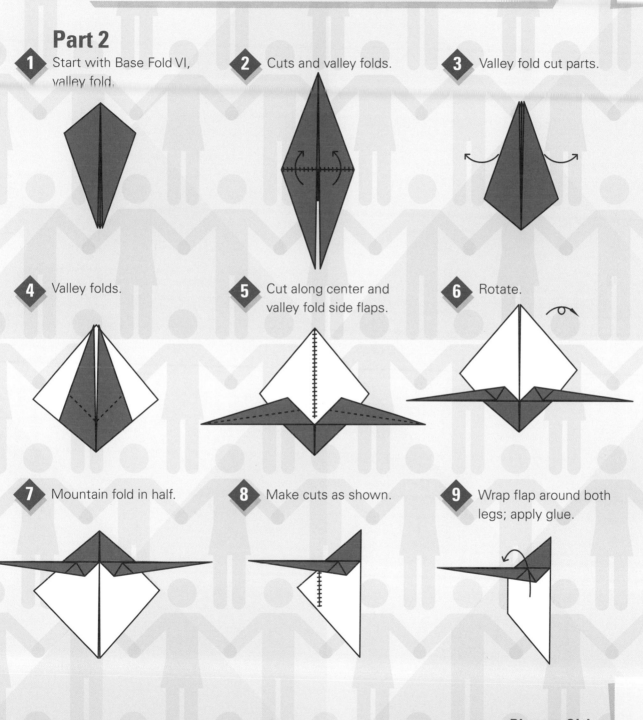

PIONEER GIRL

10 Outside reverse folds.

11 Completed part 2 (lower body) of pioneer girl.

Part 3 (hat)

1 Make Betsy Ross hat (pages 314–315) for pioneer girl.

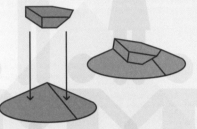

Part 4 (fence)

1 Cut large square apart; roll into tubes.

2 Completed log lengths.

3 Position long and shorter logs as shown, and glue.

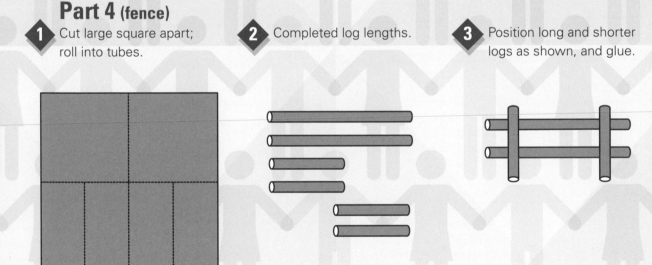

PIONEER GIRL

4 Place two remaining short logs into opening; and apply glue to attach.

5 Completed part 4 (fence).

To Attach

1 Add coloring to pioneer girl (shirt, hair) before joining body parts (1 and 2) together.

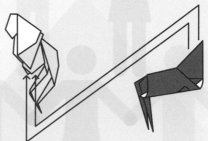

2 Add hat; apply glue to hold.

3 Position sitting pioneer girl on fence, and glue to hold.

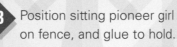

4 Completed Pioneer Girl.

Pioneer Girl

ABRAHAM LINCOLN

Part 1

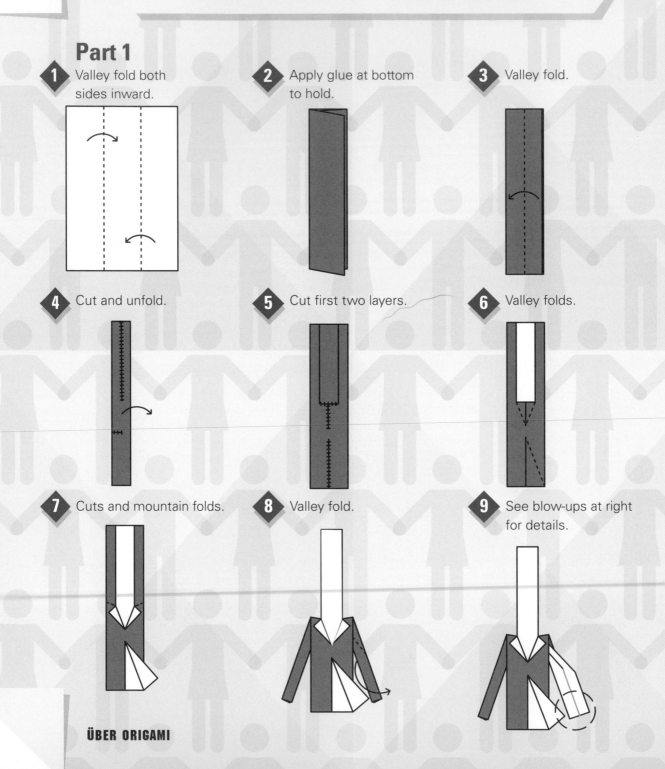

1 Valley fold both sides inward.

2 Apply glue at bottom to hold.

3 Valley fold.

4 Cut and unfold.

5 Cut first two layers.

6 Valley folds.

7 Cuts and mountain folds.

8 Valley fold.

9 See blow-ups at right for details.

ÜBER ORIGAMI

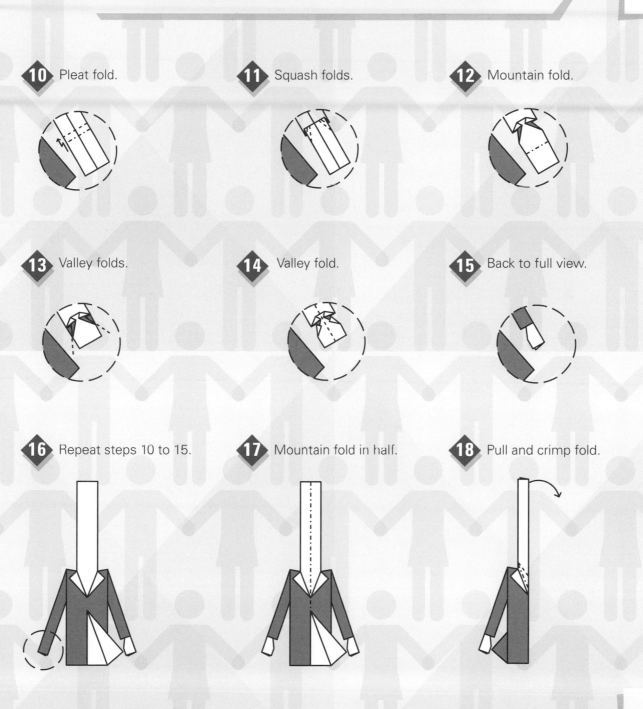

10 Pleat fold.

11 Squash folds.

12 Mountain fold.

13 Valley folds.

14 Valley fold.

15 Back to full view.

16 Repeat steps 10 to 15.

17 Mountain fold in half.

18 Pull and crimp fold.

Abraham Lincoln

ABRAHAM LINCOLN

19 Outside reverse fold.

20 Repeat outside reverse fold.

21 Inside reverse fold.

22 Outside reverse fold.

23 Tuck between layers.

24 Valley fold and add color to "hair."

25 Open out.

26 Valley fold.

27 Valley fold.

28 Apply glue to hold.

29 Completed part 1 (upper body) of Abraham Lincoln.

Part 2

1 Start with Base Fold IV. Valley folds, front and back.

2 Valley folds.

3 Inside reverse folds.

4 Completed part 2 (lower body) of Abraham Lincoln.

ABRAHAM LINCOLN

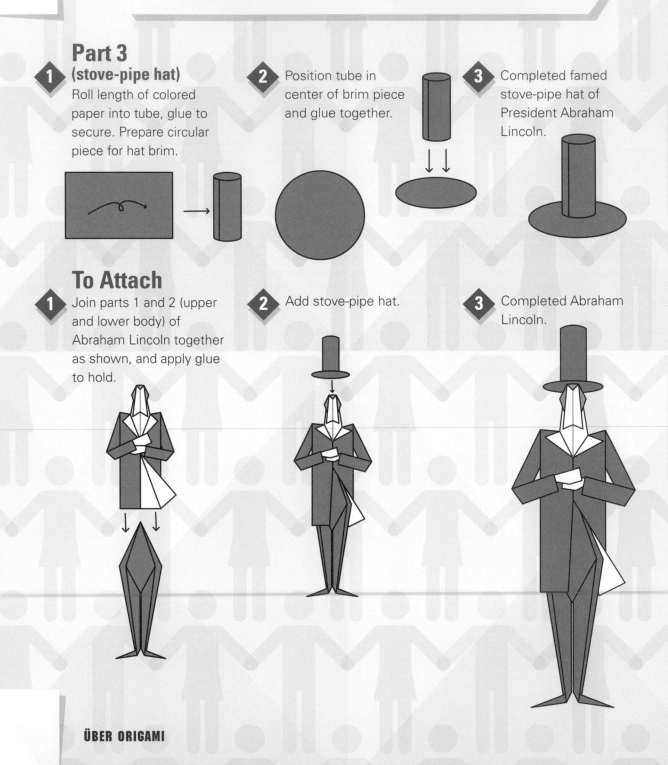

Part 3
(stove-pipe hat)

1 Roll length of colored paper into tube, glue to secure. Prepare circular piece for hat brim.

2 Position tube in center of brim piece and glue together.

3 Completed famed stove-pipe hat of President Abraham Lincoln.

To Attach

1 Join parts 1 and 2 (upper and lower body) of Abraham Lincoln together as shown, and apply glue to hold.

2 Add stove-pipe hat.

3 Completed Abraham Lincoln.

THE KING: ELVIS

Part 1

1 Valley fold both sides.

2 Glue to hold, at bottom only.

3 Valley fold.

4 Cut through layers, and open out.

5 Valley folds.

6 Glue and turn.

7 Cut front layer.

8 Cut as shown.

9 Valley fold loosely.

10 Cut front only.

11 Cuts as shown.

12 Mountain folds.

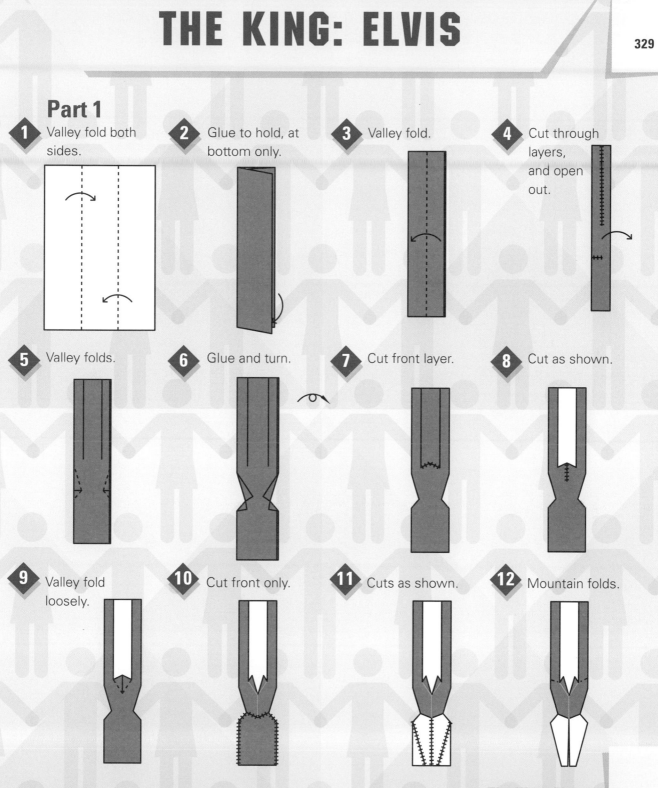

The King: Elvis

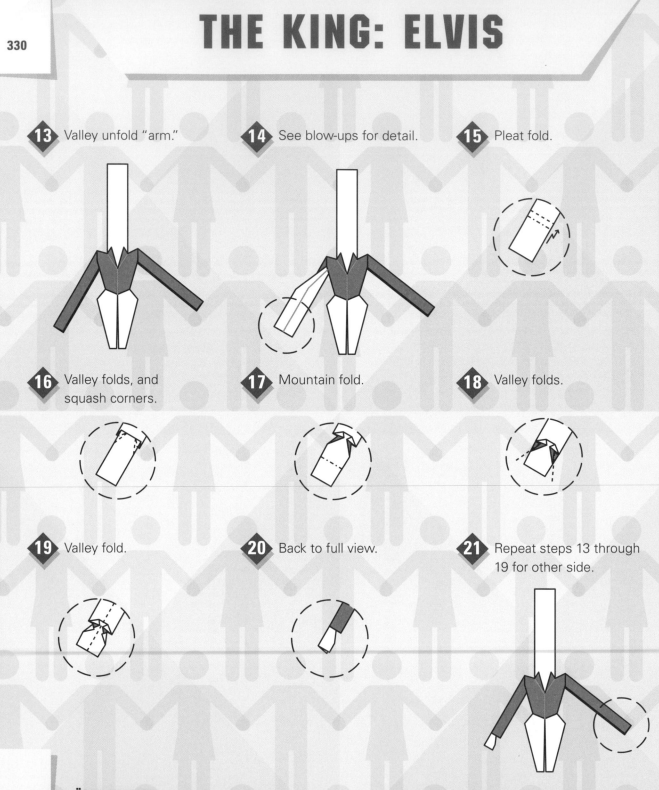

13 Valley unfold "arm."

14 See blow-ups for detail.

15 Pleat fold.

16 Valley folds, and squash corners.

17 Mountain fold.

18 Valley folds.

19 Valley fold.

20 Back to full view.

21 Repeat steps 13 through 19 for other side.

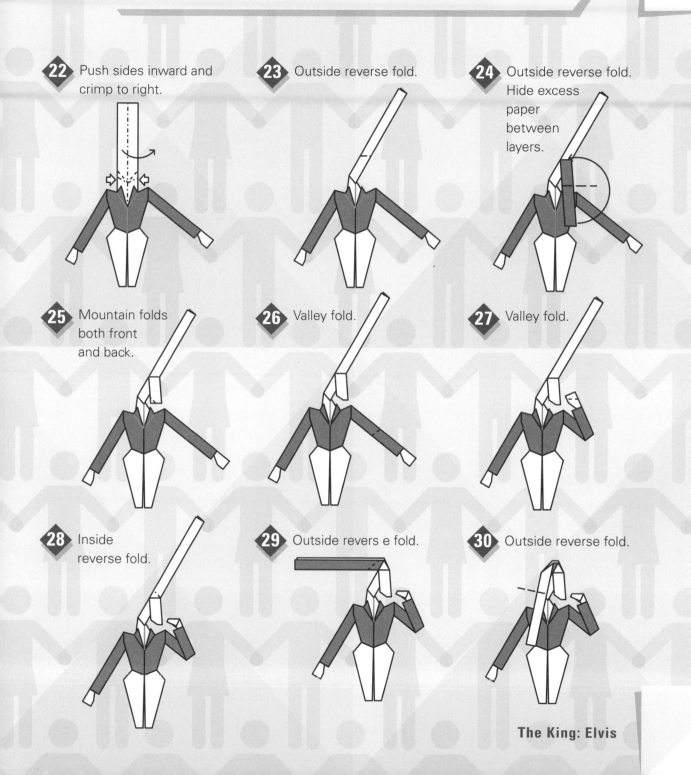

22 Push sides inward and crimp to right.

23 Outside reverse fold.

24 Outside reverse fold. Hide excess paper between layers.

25 Mountain folds both front and back.

26 Valley fold.

27 Valley fold.

28 Inside reverse fold.

29 Outside revers e fold.

30 Outside reverse fold.

The King: Elvis

THE KING: ELVIS

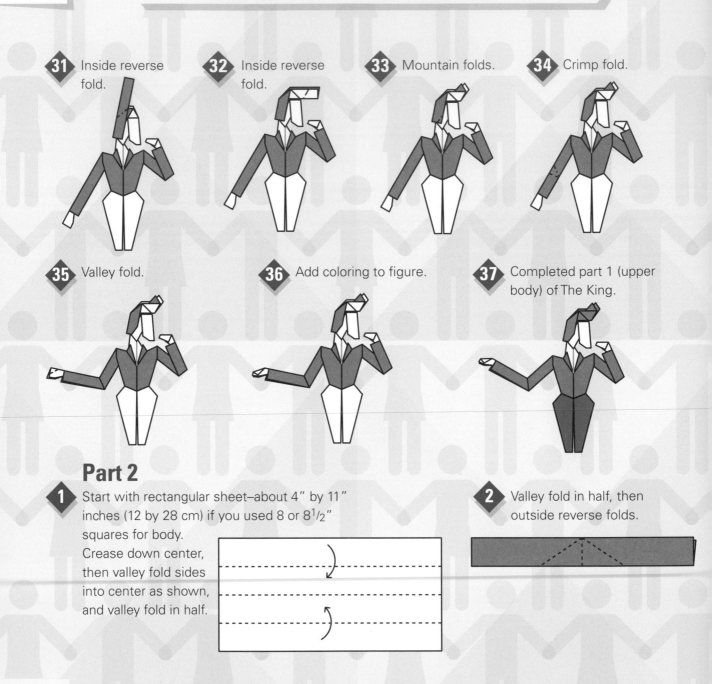

31 Inside reverse fold.

32 Inside reverse fold.

33 Mountain folds.

34 Crimp fold.

35 Valley fold.

36 Add coloring to figure.

37 Completed part 1 (upper body) of The King.

Part 2

1 Start with rectangular sheet—about 4″ by 11″ inches (12 by 28 cm) if you used 8 or 8½″ squares for body. Crease down center, then valley fold sides into center as shown, and valley fold in half.

2 Valley fold in half, then outside reverse folds.

3 Crimp fold both sides.

4 Mountain fold both front and back.

5 Valley folds, then apply color.

6 Completed part 2 (legs) of The King.

To Attach

1 Join both parts together as shown, apply glue to hold.

2 Add a small roll of paper (to serve as microphone) and glue.

3 The King! Completed Elvis.

The King: Elvis

1 Start with Base Fold II. Make cuts as shown.

2 Outside reverse fold all four corners.

3 Valley fold both sides.

4 Valley fold both sides.

5 Valley folds.

6 Valley fold both sides.

7 Valley folds.

8 Valley fold both sides.

9 Valley folds.

RUSSIAN MiG-21

 10 Valley fold both front and back.

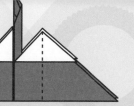

11 Valley fold both sides.

12 Valley fold both sides.

 13 Valley folds.

14 Rotate.

15 Valley fold wings front and back to balance.

16 Valley fold and balance wings to sides.

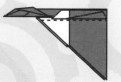

17 Add coloring if you wish.

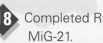

18 Completed Russian MiG-21.

Front View

Overhead View

Russian MiG-21

F-16 FALCON

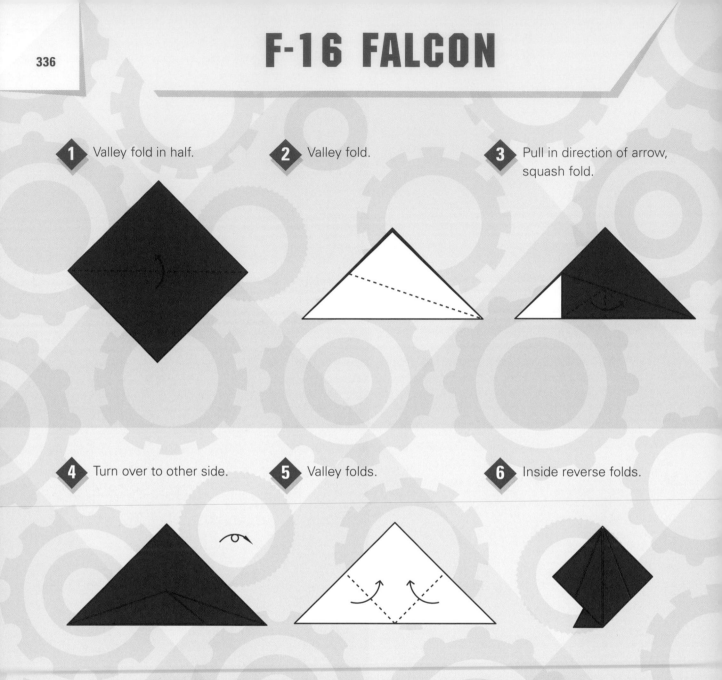

1 Valley fold in half.

2 Valley fold.

3 Pull in direction of arrow, squash fold.

4 Turn over to other side.

5 Valley folds.

6 Inside reverse folds.

F-16 FALCON

7 Inside reverse folds.

8 Make cuts to front layers only, then valley fold cut parts.

9 Valley fold both sides.

10 Inside reverse folds, left and right, as shown.

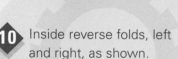

11 Turn over to other side.

12 Cuts to front layer only, as shown, and valley fold tail fin.

13 Valley fold in half (mountain fold cut flap). Rotate.

14 Cuts and valley fold cut parts.

15 Valley fold outward, balancing sides.

F-16 Falcon

F-16 FALCON

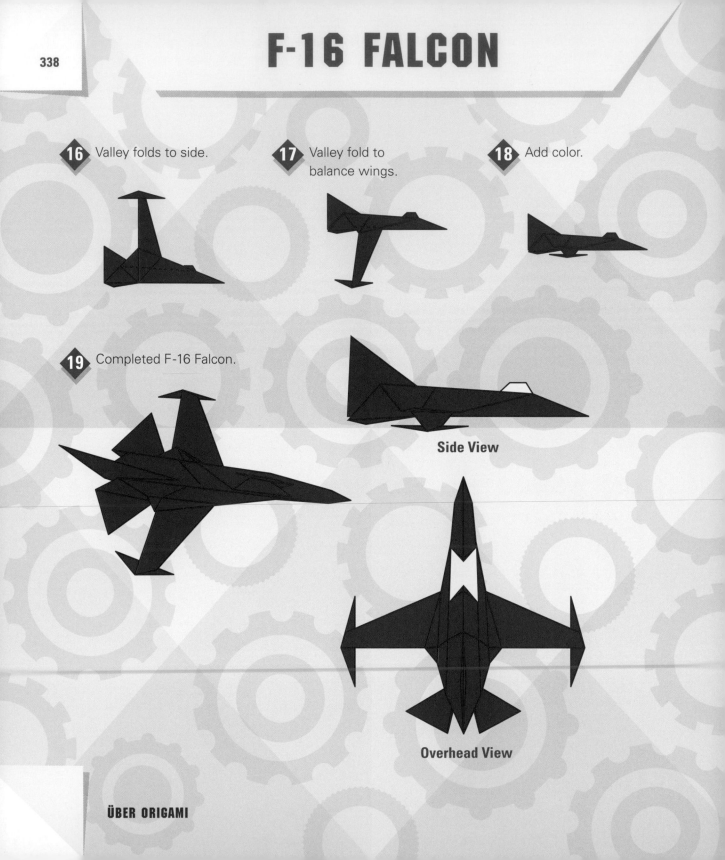

16 Valley folds to side.

17 Valley fold to balance wings.

18 Add color.

19 Completed F-16 Falcon.

Side View

Overhead View

PHANTOM

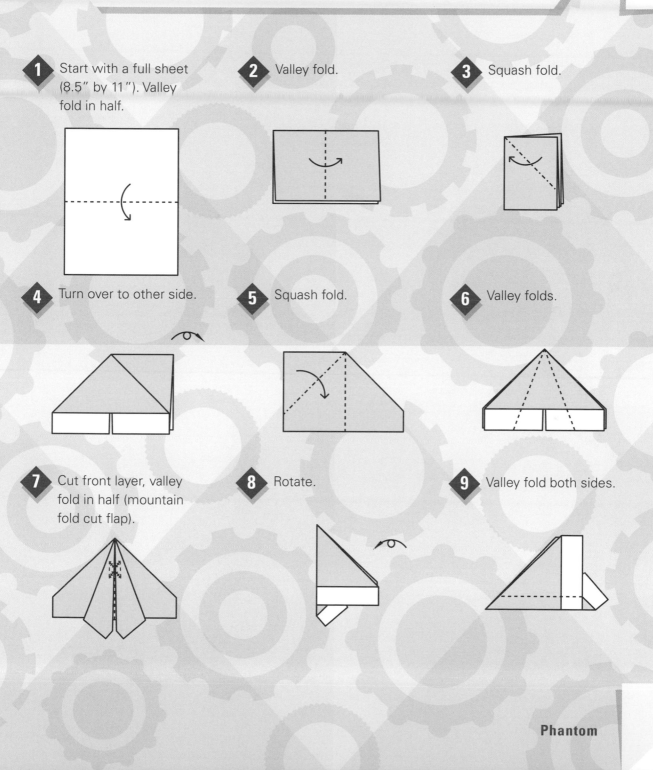

1 Start with a full sheet (8.5" by 11"). Valley fold in half.

2 Valley fold.

3 Squash fold.

4 Turn over to other side.

5 Squash fold.

6 Valley folds.

7 Cut front layer, valley fold in half (mountain fold cut flap).

8 Rotate.

9 Valley fold both sides.

PHANTOM

10 Valley fold out to sides.

11 Squash fold to sides.

12 Mountain fold both sides.

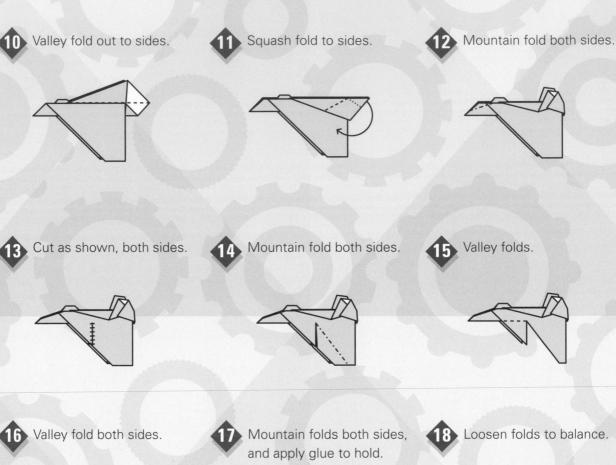

13 Cut as shown, both sides.

14 Mountain fold both sides.

15 Valley folds.

16 Valley fold both sides.

17 Mountain folds both sides, and apply glue to hold.

18 Loosen folds to balance.

PHANTOM

 19 Valley fold to balance wings.

20 Add color.

21 Completed Phantom.

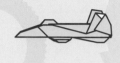

Front View

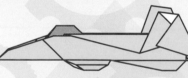

SideView

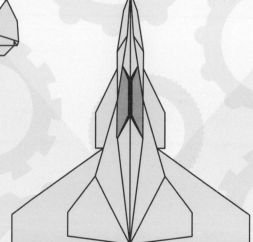

Overhead View

Phantom

B-2 BOMBER

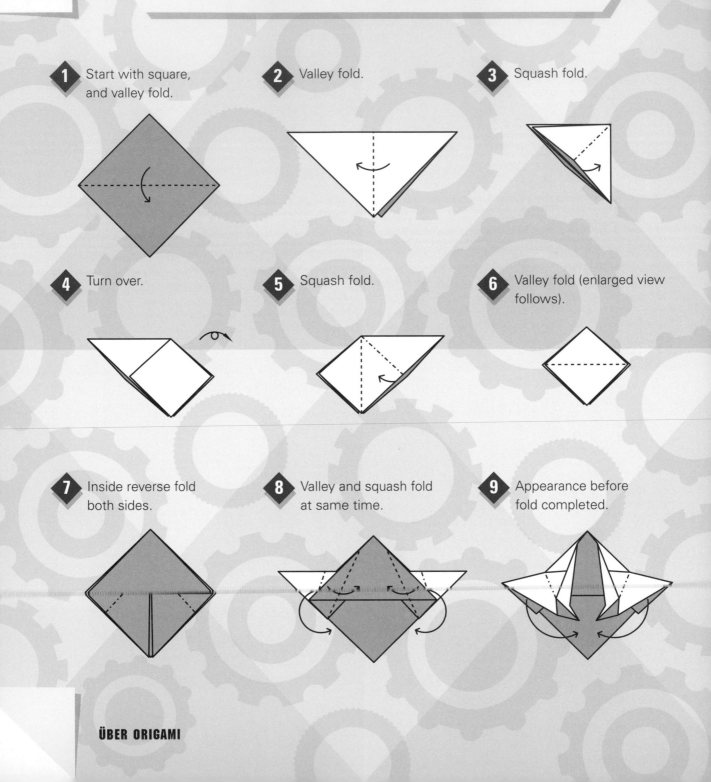

1 Start with square, and valley fold.

2 Valley fold.

3 Squash fold.

4 Turn over.

5 Squash fold.

6 Valley fold (enlarged view follows).

7 Inside reverse fold both sides.

8 Valley and squash fold at same time.

9 Appearance before fold completed.

B-2 BOMBER

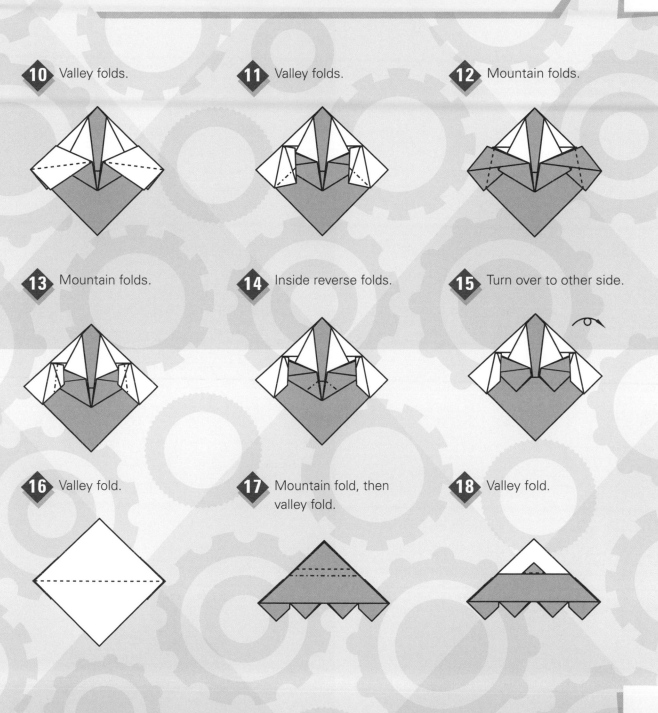

10 Valley folds.

11 Valley folds.

12 Mountain folds.

13 Mountain folds.

14 Inside reverse folds.

15 Turn over to other side.

16 Valley fold.

17 Mountain fold, then valley fold.

18 Valley fold.

B-2 BOMBER

19 Valley fold in half.

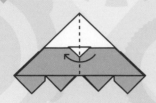

20 Valley fold both sides.

21 Valley fold both sides.

22 Open out.

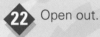

23 Press lightly on the existing creases, folding as shown.

24 Completed B-2 Bomber (overhead view).

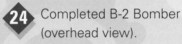

Front View

Ground View

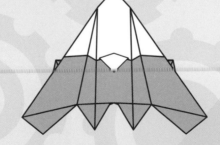

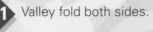

Part 1

1 Start with Base Fold III. Valley fold both sides.

2 Valley fold and squash fold.

3 Turn over to other side.

4 Repeat step 2.

5 Valley fold.

6 Valley fold.

7 Cut as shown.

8 Valley fold.

9 Valley fold.

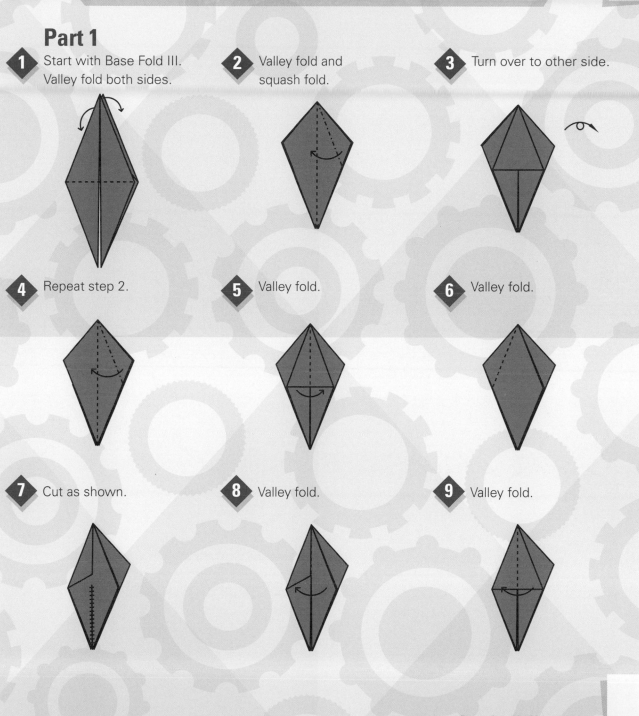

APACHE HELICOPTER

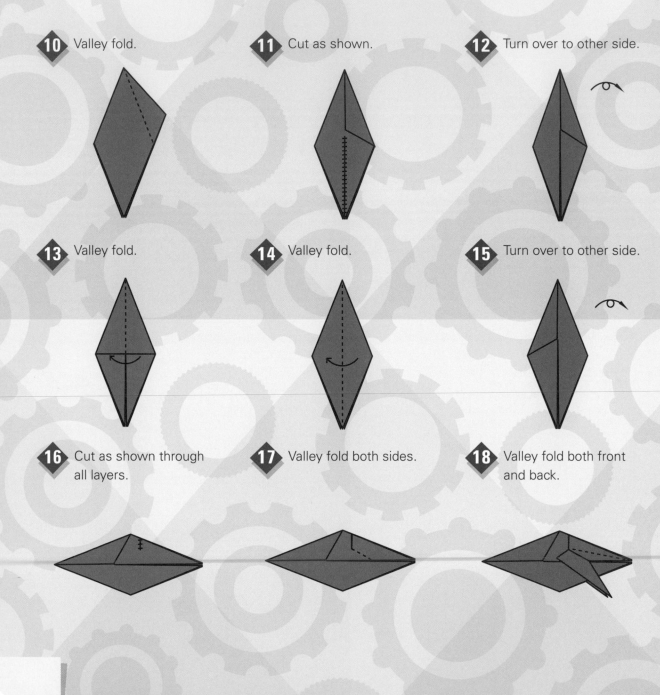

10 Valley fold.

11 Cut as shown.

12 Turn over to other side.

13 Valley fold.

14 Valley fold.

15 Turn over to other side.

16 Cut as shown through all layers.

17 Valley fold both sides.

18 Valley fold both front and back.

APACHE HELICOPTER

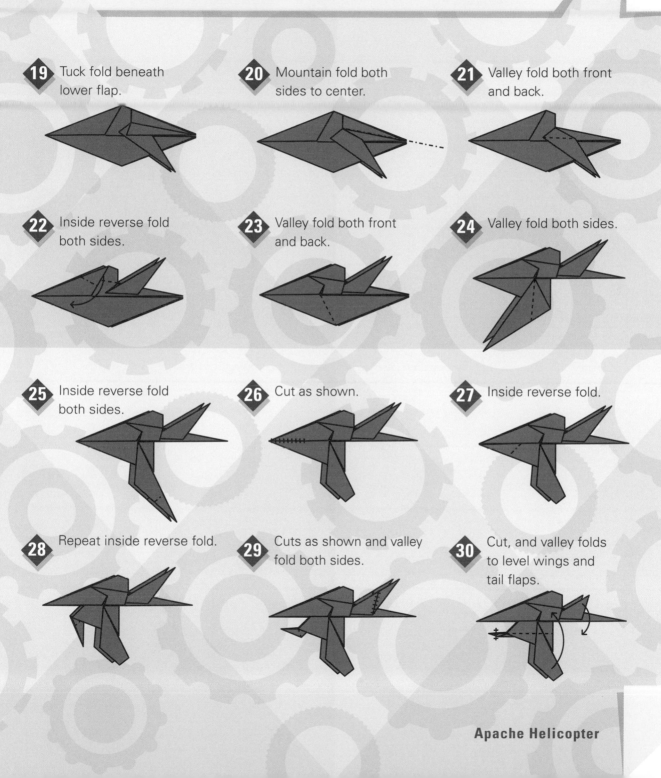

19 Tuck fold beneath lower flap.

20 Mountain fold both sides to center.

21 Valley fold both front and back.

22 Inside reverse fold both sides.

23 Valley fold both front and back.

24 Valley fold both sides.

25 Inside reverse fold both sides.

26 Cut as shown.

27 Inside reverse fold.

28 Repeat inside reverse fold.

29 Cuts as shown and valley fold both sides.

30 Cut, and valley folds to level wings and tail flaps.

Apache Helicopter

APACHE HELICOPTER

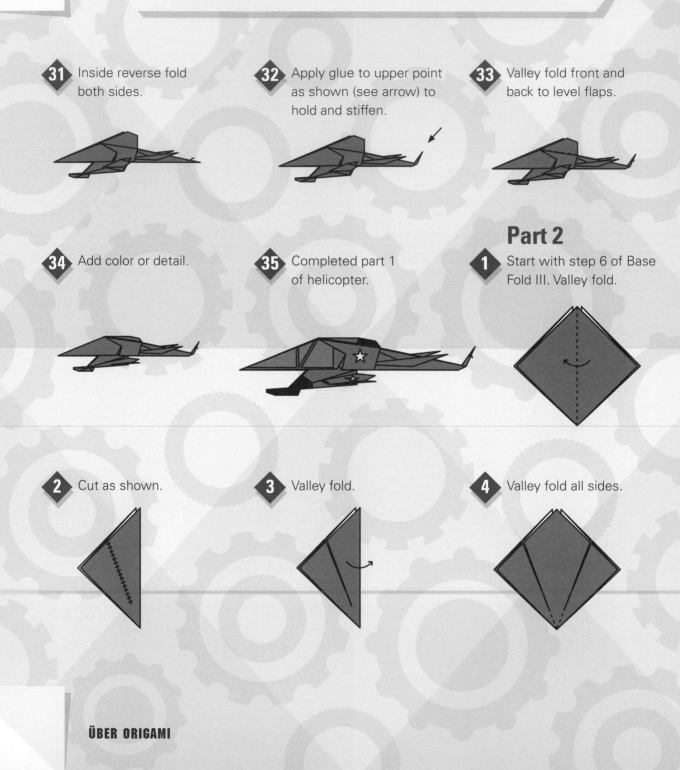

31 Inside reverse fold both sides.

32 Apply glue to upper point as shown (see arrow) to hold and stiffen.

33 Valley fold front and back to level flaps.

34 Add color or detail.

35 Completed part 1 of helicopter.

Part 2

1 Start with step 6 of Base Fold III. Valley fold.

2 Cut as shown.

3 Valley fold.

4 Valley fold all sides.

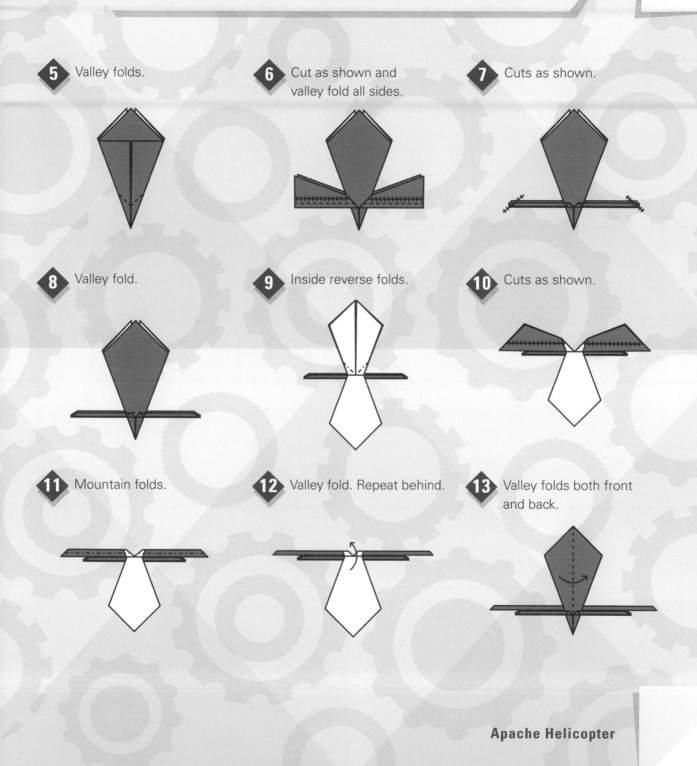

5 Valley folds.

6 Cut as shown and valley fold all sides.

7 Cuts as shown.

8 Valley fold.

9 Inside reverse folds.

10 Cuts as shown.

11 Mountain folds.

12 Valley fold. Repeat behind.

13 Valley folds both front and back.

APACHE HELICOPTER

 14 Inside reverse folds.

 **15** Cuts as shown.

16 Mountain folds.

 17 Cuts, valley folds, and open all four sides.

18 Completed part 2 of helicopter.

NOTE: *Make a second, smaller-size propeller for tail rotor.*

To Attach

1 Apply glue to outer part of a small tube (or roll a section of paper into a small tube). Insert tube into top of helicopter as shown and let dry. This will allow propeller to turn. Join parts together. Glue tail rotor onto tail to hold.

Overhead View

 2 Completed Apache Helicopter.

Part 1

1 Start at step 6 of Base Fold III. Valley fold and unfold.

2 Valley fold.

3 Valley fold.

4 Valley fold.

5 Valley fold.

6 Valley and squash folds.

7 Make cuts as shown.

8 Valley folds.

9 Valley fold.

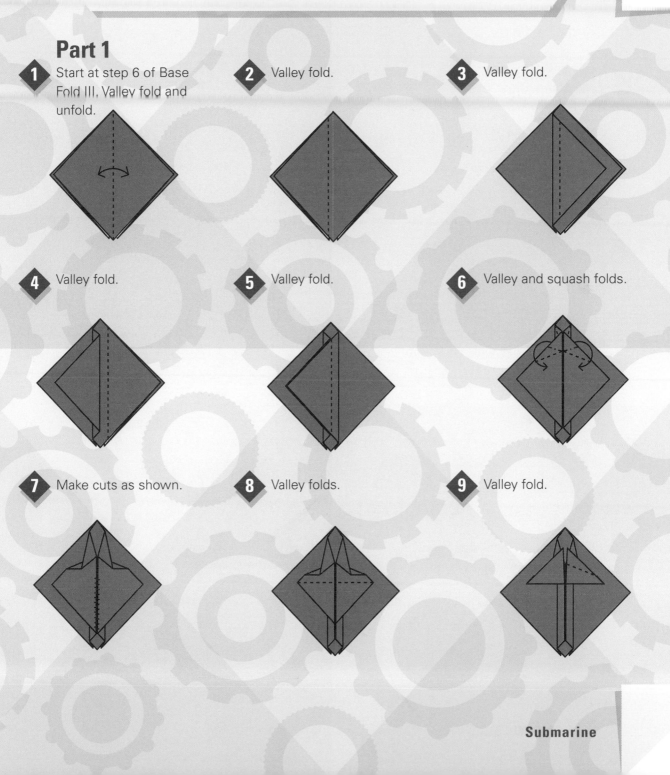

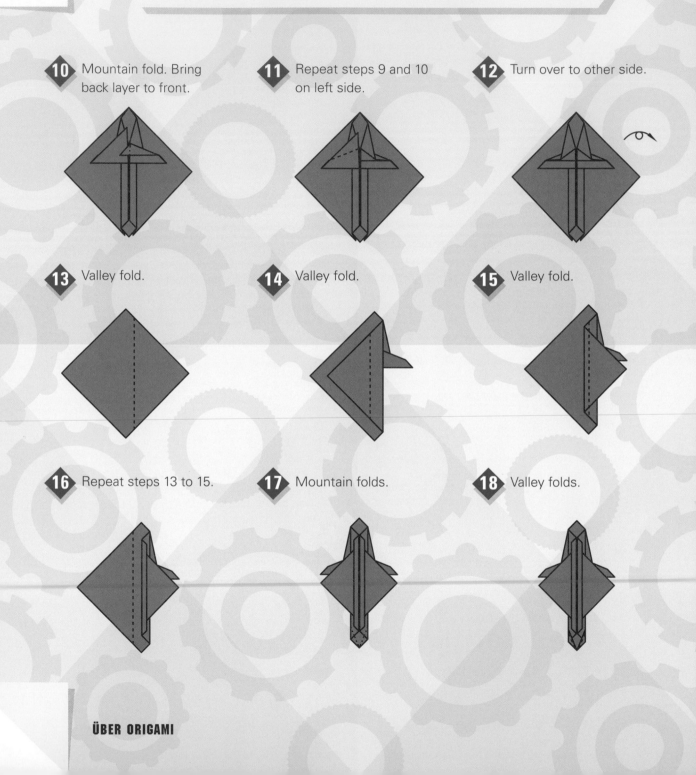

10 Mountain fold. Bring back layer to front.

11 Repeat steps 9 and 10 on left side.

12 Turn over to other side.

13 Valley fold.

14 Valley fold.

15 Valley fold.

16 Repeat steps 13 to 15.

17 Mountain folds.

18 Valley folds.

SUBMARINE

 19 Valley fold to standing position (90°).

20 Glue to hold, and rotate.

21 Valley fold layers together and glue.

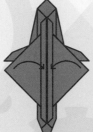

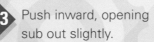

22 Cut and mountain fold cut parts.

23 Push inward, opening sub out slightly.

24 Completed part 1 of submarine.

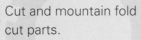

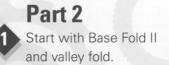

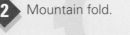

Part 2

1 Start with Base Fold II and valley fold.

2 Mountain fold.

3 Valley fold.

4 Repeat steps 1 and 2.

5 Valley fold.

6 Valley fold.

7 Repeat steps 1 and 2.

8 Valley fold and turn over.

9 Repeat steps 1 and 2.

10 Cut as shown.

11 Push tip, mountain folding in to sink.

12 Rotate.

SUBMARINE

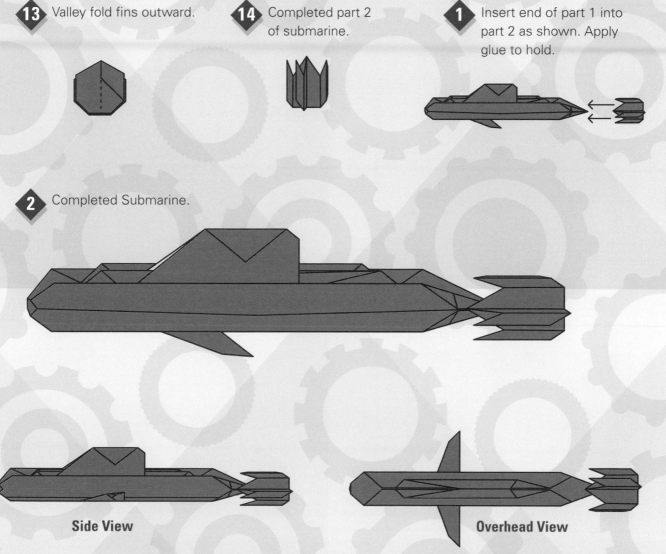

13 Valley fold fins outward.

14 Completed part 2 of submarine.

To Attach

1 Insert end of part 1 into part 2 as shown. Apply glue to hold.

2 Completed Submarine.

Side View

Overhead View

Submarine

AIRCRAFT CARRIER

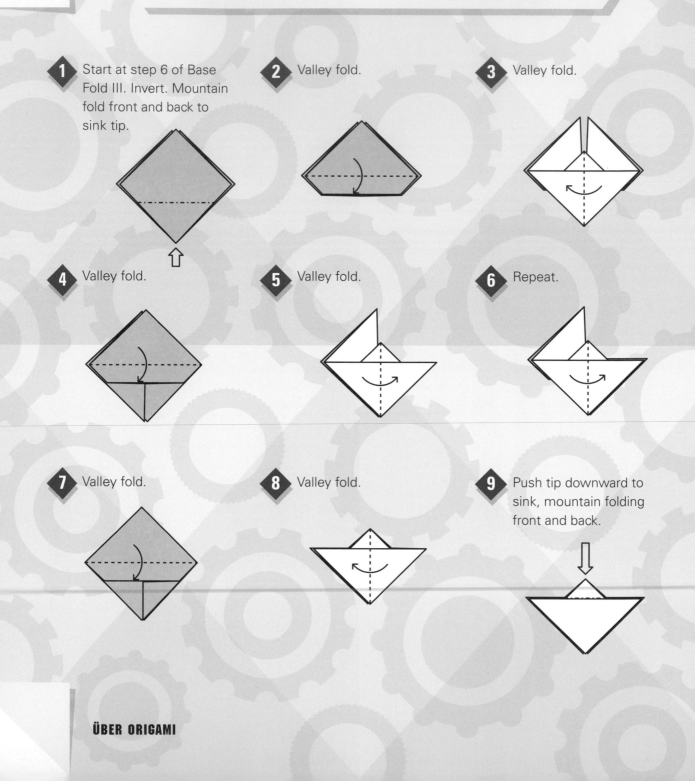

1 Start at step 6 of Base Fold III. Invert. Mountain fold front and back to sink tip.

2 Valley fold.

3 Valley fold.

4 Valley fold.

5 Valley fold.

6 Repeat.

7 Valley fold.

8 Valley fold.

9 Push tip downward to sink, mountain folding front and back.

10 Valley fold both sides.

11 Mountain fold tips to inside, front and back.

12 Valley fold.

13 Valley fold.

14 Valley fold.

15 Valley fold.

16 Valley fold.

17 Valley fold.

18 Inside reverse folds.

AIRCRAFT CARRIER

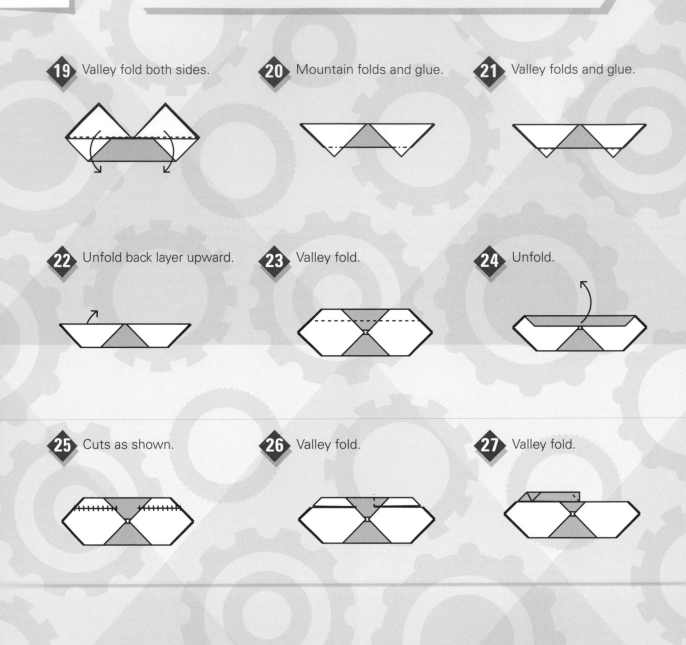

19 Valley fold both sides.

20 Mountain folds and glue.

21 Valley folds and glue.

22 Unfold back layer upward.

23 Valley fold.

24 Unfold.

25 Cuts as shown.

26 Valley fold.

27 Valley fold.

AIRCRAFT CARRIER

28 Valley fold.

29 Valley fold.

30 Valley fold.

31 Squash fold.

32 Inside reverse fold.

33 Valley fold.

34 Unfold to a right angle, 90°.

35 Add color to tower, and rotate.

36 Completed Aircraft Carrier (see page 360 for jets).

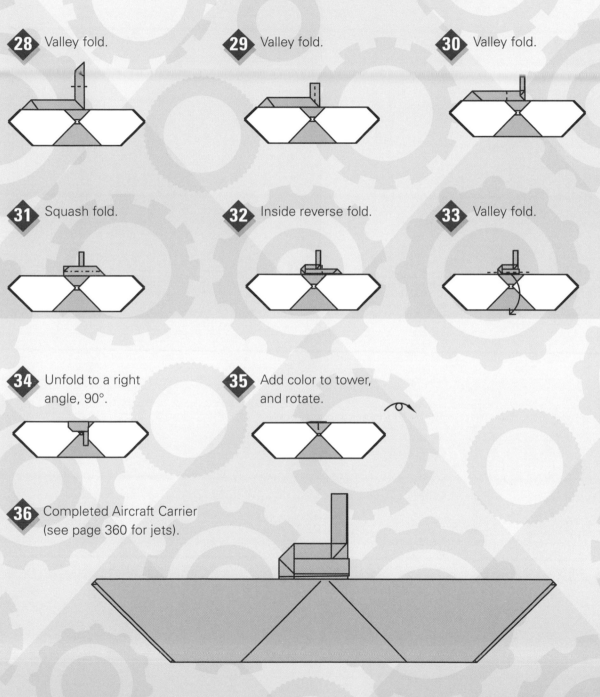

Aircraft Carrier

CARRIER JET

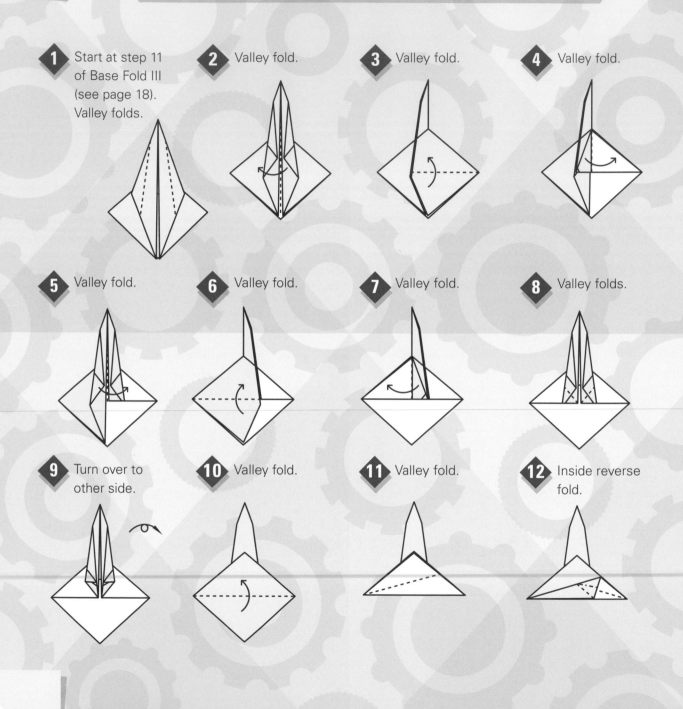

1 Start at step 11 of Base Fold III (see page 18). Valley folds.

2 Valley fold.

3 Valley fold.

4 Valley fold.

5 Valley fold.

6 Valley fold.

7 Valley fold.

8 Valley folds.

9 Turn over to other side.

10 Valley fold.

11 Valley fold.

12 Inside reverse fold.

CARRIER JET

 13 Add details: color and text.

 **14** Fold in half.

 **15** Rotate.

 16 Valley fold wings into balanced position.

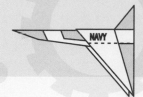

 17 Completed Carrier Jet.

To Attach

1 Place a piece of stiff cardboard against the carrier top, and cut to fit. Add detail as indicated, then position the cardboard, and glue to hold.

2 Add as many carrier jets as you wish for a fully outfitted Aircraft Carrier.

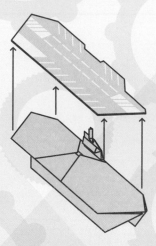

Carrier Jet

'TIS THE SEASON
FOR ORIGAMI

Holiday origami figures will add
a personal touch to Christmas decorations.

STOCKING

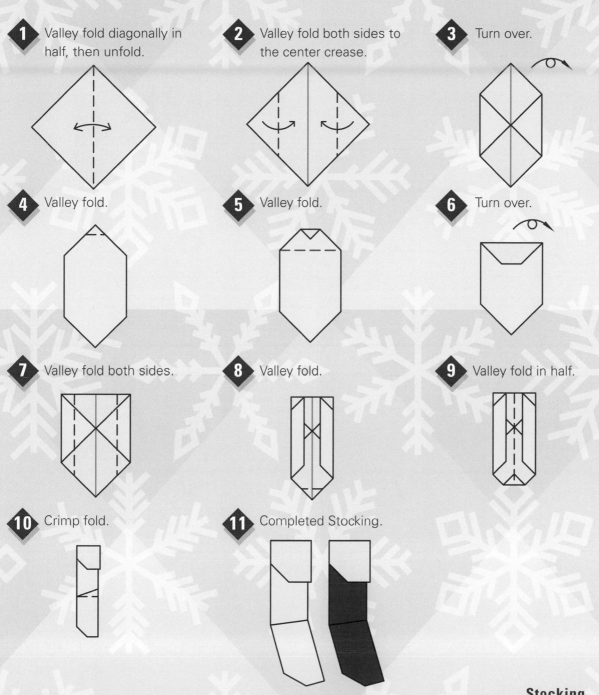

1 Valley fold diagonally in half, then unfold.

2 Valley fold both sides to the center crease.

3 Turn over.

4 Valley fold.

5 Valley fold.

6 Turn over.

7 Valley fold both sides.

8 Valley fold.

9 Valley fold in half.

10 Crimp fold.

11 Completed Stocking.

Stocking

CHRISTMAS CANDLE

Part 1

1 Valley fold and unfold.

2 Make valley folds.

3 Make valley folds.

4 Make valley folds.

5 Make squash folds.

6 Appearance before completion of squash folds.

7 Mountain fold.

8 Pleat fold.

9 Make squash folds.

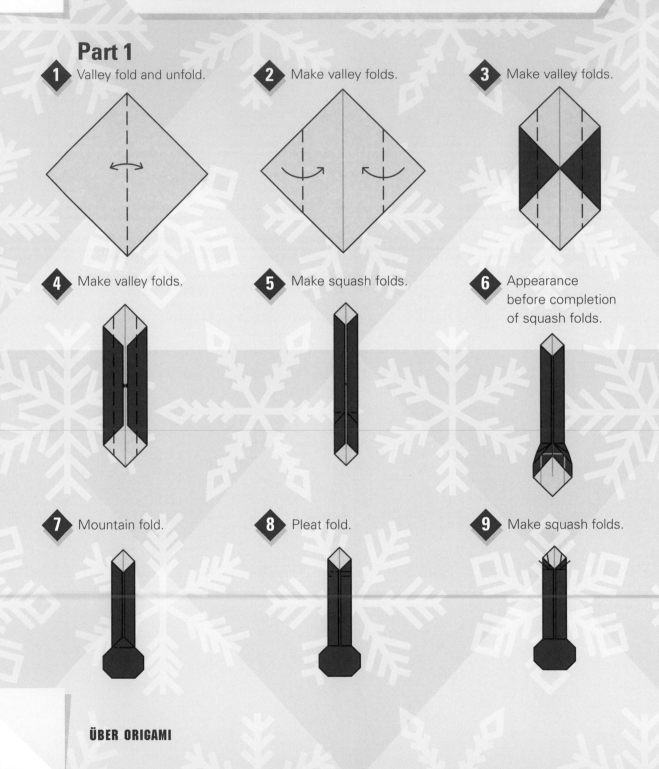

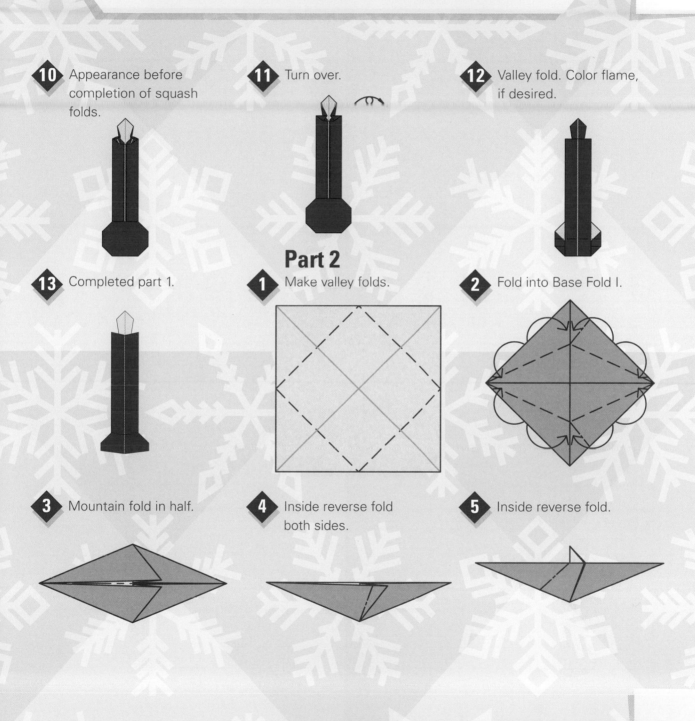

10 Appearance before completion of squash folds.

11 Turn over.

12 Valley fold. Color flame, if desired.

13 Completed part 1.

Part 2

1 Make valley folds.

2 Fold into Base Fold I.

3 Mountain fold in half.

4 Inside reverse fold both sides.

5 Inside reverse fold.

CHRISTMAS CANDLE

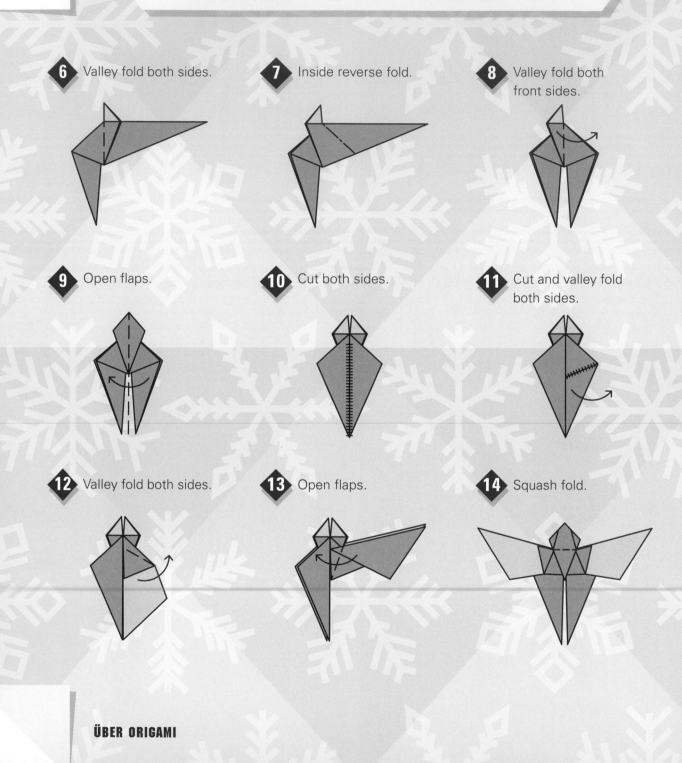

6 Valley fold both sides.

7 Inside reverse fold.

8 Valley fold both front sides.

9 Open flaps.

10 Cut both sides.

11 Cut and valley fold both sides.

12 Valley fold both sides.

13 Open flaps.

14 Squash fold.

CHRISTMAS CANDLE

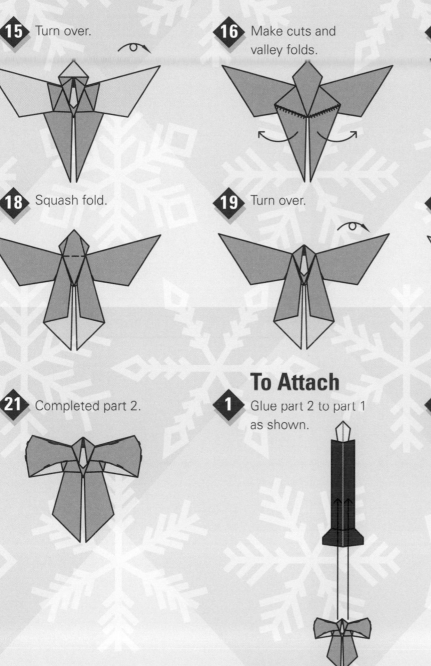

15 Turn over.

16 Make cuts and valley folds.

17 Make valley folds.

18 Squash fold.

19 Turn over.

20 Curve tips to center and glue to hold.

21 Completed part 2.

To Attach

1 Glue part 2 to part 1 as shown.

2 Completed Christmas Candle.

Christmas Candle

SANTA'S SLED

Part 1

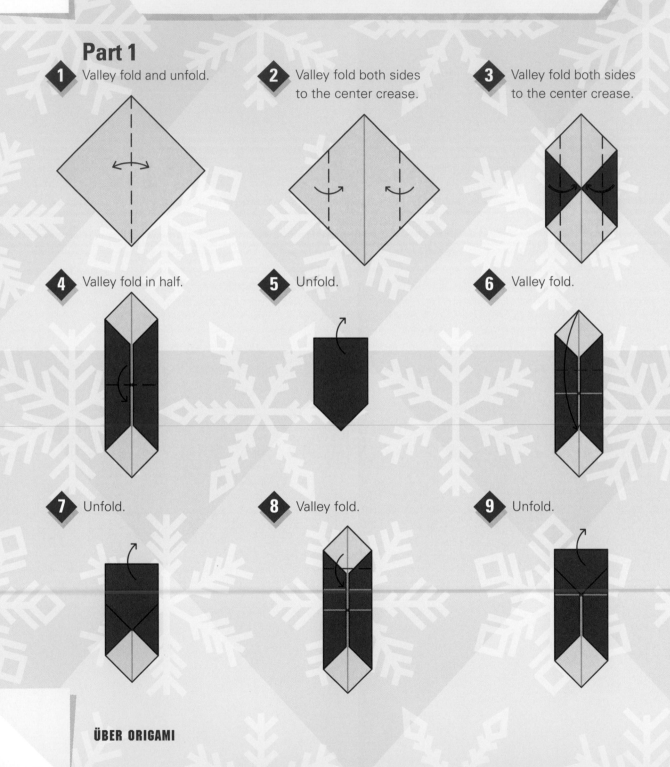

1 Valley fold and unfold.

2 Valley fold both sides to the center crease.

3 Valley fold both sides to the center crease.

4 Valley fold in half.

5 Unfold.

6 Valley fold.

7 Unfold.

8 Valley fold.

9 Unfold.

SANTA'S SLED

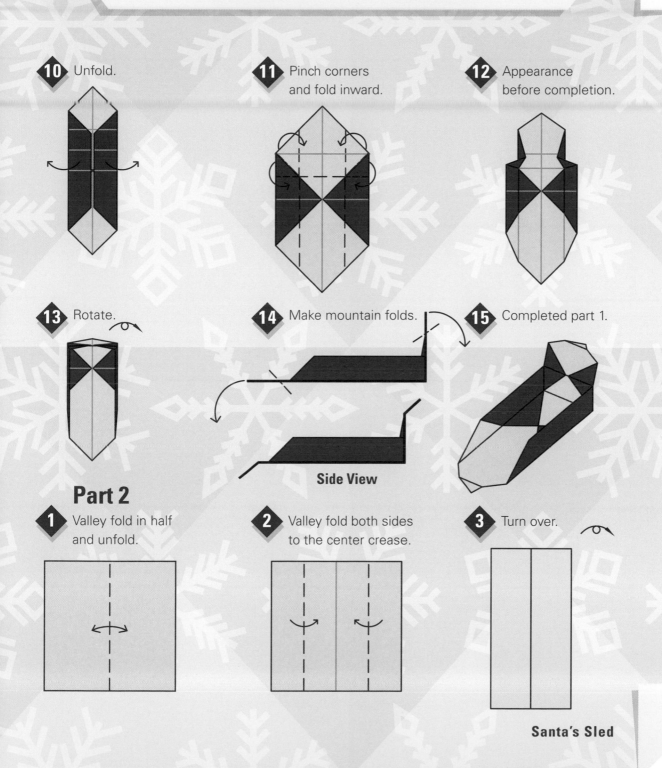

10 Unfold.

11 Pinch corners and fold inward.

12 Appearance before completion.

13 Rotate.

14 Make mountain folds.

Side View

15 Completed part 1.

Part 2

1 Valley fold in half and unfold.

2 Valley fold both sides to the center crease.

3 Turn over.

Santa's Sled

SANTA'S SLED

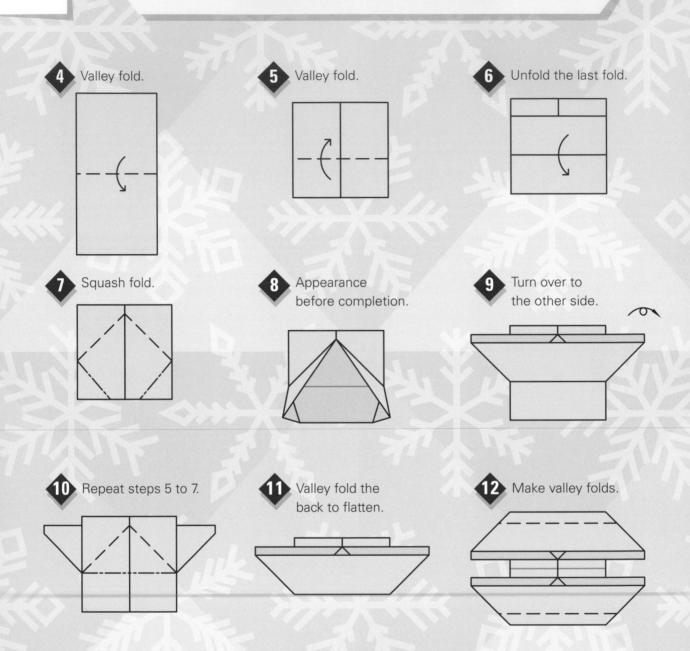

4 Valley fold.

5 Valley fold.

6 Unfold the last fold.

7 Squash fold.

8 Appearance before completion.

9 Turn over to the other side.

10 Repeat steps 5 to 7.

11 Valley fold the back to flatten.

12 Make valley folds.

13 Make mountain folds.

14 Turn to the side.

15 Completed part 2.

To Attach

1 Glue both parts together as shown.

2 Completed Santa's Sled.

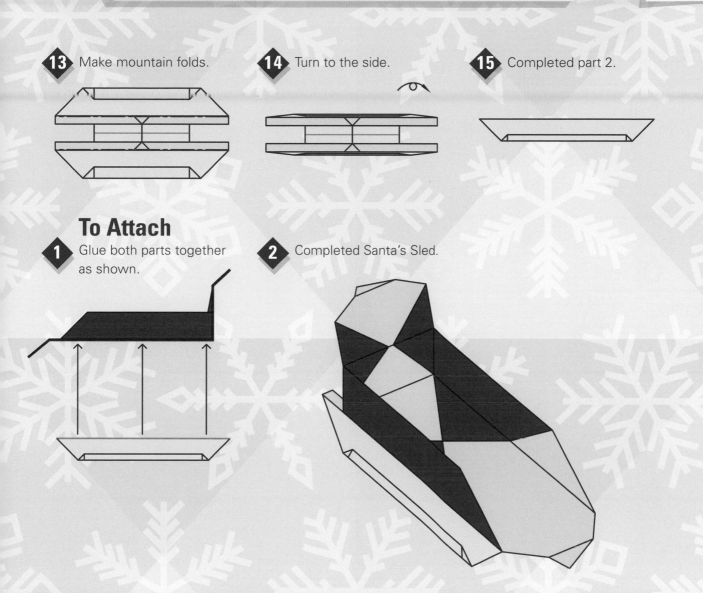

REINDEER

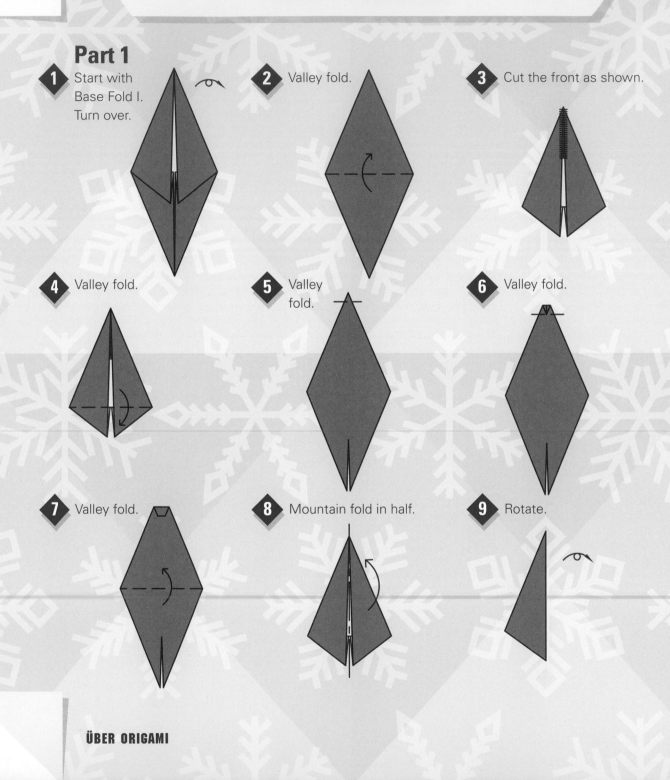

Part 1

1 Start with Base Fold I. Turn over.

2 Valley fold.

3 Cut the front as shown.

4 Valley fold.

5 Valley fold.

6 Valley fold.

7 Valley fold.

8 Mountain fold in half.

9 Rotate.

REINDEER

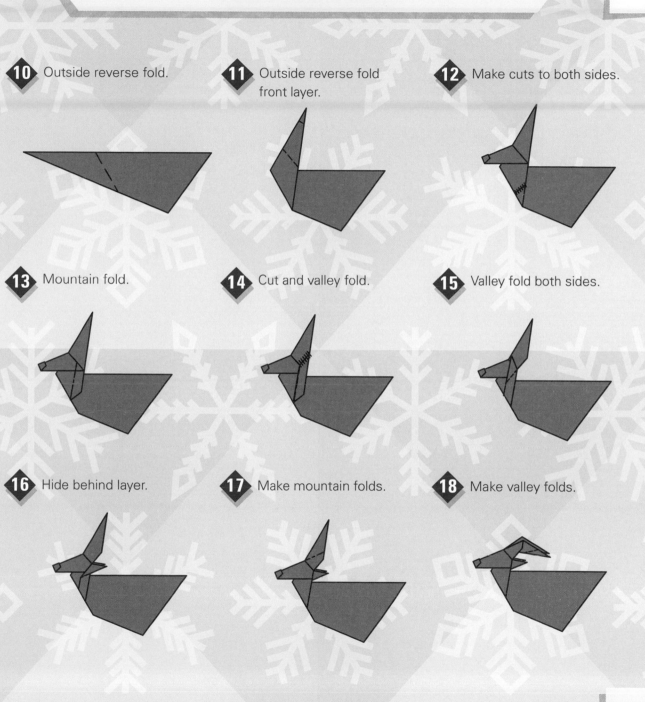

10 Outside reverse fold.

11 Outside reverse fold front layer.

12 Make cuts to both sides.

13 Mountain fold.

14 Cut and valley fold.

15 Valley fold both sides.

16 Hide behind layer.

17 Make mountain folds.

18 Make valley folds.

REINDEER

19 Make mountain folds.

20 Mountain fold.

21 Valley fold.

22 Hide behind layer.

23 Make mountain folds.

24 Completed part 1.

Part 2

1 Start with Base Fold I. Make cuts and valley folds.

2 Make squash folds.

3 Make outside reverse folds.

REINDEER

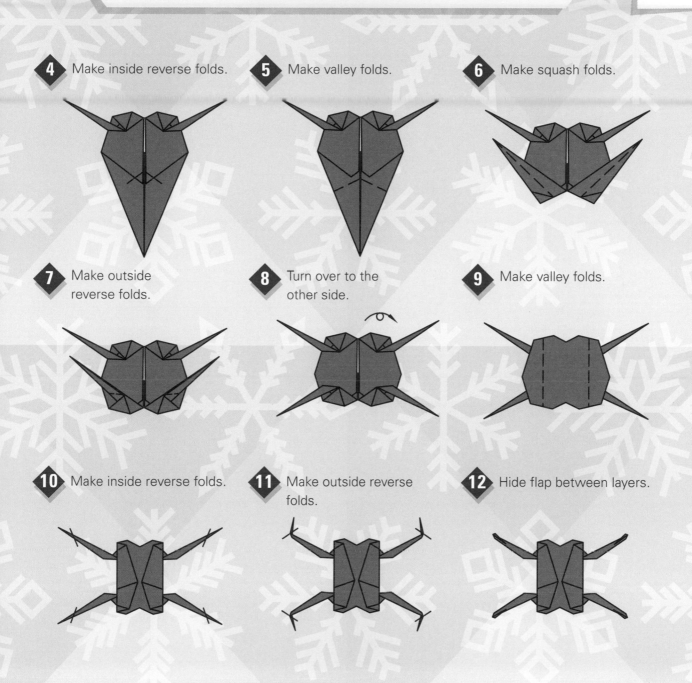

4 Make inside reverse folds.

5 Make valley folds.

6 Make squash folds.

7 Make outside reverse folds.

8 Turn over to the other side.

9 Make valley folds.

10 Make inside reverse folds.

11 Make outside reverse folds.

12 Hide flap between layers.

REINDEER

13 Valley fold in half.

14 Rotate.

15 Completed part 2.

To Attach

1 Join both parts together as shown and apply glue to hold.

2 Completed Reindeer.

MRS. CLAUS

Part 1

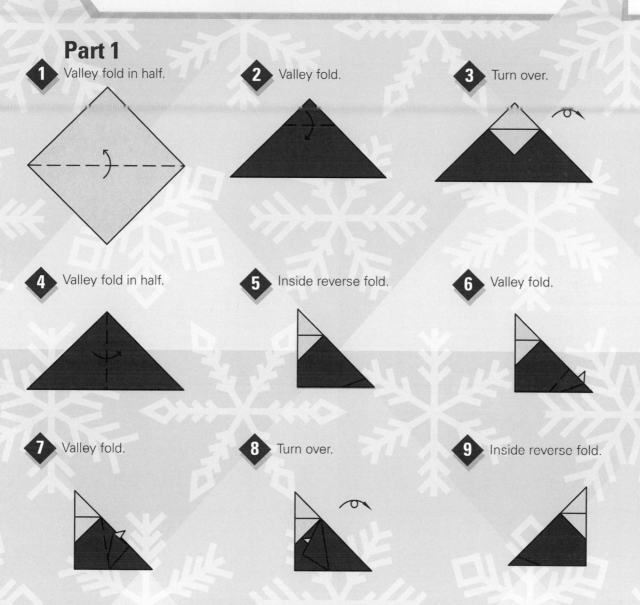

1 Valley fold in half.

2 Valley fold.

3 Turn over.

4 Valley fold in half.

5 Inside reverse fold.

6 Valley fold.

7 Valley fold.

8 Turn over.

9 Inside reverse fold.

MRS. CLAUS

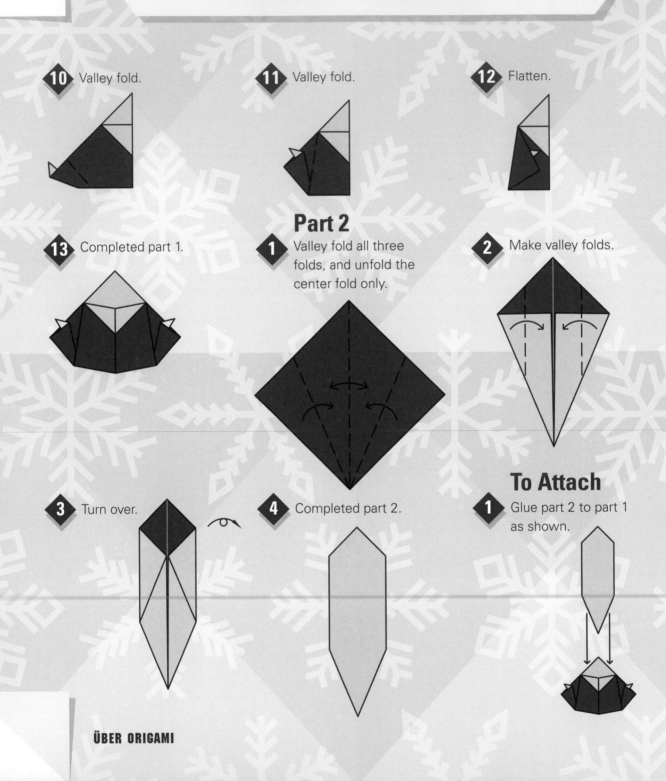

10 Valley fold.

11 Valley fold.

12 Flatten.

13 Completed part 1.

Part 2

1 Valley fold all three folds, and unfold the center fold only.

2 Make valley folds.

3 Turn over.

4 Completed part 2.

To Attach

1 Glue part 2 to part 1 as shown.

2 Valley fold.

3 Hide behind layer.

4 Make cuts and then mountain folds.

5 Pleat fold.

6 Make valley folds.

7 Valley fold.

8 Completed first assembly.

Part 3

1 Valley fold and unfold.

2 Make valley folds.

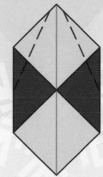

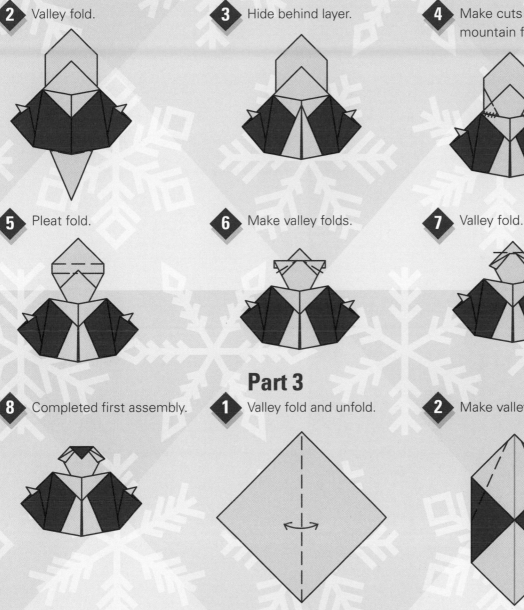

3 Valley fold.

4 Turn over.

5 Make valley folds.

6 Mountain fold to crease.

7 Completed part 3.

To Attach

1 Insert part 3 into the assembled parts 1 and 2 as shown and apply glue to hold.

2 Completed Mrs. Claus.

NUTCRACKER SOLDIER

Part 1

1 Valley fold in half diagonally.

2 Make valley folds.

3 Make inside reverse folds.

4 Valley fold both sides.

5 Make cuts as shown to the top layer only.

6 Make valley folds.

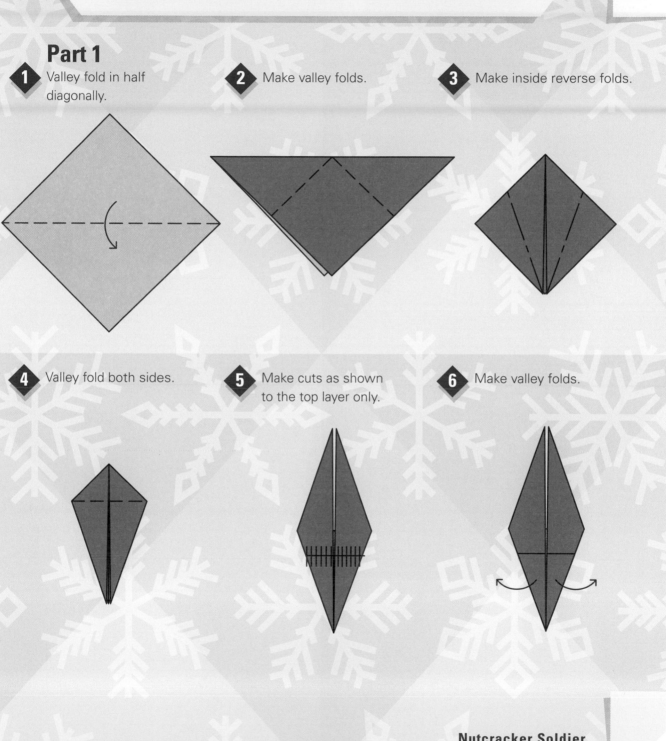

NUTCRACKER SOLDIER

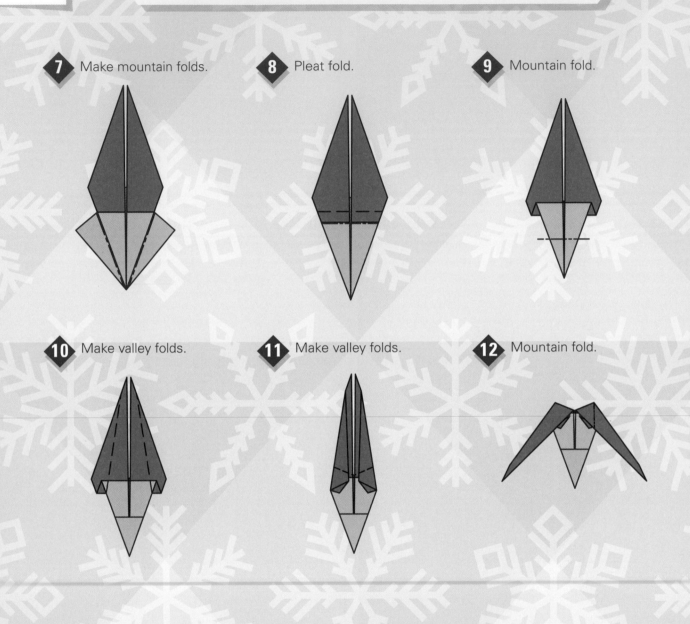

7 Make mountain folds.

8 Pleat fold.

9 Mountain fold.

10 Make valley folds.

11 Make valley folds.

12 Mountain fold.

NUTCRACKER SOLDIER

13 Mountain fold.

14 Turn over.

15 Valley fold.

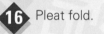

16 Pleat fold.

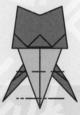

17 Tuck flap behind layer.

18 Completed part 1.

Part 2

1 Start with Base Fold III. Open the flaps.

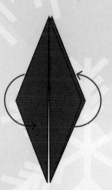

2 Make inside reverse folds.

3 Valley fold both sides.

Nutcracker Soldier

NUTCRACKER SOLDIER

4 Mountain fold.

5 Make outside reverse folds.

6 Valley fold.

7 Mountain fold.

8 Make cuts and valley folds.

9 Make cuts as shown and valley fold both sides.

10 Make mountain folds.

11 Fold in half and unfold.

12 Completed part 2.

To Attach

1 Insert part 1 into part 2 as shown and apply glue to hold.

2 Completed first assembly.

Part 3

1 Start with Base Fold III and make mountain folds.

2 Make valley folds.

3 Tuck behind layers.

4 Valley fold.

5 Valley fold.

6 Turn over.

7 Valley fold.

NUTCRACKER SOLDIER

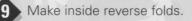

8 Valley fold.

9 Make inside reverse folds.

10 Fold in half to crease and add color.

11 Completed part 3.

To Attach

1 Insert part 3 into the assembly of parts 1 and 2 and apply glue to hold.

2 Completed Nutcracker Soldier.

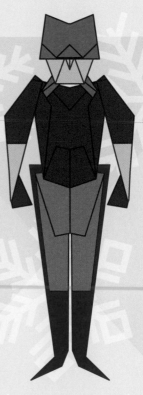

KRIS KRINGLE

Part 1

1 Start with Base Fold I. Turn over.

2 Valley fold.

3 Make outside reverse folds.

4 Make outside reverse folds.

5 Make pleat folds.

6 Make cuts as shown.

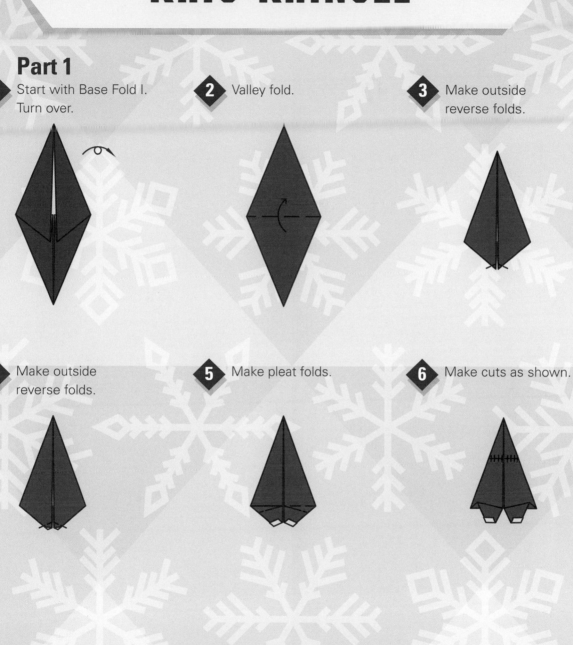

Kris Kringle

KRIS KRINGLE

7 Make valley folds.

8 Valley fold.

9 Valley fold.

10 Make valley folds.

11 Valley fold.

12 Turn over.

13 Make valley folds.

14 Cut as shown.

15 Make valley folds.

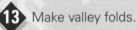
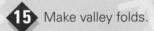

KRIS KRINGLE

16 Turn over.

17 Valley fold.

18 Completed part 1.

Part 2

1 Start with Base Fold I. Turn over.

2 Valley fold.

3 Make valley folds.

4 Make outside reverse folds.

5 Make outside reverse folds.

6 Cut as shown.

KRIS KRINGLE

7 ▸ Make pleat folds.

8 ▸ Make cuts and valley folds.

9 ▸ Valley fold.

10 ▸ Pleat fold.

11 ▸ Pleat fold.

12 ▸ Fold in half.

13 ▸ Pull and fold.

14 ▸ Flatten.

15 ▸ Make valley folds.

KRIS KRINGLE

16 Completed part 2.

To Attach

1 Join parts 1 and 2 together and apply glue to hold.

2 Pinch the top of the cap in half.

3 Completed first assembly of Kris Kringle.

Part 3

1 Valley fold and unfold.

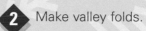

2 Make valley folds.

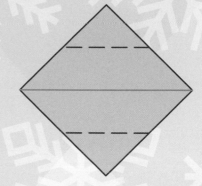

KRIS KRINGLE

3 Make valley folds.

4 Turn over to the other side.

5 Make valley folds.

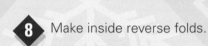

6 Valley fold in half.

7 Valley fold and unfold.

8 Make inside reverse folds.

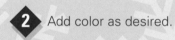

9 Completed part 3.

To Attach

1 Join part 3 to the first assembly and apply glue to hold.

2 Add color as desired.

KRIS KRINGLE

3 Completed Kris Kringle second assembly.

Part 4

1 Valley fold and unfold.

2 Make valley folds.

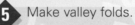

3 Valley fold.

4 Tuck flap behind the layer.

5 Make valley folds.

Kris Kringle

KRIS KRINGLE

6 Make valley folds.

7 Valley fold.

8 Completed part 4.

To Attach

1 Join part 4 to the second assembly and apply glue to hold.

2 Valley fold.

3 Valley fold and apply glue.

4 Completed Kris Kringle.

Part 1

1 Valley fold and unfold.

2 Valley fold both sides to the center crease.

3 Valley fold and unfold.

4 Make valley folds.

5 Make valley folds.

6 Valley fold.

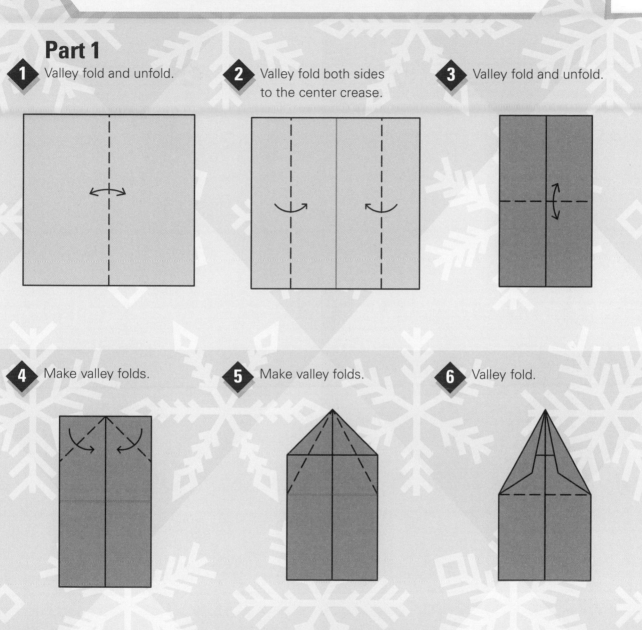

CHRISTMAS TREE

7 Valley fold.

8 Squash fold.

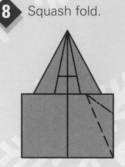

9 Appearance before completion of step 8.

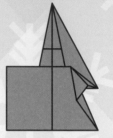

10 Squash fold.

11 Appearance before completion of step 10.

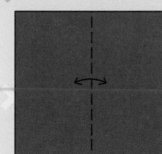

12 Turn over.

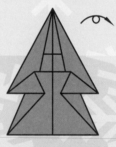

13 Completed part 1.

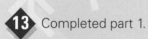

Part 2

1 Valley fold and unfold.

2 Make valley folds.

CHRISTMAS TREE

 3 Valley fold and unfold.

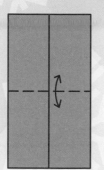

4 Make valley folds.

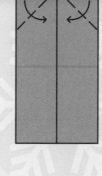

5 Make valley folds.

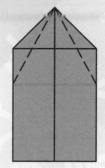

6 Valley fold.

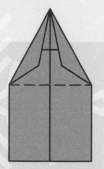

7 Valley fold.

8 Make cuts and then valley folds.

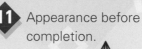

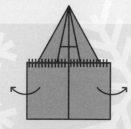

9 Make mountain folds.

10 Squash folds.

11 Appearance before completion.

Christmas Tree

CHRISTMAS TREE

12 Make valley folds.

13 Turn over.

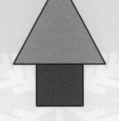

14 Completed part 2.

To Attach

1 Insert part 1 into part 2 as shown and apply glue to hold.

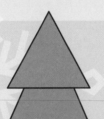

2 Fold in half and unfold to crease.

3 Completed Christmas Tree.

MARY

Part 1

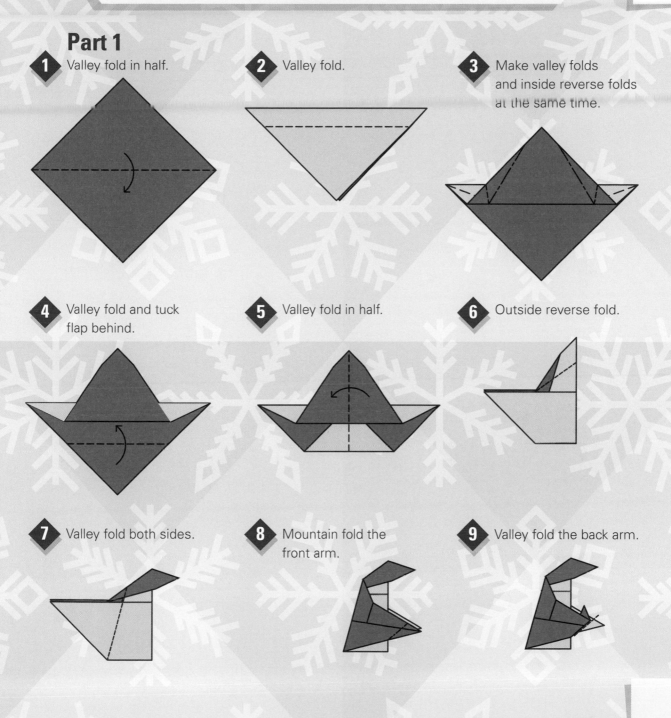

1 Valley fold in half.

2 Valley fold.

3 Make valley folds and inside reverse folds at the same time.

4 Valley fold and tuck flap behind.

5 Valley fold in half.

6 Outside reverse fold.

7 Valley fold both sides.

8 Mountain fold the front arm.

9 Valley fold the back arm.

Mary

MARY

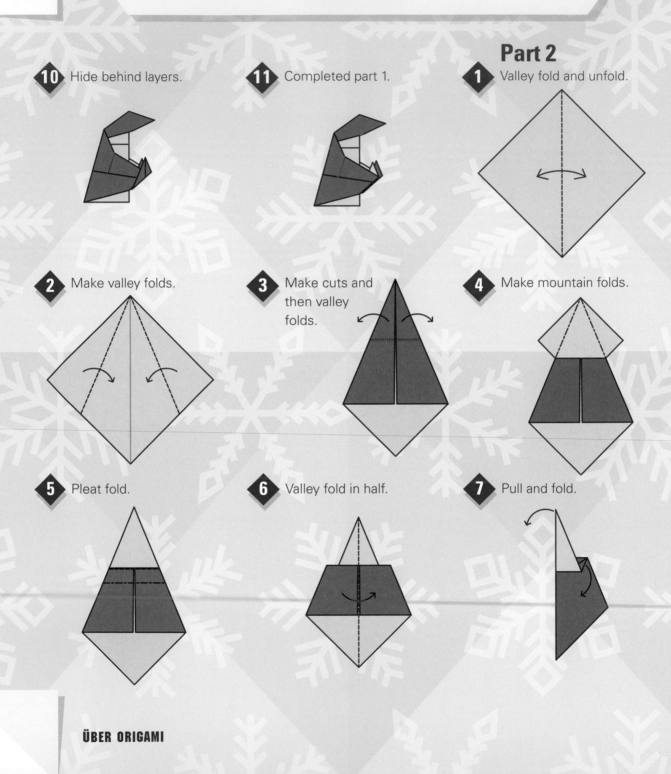

10 Hide behind layers.

11 Completed part 1.

Part 2

1 Valley fold and unfold.

2 Make valley folds.

3 Make cuts and then valley folds.

4 Make mountain folds.

5 Pleat fold.

6 Valley fold in half.

7 Pull and fold.

8 Outside reverse fold.

9 Outside reverse fold.

10 Crimp fold.

11 Inside reverse fold.

12 Inside reverse fold.

13 Completed part 2.

To Attach

1 Insert part 1 into part 2 as shown and apply glue to hold.

2 Completed Mary.

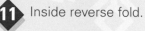

JOSEPH

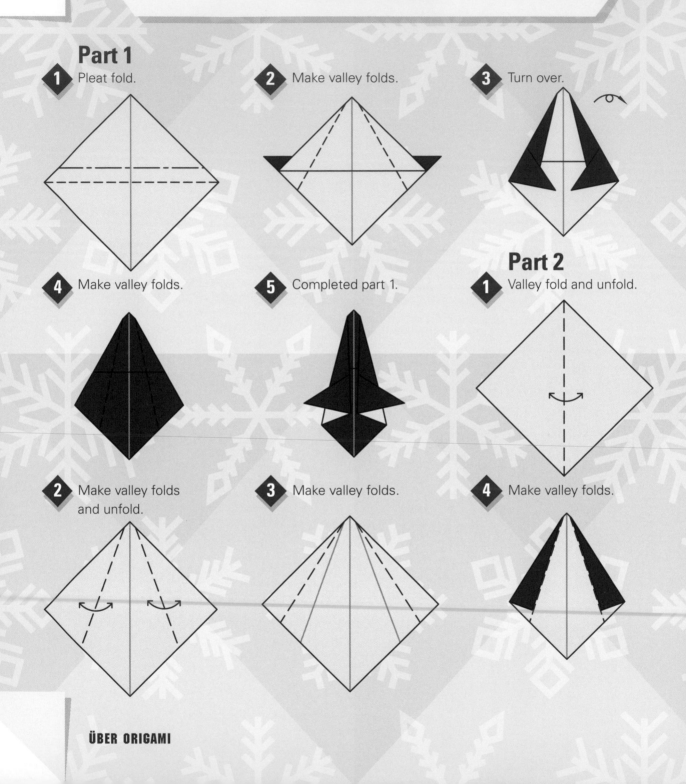

Part 1

1 Pleat fold.

2 Make valley folds.

3 Turn over.

4 Make valley folds.

5 Completed part 1.

Part 2

1 Valley fold and unfold.

2 Make valley folds and unfold.

3 Make valley folds.

4 Make valley folds.

ÜBER ORIGAMI

JOSEPH

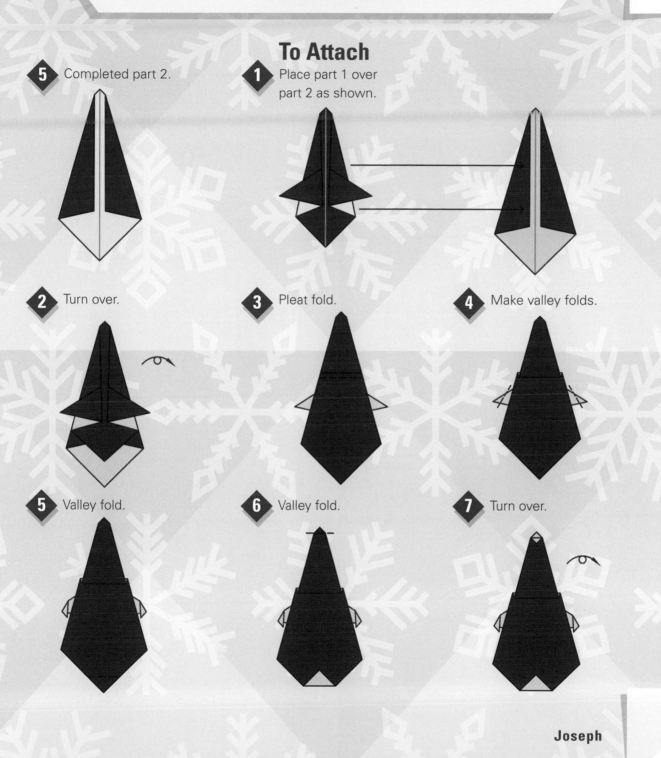

5 Completed part 2.

To Attach

1 Place part 1 over part 2 as shown.

2 Turn over.

3 Pleat fold.

4 Make valley folds.

5 Valley fold.

6 Valley fold.

7 Turn over.

Joseph

8 Valley fold.

9 Turn over.

10 Valley fold.

11 Inside reverse fold.

12 Unfold first layer only.

13 Outside reverse fold.

14 Squash fold.

15 Squash fold.

16 Valley fold.

17 Completed Joseph.

BABY JESUS

Part 1

1 Valley fold.

2 Make valley folds.

3 Make inside reverse folds.

4 Make valley folds.

5 Make inside reverse folds.

6 Turn over.

7 Make valley folds.

8 Valley fold in half.

9 Crimp fold.

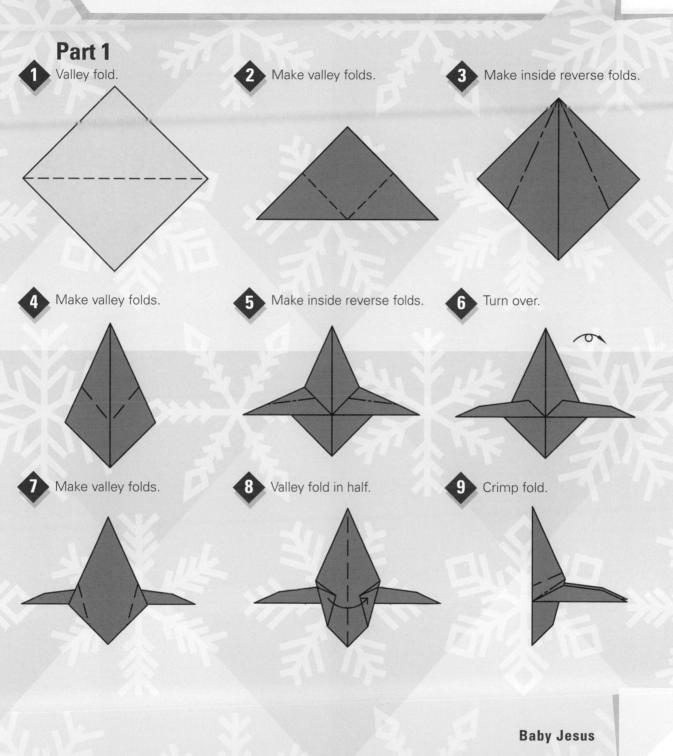

Baby Jesus

BABY JESUS

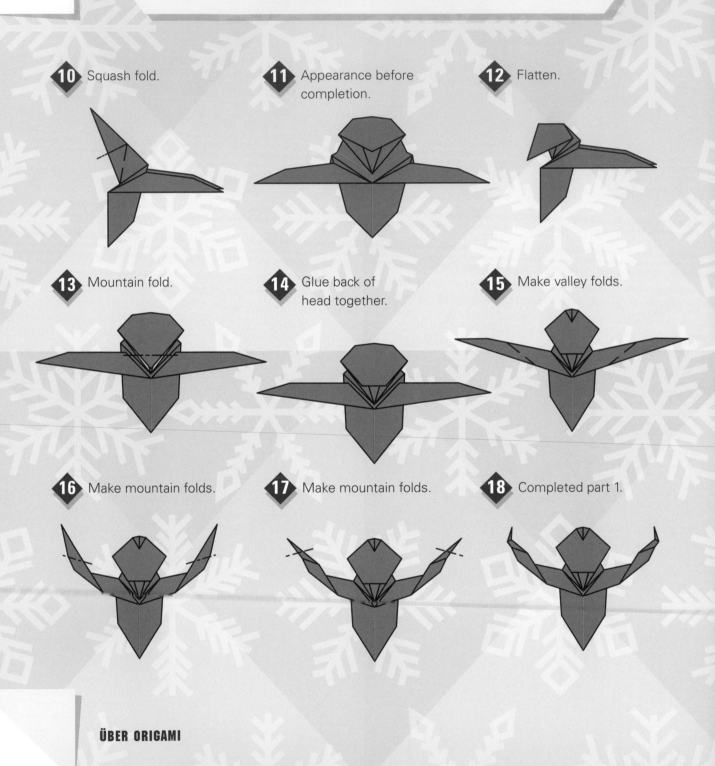

10 Squash fold.

11 Appearance before completion.

12 Flatten.

13 Mountain fold.

14 Glue back of head together.

15 Make valley folds.

16 Make mountain folds.

17 Make mountain folds.

18 Completed part 1.

Part 2

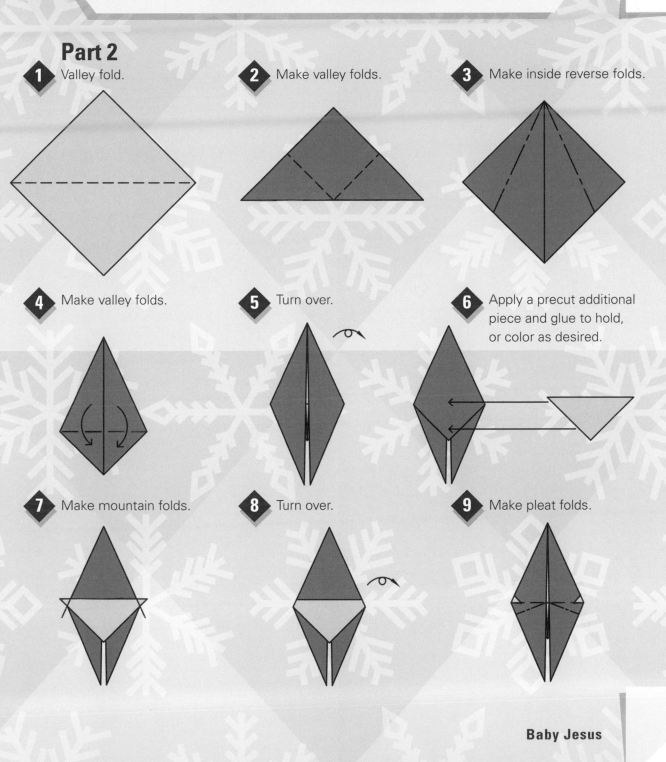

1 Valley fold.

2 Make valley folds.

3 Make inside reverse folds.

4 Make valley folds.

5 Turn over.

6 Apply a precut additional piece and glue to hold, or color as desired.

7 Make mountain folds.

8 Turn over.

9 Make pleat folds.

Baby Jesus

BABY JESUS

10 Pleat fold.

11 Valley fold.

12 Valley fold in half.

13 Inside reverse fold.

14 Inside reverse fold.

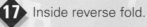

15 Inside reverse fold.

16 Inside reverse fold and turn over.

17 Inside reverse fold.

18 Valley fold.

19 Turn over.

20 Valley fold.

21 Completed part 2.

Part 2

1 Insert part 1 into part 2 as shown and apply glue to hold.

2 Completed Baby Jesus.

WISEMAN 1

Part 1

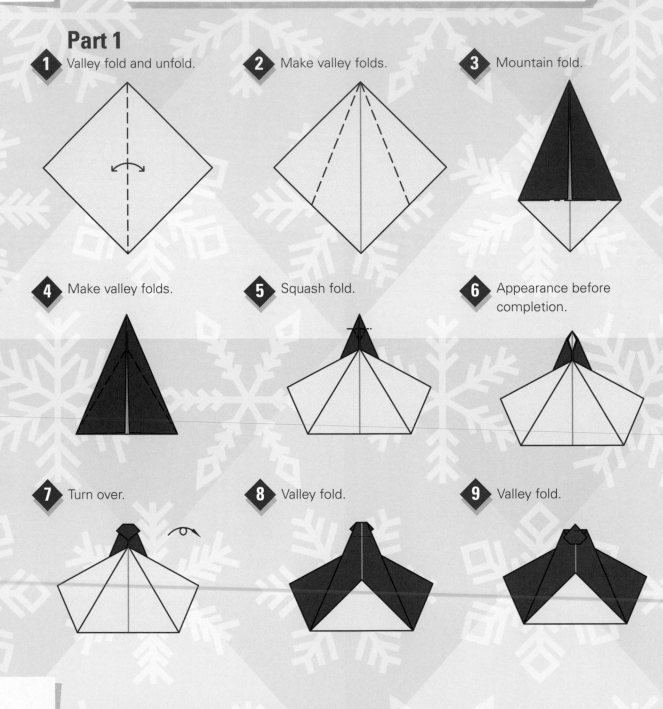

1 Valley fold and unfold.

2 Make valley folds.

3 Mountain fold.

4 Make valley folds.

5 Squash fold.

6 Appearance before completion.

7 Turn over.

8 Valley fold.

9 Valley fold.

10 Turn over.

11 Make valley folds.

12 Turn over.

13 Valley fold.

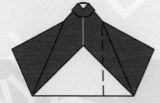

14 Mountain fold in half and unfold.

15 Valley fold.

Part 2

16 Completed part 1.

1 Start with Base Fold I. Turn over.

2 Valley fold.

WISEMAN 1

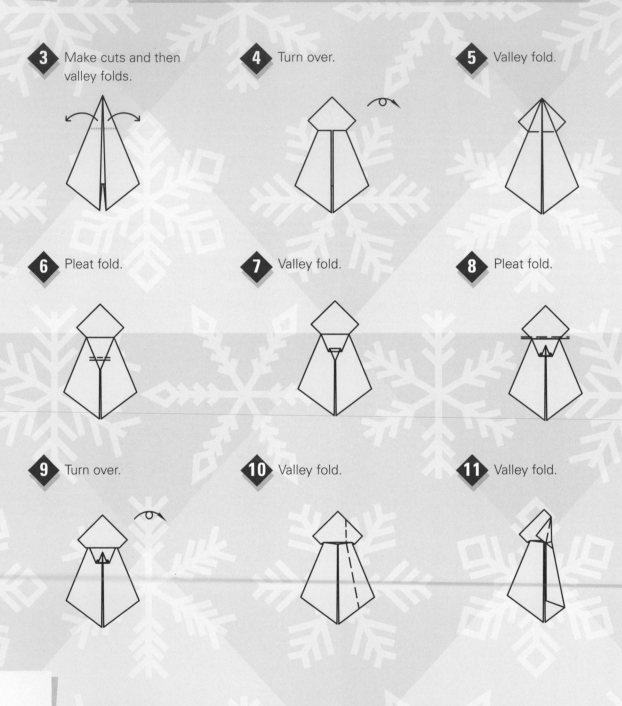

3 Make cuts and then valley folds.

4 Turn over.

5 Valley fold.

6 Pleat fold.

7 Valley fold.

8 Pleat fold.

9 Turn over.

10 Valley fold.

11 Valley fold.

12 Repeat steps 10 and 11.

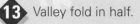 **13** Valley fold in half.

14 Pull, fold, and flatten.

 15 Completed part 2.

To Attach

1 Join parts 1 and 2 together as shown and apply glue to hold.

2 Completed Wise Man 1.

WISEMAN 2

Part 1

1 Valley fold and unfold.

2 Make valley folds.

3 See close up for better detail.

4 Make cuts as shown.

5 Make valley folds.

6 Make cuts as shown.

7 Make valley folds.

8 Return to full view.

9 Make valley folds.

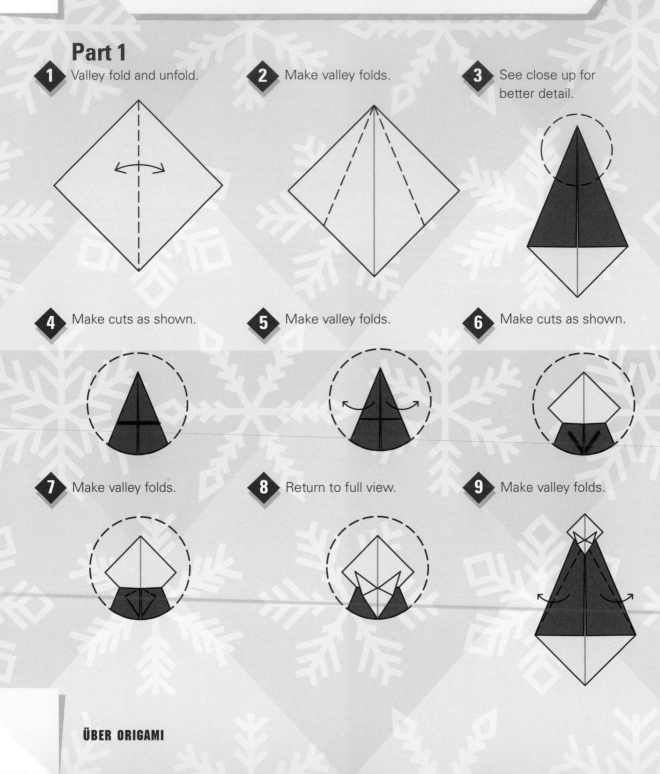

10 Turn over.

11 Valley fold the front.

12 Make mountain folds to the back.

13 Make valley folds.

14 Valley fold.

15 Completed part 1.

WISEMAN 2

Part 2

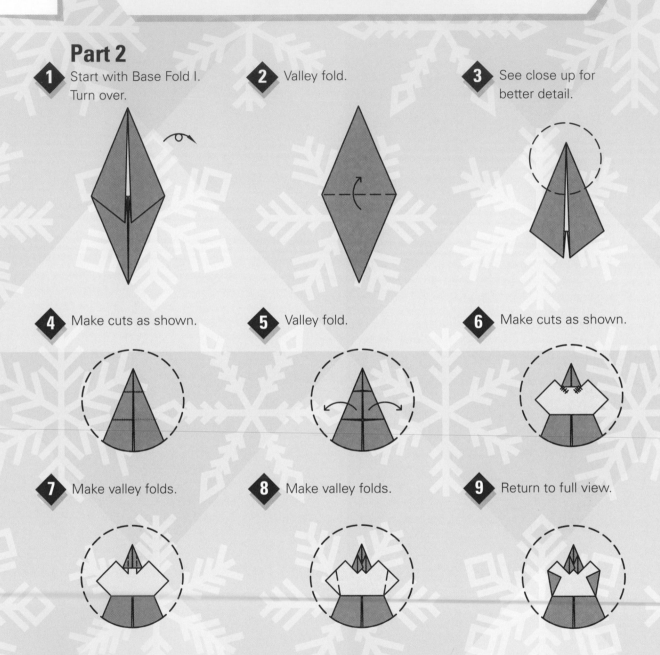

1 Start with Base Fold I. Turn over.

2 Valley fold.

3 See close up for better detail.

4 Make cuts as shown.

5 Valley fold.

6 Make cuts as shown.

7 Make valley folds.

8 Make valley folds.

9 Return to full view.

10 Turn over.

11 Make cuts and then valley folds.

12 Make mountain folds.

13 Valley fold.

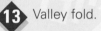

14 Pleat fold.

15 Valley fold.

To Attach

16 Make valley folds.

17 Completed part 2.

1 Insert part 1 into part 2 and apply glue to hold.

Wiseman 2

WISEMAN 2

2 Mountain fold in half.

3 Make valley folds.

4 Flatten.

5 Pleat fold.

6 Completed Wise Man 2.

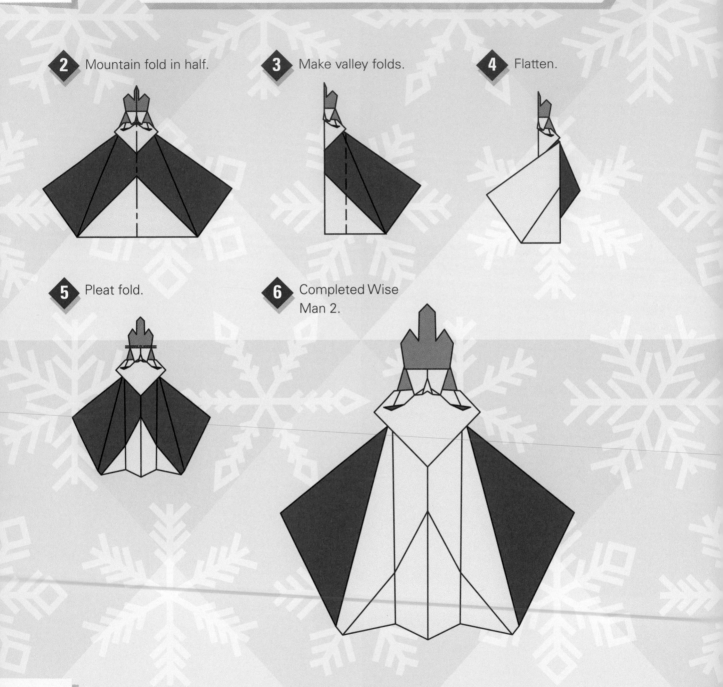

Part 1

1 Valley fold and unfold.

2 Make valley folds.

3 Make valley folds.

4 Turn over to the other side.

5 Valley fold.

6 Turn over.

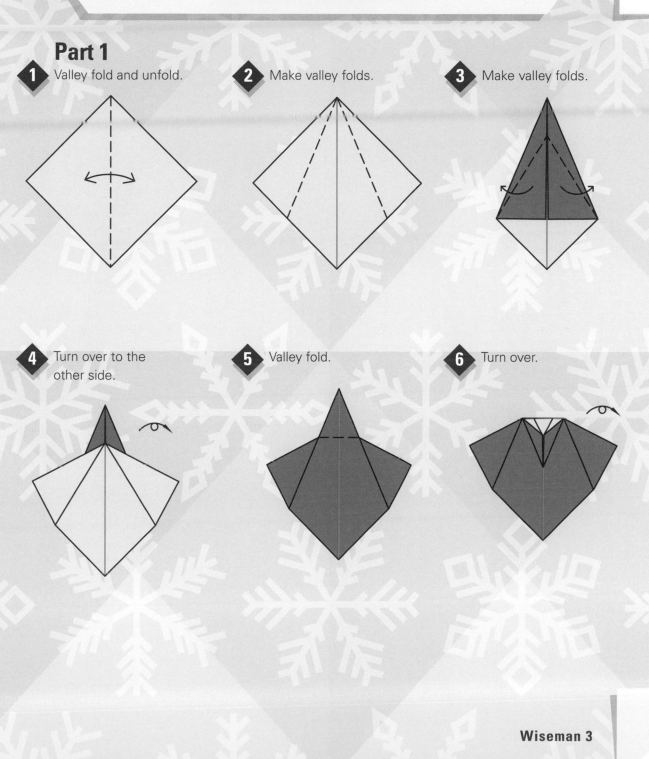

WISEMAN 3

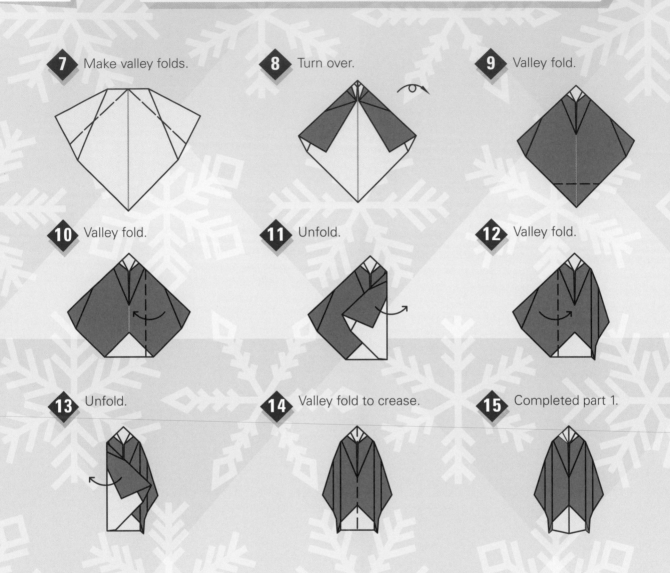

7 Make valley folds.

8 Turn over.

9 Valley fold.

10 Valley fold.

11 Unfold.

12 Valley fold.

13 Unfold.

14 Valley fold to crease.

15 Completed part 1.

Part 2

1 Start with Base Fold 1. Turn over.

2 Valley fold.

3 Valley fold.

4 Valley fold.

5 Pleat fold.

6 Valley fold.

7 Turn over.

8 Valley fold.

9 Valley fold.

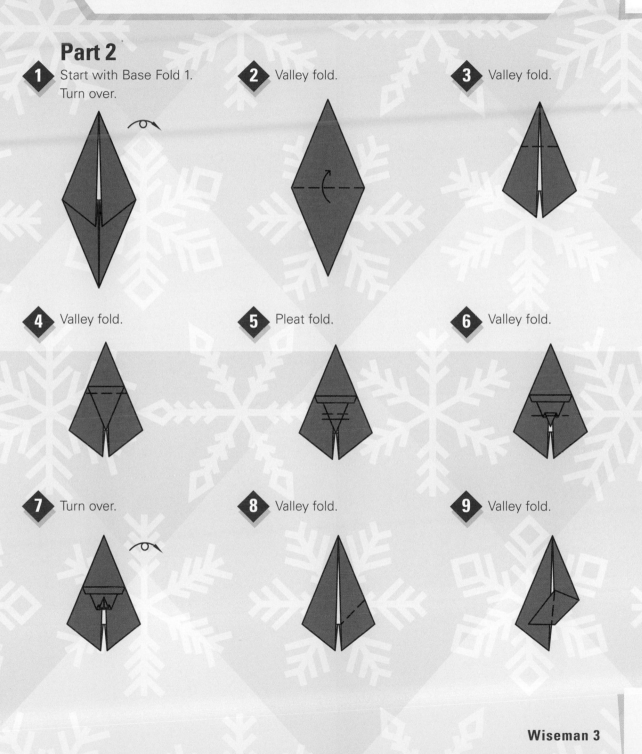

10 Valley fold.

11 Valley fold.

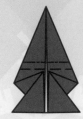

12 Pleat fold.

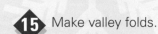

13 Make valley folds.

14 Turn over.

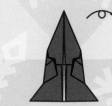

15 Make valley folds.

16 Make valley folds.

17 Mountain fold in half.

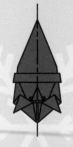

18 View close up for better detail.

WISEMAN 3

WISEMAN 3

WISEMAN 3

19 Make pulls and folds.

20 Flatten and return to full view.

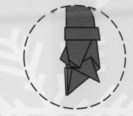

21 Completed part 2.

To Attach

1 Insert part 1 into part 2 and apply glue to hold.

2 Completed Wise Man 3.

DOLLAR BILLS

By now you're a pro at classic origami,
so try your hand folding dollar bills!

SEA LION

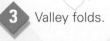

1 Valley fold in half and unfold.

2 Repeat.

3 Valley folds.

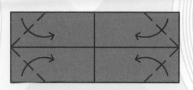

4 Turn over to the other side.

5 Valley folds.

6 Repeat.

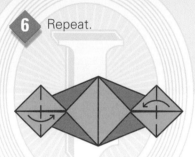

7 Valley fold.

8 Repeat.

9 Valley folds and squash folds.

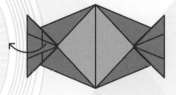

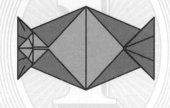

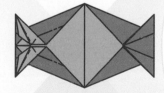

SEA LION

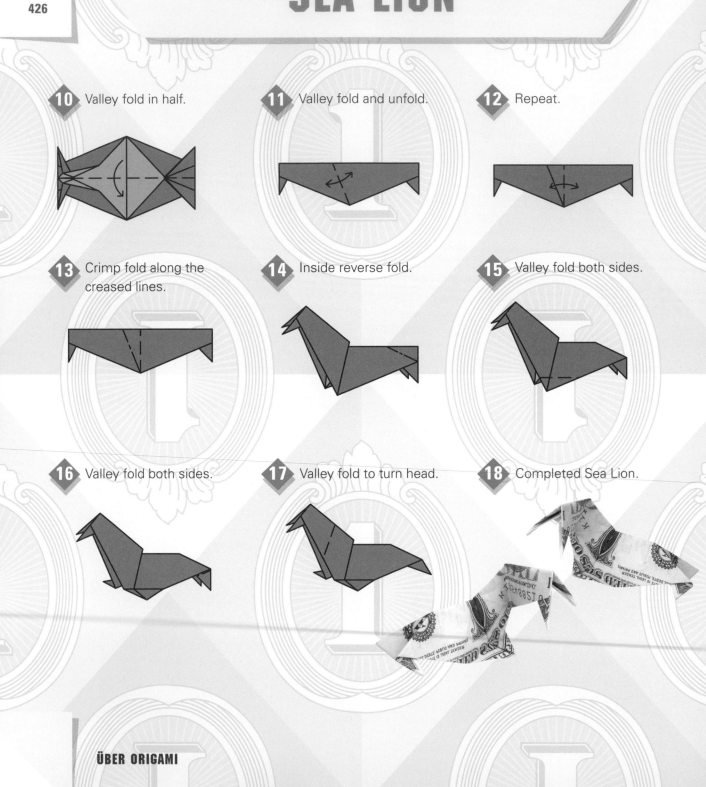

10 Valley fold in half.

11 Valley fold and unfold.

12 Repeat.

13 Crimp fold along the creased lines.

14 Inside reverse fold.

15 Valley fold both sides.

16 Valley fold both sides.

17 Valley fold to turn head.

18 Completed Sea Lion.

KLINGON BIRD OF PREY

1 Valley fold then unfold.

2 Valley folds.

3 Valley folds.

4 Unfold.

5 Pull and folds along the crease lines.

6 Mountain fold.

7 Turn over to the other side.

8 Valley fold and squash fold.

9 Valley fold.

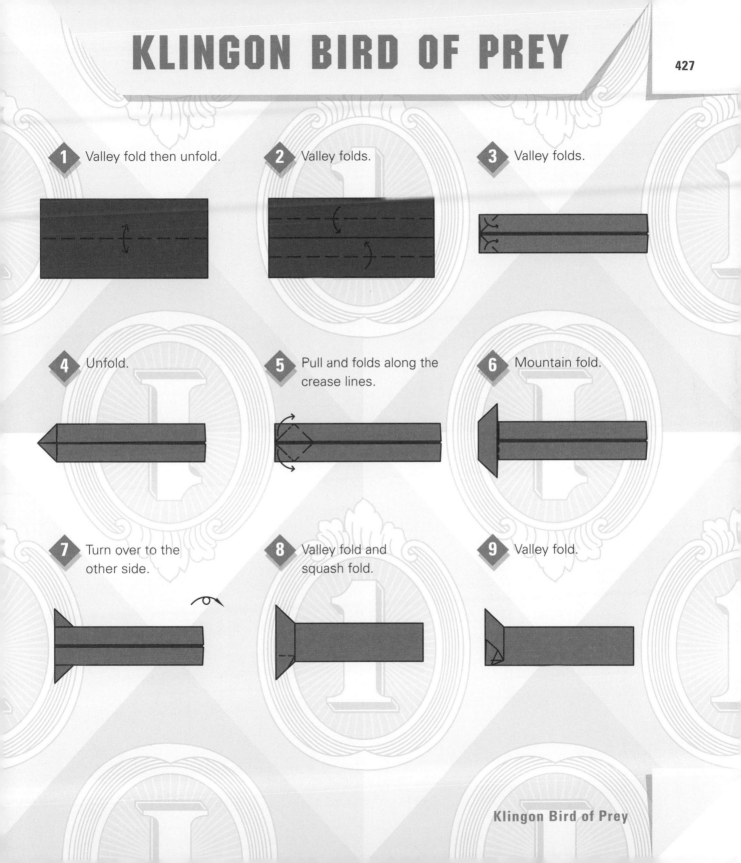

KLINGON BIRD OF PREY

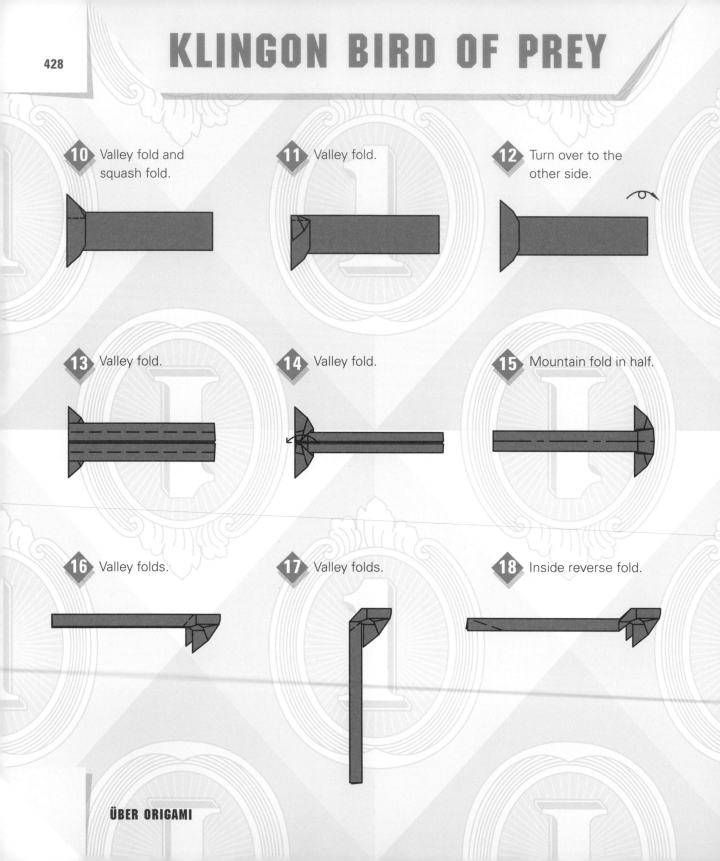

10 Valley fold and squash fold.

11 Valley fold.

12 Turn over to the other side.

13 Valley fold.

14 Valley fold.

15 Mountain fold in half.

16 Valley folds.

17 Valley folds.

18 Inside reverse fold.

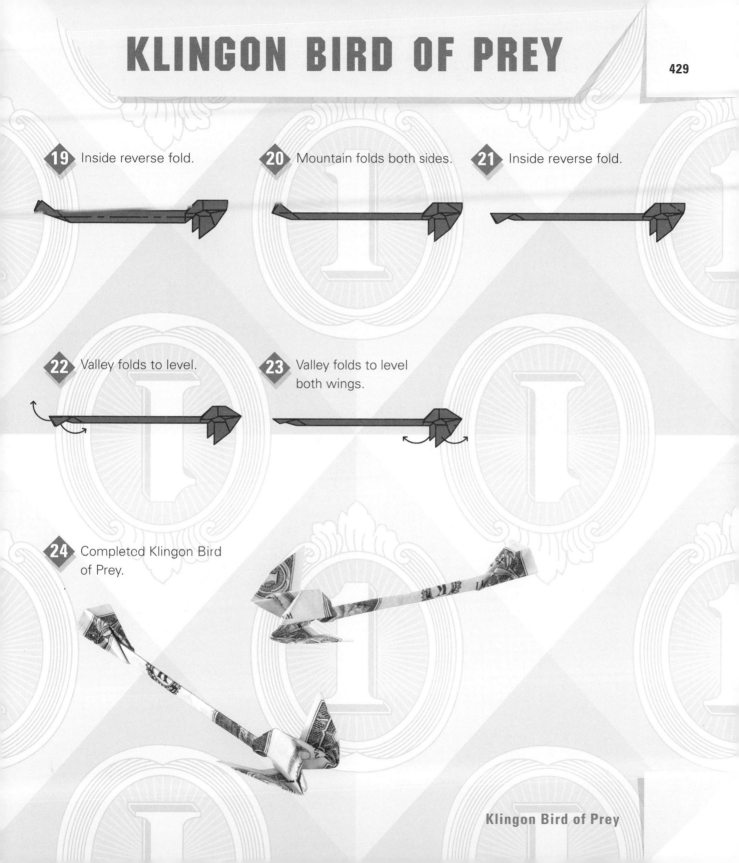

19 Inside reverse fold.

20 Mountain folds both sides.

21 Inside reverse fold.

22 Valley folds to level.

23 Valley folds to level both wings.

24 Completed Klingon Bird of Prey.

Klingon Bird of Prey

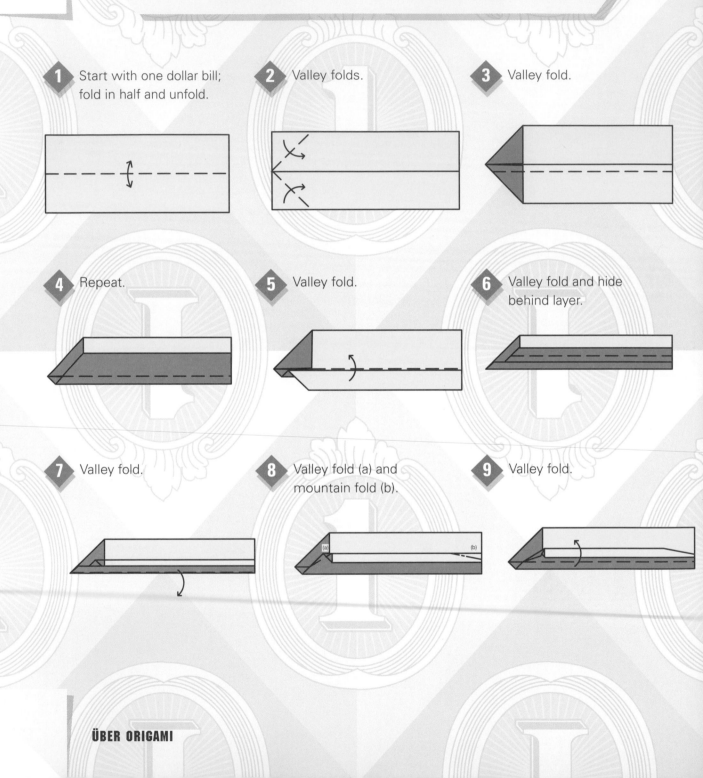

1 Start with one dollar bill; fold in half and unfold.

2 Valley folds.

3 Valley fold.

4 Repeat.

5 Valley fold.

6 Valley fold and hide behind layer.

7 Valley fold.

8 Valley fold (a) and mountain fold (b).

9 Valley fold.

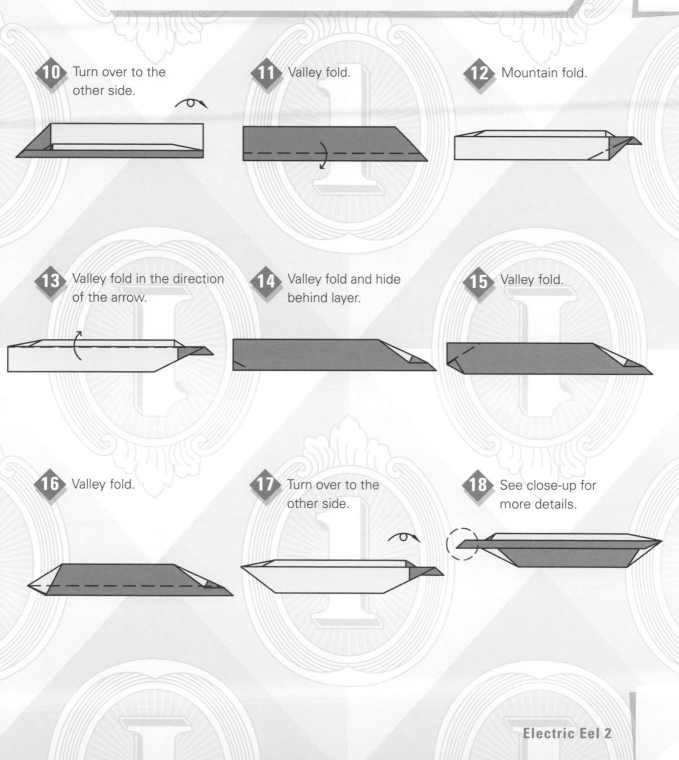

10 Turn over to the other side.

11 Valley fold.

12 Mountain fold.

13 Valley fold in the direction of the arrow.

14 Valley fold and hide behind layer.

15 Valley fold.

16 Valley fold.

17 Turn over to the other side.

18 See close-up for more details.

ELECTRIC EEL 2

19 Crimp folds.

20 Pull down as shown.

21 Valley folds.

22 Valley folds.

23 Valley fold.

24 Turn over.

25 Valley fold.

26 Valley fold.

27 Pleat fold.

28 Valley fold.

29 Press and pull firmly
at the bended parts
to form a curve.

30 Completed Electric Eel 2.

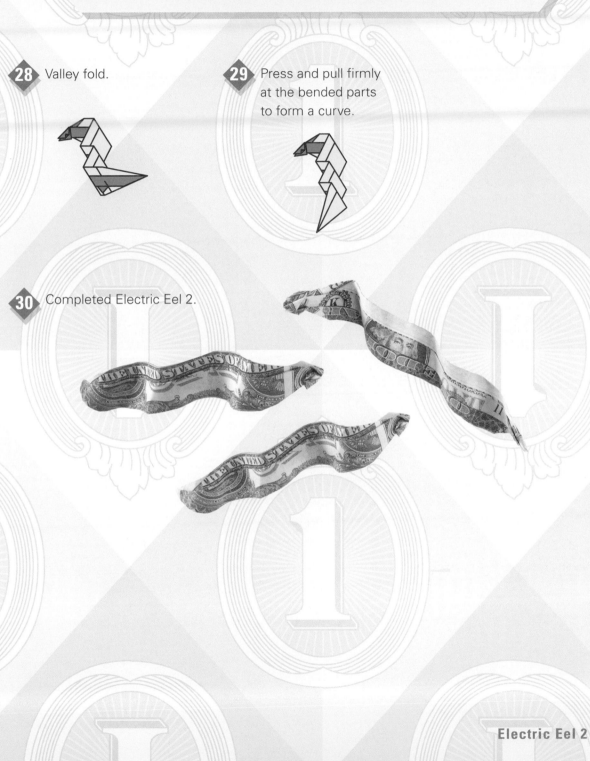

434

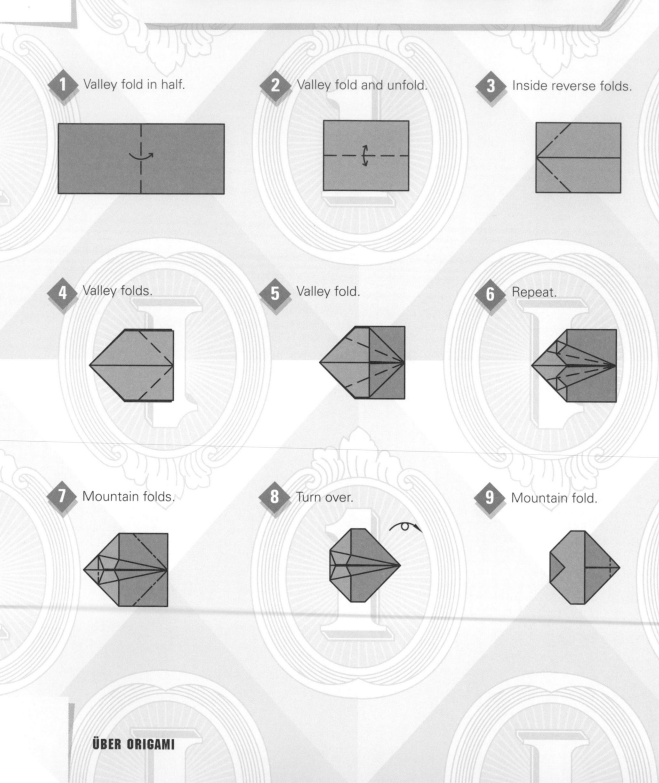

1 Valley fold in half.

2 Valley fold and unfold.

3 Inside reverse folds.

4 Valley folds.

5 Valley fold.

6 Repeat.

7 Mountain folds.

8 Turn over.

9 Mountain fold.

HORSESHOE CRAB 2

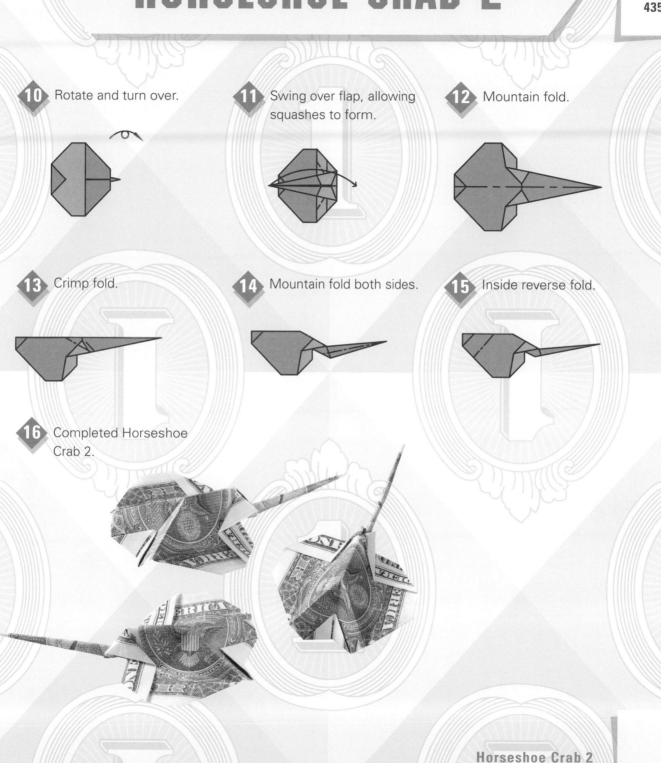

10 Rotate and turn over.

11 Swing over flap, allowing squashes to form.

12 Mountain fold.

13 Crimp fold.

14 Mountain fold both sides.

15 Inside reverse fold.

16 Completed Horseshoe Crab 2.

PHOENIX 2

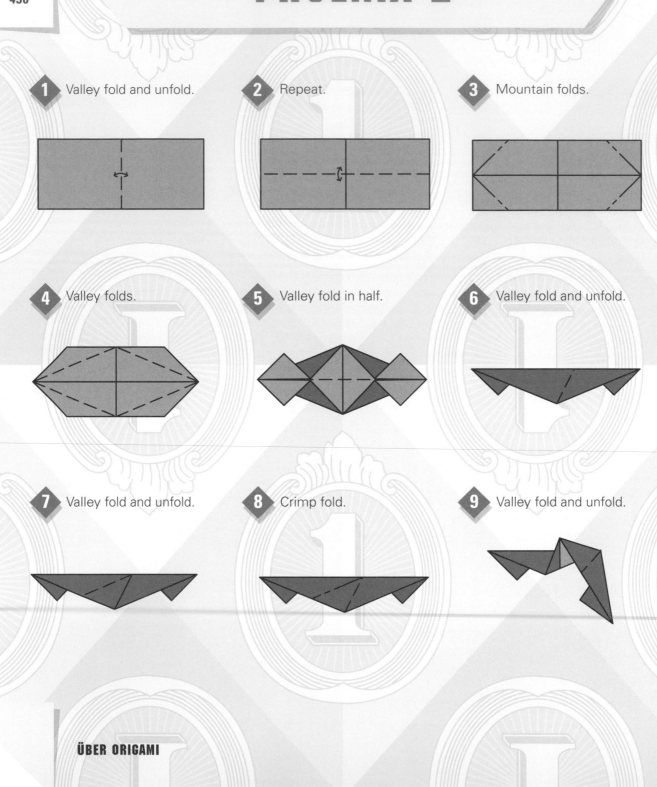

1 Valley fold and unfold.

2 Repeat.

3 Mountain folds.

4 Valley folds.

5 Valley fold in half.

6 Valley fold and unfold.

7 Valley fold and unfold.

8 Crimp fold.

9 Valley fold and unfold.

10 Repeat.

11 Crimp fold.

12 Valley folds.

13 Inside reverse fold.

14 Squash folds.

15 Crimp fold.

16 Inside reverse fold.

17 Rotate.

18 Completed Phoenix 2.

ABOUT THE AUTHOR

Dan Nguyen is the creator of
many origami books and kits,
including everything from
Cocktail Napkin Origami
to *Zombigami*.